BORN OF ADVERSITY

BORN OF ADVERSITY

BRITAIN'S AIRLINES
1919–1963

GUY HALFORD-MacLEOD

AMBERLEY

First published 2014

Amberley Publishing
The Hill, Stroud
Gloucestershire, GL5 4EP

www.amberley-books.com

British Library Cataloguing in Publication Data.
A catalogue record for this book is available from the British Library.

ISBN 978 1 84868 993 0
E-book ISBN 978 1 4456 3698 6

Typeset in 10pt on 12pt Minion Pro.
Typesetting and Origination by Amberley Publishing.
Printed in the UK.

Contents

The best results in any form of activity are usually born of adversity and not from over-indulgence.
John Longhurst, *Nationalisation in Practice*

Each new Fashion had been hailed as a panacea: 'Now we shall vanquish, now the machine will work!' Each had gone out with a whimper, leaving behind it the familiar English muddle.
John Le Carré, *Smiley's People*

It must be accepted that British air transport does not exist for its own sake, nor to fly the flag, nor to provide a market for British aircraft manufacturers. It exists solely and exclusively to serve the public…No one has suffered more than the corporations from confusion in government as to what the air transport industry is for.
J. E. D. Williams, June 1967 Barnwell lecture

I am very surprised at the argument that is going on, and very upset about it, because I never believed that it was the Corporation's job to make profits. The Corporation was there to support the British aircraft industry, to develop the routes round the world, and so on.
Sir Matthew Slattery, quoting Sir Gerard d'Erlanger, 1964 Select Committee

I have sometimes been told that there is uncertainty on the part of the British Overseas Airways Corporation as to how far its role is commercial and how far it should take account of considerations such as public service and national prestige which might conflict with a purely national interest. The Government do not consider that there is any solid justification for such uncertainty.
The Minister of Aviation, Julian Amery, to the chairman of BOAC, Sir Giles Guthrie, 1 January 1964

Preface and Acknowledgements

Who better than our parliamentarians, never short of an opinion or two, to explain and comment on the history of civil aviation in the British Isles? And of course they did more than that, they passed the laws that regulate the airline industry, they suggested improvements, they recorded events, they even sometimes changed the course of government. Many of them had a personal interest in aviation, maybe a directorship, possibly just a fascination with the subject. In using parliamentary records to help tell the story, I pray tribute to the eloquence, expert knowledge and good sense displayed by many of them as they vigorously propounded and defended their point of view, and ruthlessly cut their opponents down to size. They too had to contend with the machinery of government – as did airlines both state owned and independent – and the vested interests of other related industries, the privately owned aircraft manufacturers exercising a major influence in this regard. The history of Britain's airlines is an endearing and enduring story of muddle, heroic pioneering, lost opportunities, determined entrepreneurs, extravagant waste, commercial reality, socialism, private enterprise, to which Members of Parliament and the House of Lords contributed with enthusiasm.

I am grateful for the privilege of using Parliamentary information licensed under the Open Parliament Licence v1.0, which has allowed me to select extracts from the Official Report (Hansard), House of Commons papers and Select Committee reports. I have also had access to government records, Command Papers and other publications from Her Majesty's Stationery Office; this book contains public sector information licensed under the Open Government Licence v2.0. In all cases I acknowledge the rights of the Crown and waiver of copyright. I am also grateful to Flight International for generously making its archive material available online, to Iain Hutchinson for allowing me to quote from Captain Fresson's autobiography, and to Air-Britain (Historians), Putnam and all the other publishers who clearly and concisely record the passage of events, and explain the mechanics of the industry.

I have an enduring debt to the Smithsonian Institution's National Air and Space Museum in Washington DC, which allowed me to use its formidable library and furthermore granted me a Smithsonian Writer's Award to help me research and write this book. I also acknowledge with gratitude the support of the University of Pennsylvania, which kindly accorded me the status of visiting scholar, and offered access to its library and online resources. Thanks also to Campbell McCutcheon and Brian Pickering for allowing me to draw on their photographic archives; their images are marked (*CMcC*) and (*MAP*) respectively.

Finally, I pay tribute to my wife Johanna, always supportive and who provided me with some of the lighter moments during my research. 'What's that you're reading?' she asked one day as I made my way through another weighty parliamentary report. 'Select Committee,' I mumbled. 'What was that?' she queried, 'Sex and the City?'

CHAPTER 1

Managing Somehow to
Muddle Through

Perhaps the muddle surrounding Britain's early attempts to get airborne after the Great War came down to this, that no one could agree on the right metaphor:

> It may be questioned whether civil aviation in England is to be regarded as one of those industries which is unable to stand on its own feet, and is yet so essential to the national interest that it must be kept alive at all costs…at the beginning the British aircraft industry cannot stand on its own feet, and that to ensure its existence, although foreign to usual British practice, some form of direct Government assistance is a necessity.[1]

But Churchill held opposing views and, as one would expect, his observations were less pedestrian, more high-flown; here he is as Secretary of State for War responding good naturedly to his friend Lord Hugh Cecil in the House of Commons:

> I was very glad to hear my right hon. Friend speak so sensibly, if I may say so without presumption, on the subject of civil aviation. Civil aviation must fly by itself; the Government cannot possibly hold it up in the air. The first thing the Government have got to do is to get out of the way, and the next thing is to smooth the way. But when both these steps have been taken…it must fly on its own power, and any attempt to support it artificially by floods of State money will not ever produce a really sound commercial aviation service which the public will use, and will impose a burden of an almost indefinite amount upon the Exchequer.[2]

There is more to this response than the often quoted 'civil aviation must fly by itself'. Readers of a later generation will be stunned by the thought that the government should 'get out of the way', and that the only legitimate help the government could proffer would be to 'smooth the way'. Note also the baleful allusion to the Exchequer. Adding further to the muddle and confusion, civil aviation was parked under the wing of the Air Ministry, a service ministry which had as its prime concern the development of the fledgling Royal Air Force (RAF); it would stay there until 1945.

The government tried it Churchill's way, but the pioneering airlines quickly learned that not everyone in Europe played by the same rules. Flying by itself had its drawbacks:

> Well, that might have been all right if the same had applied to our foreign rivals; but their State assistance, compared with our unaided flying, put us in an awkward position. We had been doing quite well, all things considered, and on one or two of the routes it really looked as though the corner would soon be turned financially. But then a bombshell fell among us. Our foreign rivals, not liking the look of things, and with

their Government assistance behind them, suddenly decided to cut their air fares drastically in their endeavour to gain more traffic. That hit our British air-lines very hard. Ruin stared us in the face…there was nothing left for the British air-lines but to close down.[3]

Fortunately for Captain Olley and his employer, Handley Page Transport, a way was found to get them, and those other British airlines, back into the air early in 1921. The first of many policy changes was introduced. Now Churchill no longer stepped back; instead he 'cleared the way for civil aviation', and the airlines were all given temporary subsidies, even though they were largely competing among themselves for the sparse traffic on the main route to Paris. When that still did not work, the subsidy scheme was revised in October 1922, with cash for operations and grants towards new equipment, and the participating airlines were given sole rights on their respective routes. So Handley Page Transport was awarded the London–Paris route, which was later extended to Switzerland; the Daimler Airway was confirmed on the London–Amsterdam route, with extension to Berlin; it also operated a Manchester–London service, the first sustained domestic air service within the United Kingdom; the Instone Air Line continued on the London–Brussels–Cologne route; and an amphibian operator, British Marine Air Navigation, flew between Southampton and the Channel Islands. Other airlines managed on their own. De Havilland, an early British manufacturer, used its aircraft to fly charters, mostly around the United Kingdom, but some ventured further afield, to southern Europe and North Africa; a de Havilland DH.50 was used by pioneer Alan Cobham for two lengthy survey flights, to India in 1924–25, and South Africa in 1925–26. Surrey Flying Services started using its Avros for joy-riding in 1920, just one of many operators who took advantage of the novelty value of flying, although Surrey went on to undertake aerial photography; later the company established a flying school and survived through to the Second World War.

The government, now that it was committed to underwriting the development of British civil aviation – the inevitability of gradualness, as a later commentator put it[4]– asked Sir Herbert Hambling, a banker, to report on 'the best method of subsidising Air Transport in future'. His report[5] and its recommendations were admirably short and concise. All the present arrangements should be scrapped: a new, properly capitalised airline should be established – in the interests of fairness, it would buy out the four pioneering airlines – and the government should guarantee it subsidies for the next ten years: 'the Government should not exercise any direct control over the activities of the Company'; and the new airline would be 'a commercial organisation run entirely on business lines with a privileged position with regard to air transport subsidies'. The committee adopted a realistic position on competition. Competition had not developed traffic on the route to Paris; rather, it had reduced the numbers of passengers per machine – leading to lower load factors – and anyway, experience had shown there was quite enough competition from foreign carriers. The government accepted the report's recommendations, but added a few stipulations of its own, including the requirement that for the new airline 'all aircraft should be of British design and manufacture', and it agreed the financial figures: £1,000,000 in capital for the new organisation; £1,000,000 in guaranteed subsidy to be provided by the government, spread over ten years. The British, Foreign and Colonial Corporation put up half the capital and the rest was raised through a share issue, used in part to buy out the four airlines and some of their aircraft. The new company, Imperial Airways, was launched on 1 April 1924, hardly an auspicious date, the more so as the company had been unable to agree terms with its pilots, so that it was some weeks before services could be operated.

'Imperial Airways was created to salve the wreckage of the four previously existing companies which had been operating in competition'.[6] For all the criticism and bad press that came later – over its poor labour relations, inept handling of the government and Parliament, and the out-dated aircraft that it flew – Imperial Airways was a true pioneer, courageously developing air services throughout the Empire, far-sightedly promoting the carriage of mail by air, efficiently husbanding its slender resources, even occasionally, and controversially, returning dividends to its shareholders, and, of course, loyally supporting the British aircraft industry.

> The story of Imperial Airways is sixteen years of pioneering and development—sixteen years of glorious achievement. From its birth as a public company in 1924 to its absorption within the state-owned British Overseas Airways Corporation, this virile airline, begotten of the first generation of a new form of transport, had by the outbreak of war in September 1939 surveyed, opened and put into regular operation air services between the United Kingdom and the Dominions and Colonies of the British Commonwealth.[7]

The aeroplanes it inherited, and the routes that they flew, were quickly supplanted by a new generation of aircraft and a new sense of purpose – responding to calls raised at the Imperial Conferences throughout the 1920s – to develop air services within the British Empire and Commonwealth. With help from the intrepid Cobham, who systematically undertook the route surveys, Imperial Airways, as befitted its name, devoted its energies to the challenging task of pioneering air routes worldwide, first within the Middle East, then on to India, the Far East and Australia in one direction, to Africa and the Cape in another; and finally even meeting the daunting demands of transatlantic operation.

The Royal Air Force had opened the airmail service between Cairo and Baghdad in Iraq in 1921, following Churchill's counsel:

> Of all the places where you can bring civil aviation into effective commercial use this section between Cairo and India is the best. It has also the effect of buckling the Empire together in a very remarkable manner, because by the saving of time it ought to be possible to fly in two days, or in three days at the outside, from Cairo to Karachi, and that saves a large part of the eleven or twelve days which would be spent at sea.[8]

Imperials, as it came to be known, took over the service in 1927, extending it two years later to India, and on to Calcutta, Rangoon and Singapore in 1933, Australia in 1935. From Cairo, the route to Central Africa was opened in 1931, and reached Cape Town in 1932. Blazing the trail was not for the faint hearted:

> The landing ground at Ndola was cut out of forest. Sixty-three anthills towering between twenty and thirty feet were removed. Each one was about forty feet in diameter. Seven hundred Africans spent almost five months manually clearing and levelling 25,000 tons of ant heap sand. At another site, 90,000 trees were felled and removed. Elsewhere, workers carted away a thousand wagonloads of stone and rock.[9]

Aircraft progressed from small, single and twin-engine biplanes to much larger multi-engine landplanes and flying boats, the Handley Page HP.42, the Armstrong Whitworth Atalanta, the Short Kent and its landplane sibling, the Short Scylla, the latter able to carry thirty-nine passengers. Reliability improved: almost a quarter of the services had been cancelled in 1925; by 1934, that figure was down to 1.56 per cent. 11,395 passengers were carried in 1925; the numbers were up to 58,071 in 1934. More impressive was the carriage of mail by air, up almost tenfold in the same period: 46,110 lbs in 1925, up to 423,725 lbs in 1934, over 210 tonnes. In 1934 Imperials, which continuously renegotiated its subsidy payments, showed a profit of £133,769, paid a 7 per cent dividend, and received £543,694 in subsidy. That same year Air France was paid a subsidy of £1,315,555, and Deutsche Lufthansa £1,010,764.[10] The comparative subsidy amounts underline the political underpinning of British civil aviation policy, unwittingly summarised thus in later years: 'We have considered how such an experiment could be made on a sufficiently large scale, and yet with the smallest possible outlay of money.'[11]

What has been missing so far is the final link, the air connection with the British Isles. The so-called 'freedoms of the air' were not recognised at this stage, but the British assumed that there would be no problem for their aircraft to land in, or fly over, the countries in their path. Instead, Imperial Airways had to reroute its services from 1932 through the Gulf and Trucial States because of the problems it faced overflying Persia; in India at least half the transit passengers had to switch to Indian Trans-Continental Airways if they wanted to continue on to the Far East; at Singapore Imperials' passengers transferred to the Australian airline, Qantas Empire Airways, for the final leg to Australia; and in South Africa, Imperials had to withdraw from Cape Town in 1936, although the South African government reluctantly allowed the airline to fly as far south as Johannesburg.

Almost every European country gave the British a hard time. The Italians were the most trouble, trailed closely by the French and Spanish. Imperials had to experiment with many permutations of rail and air connections to avoid overflying Italy on its way to Egypt, before settling in 1931 for a laborious routeing that involved a short flight from London's Croydon Airport to Paris, followed by a long train journey to Brindisi, in the heel of Italy, 32 hours. At Brindisi passengers joined a flying boat for the sectors to Alexandria, with stops in the Greek islands and Athens – readers may recall Gerald Durrell's description of the flying boats landing at Corfu in *My Family and Other Animals* – before transferring to a Handley Page HP.42 for the long, and hot, flight to Karachi. There they continued in an Atalanta of Indian Trans-Continental Airways to Calcutta, and on to Rangoon and Singapore. What was it like to fly under those conditions? This extract from an account of a journey from Singapore to London made in 1934 was first published in the *Sydney Morning Herald*.

At Karachi we started on the second stage of our journey. The first sight we had of the great *Hanno* (HP.42) was at 2 a.m. There she stood on the runway, with half a dozen spotlights focussed on her. She looked magnificent, her size accentuated by the blackness of the background, and her long lizard-like fuselage shimmering like beaten silver.

We took off at 2.30. Another thrilling experience. As soon as we were in the air the steward came round and turned out the lights, and as it were, tucked us in for the night. We landed at Gwadar to refuel, and a little later at an out-of-the-way place named Jiwani, where we took on a little extra petrol, for head winds were expected and we had a long run ahead of us.

Soon we were in the air again and heading for Sharjah. We flew low over the Persian Gulf, and at 300 ft. could clearly see hundreds of sharks, stingrays, sea snakes, and a few tortoises. Breakfast was served on board by the steward and a very good meal it was. We continued to fly very low throughout the morning, for a very strong head wind was blowing at 1,000 ft. At 12.30 the *Hanno* landed at Sharjah, which is a little self-contained fort, hot and cold running water, and all modern conveniences.

After we left Sharjah lunch was served, consisting of soup, fried fish, cold meats and salad and fruit salad. It is remarkable to think that a meal like this could be served in the air, out of sight of land, flying over the Persian Gulf. It is this kind of attention that brings added comfort to air travel.

The country from Basra to Baghdad is mostly desert, cultivated only for a short distance on either side of the River Euphrates. The aerodrome at Baghdad is very fine indeed. In the air once more, we soon left all civilisation behind and were flying over the Syrian desert, mile upon mile of rolling sandhills as far as the eye can see in all directions. At 9.30 we landed at Rutbah Wells. Half an hour later we were on our way again, and landed at 1.30 pm at Amman, which is just this side of the Dead Sea. The aerodrome is an R.A.F. post, and is quite a busy place.

The run to Cairo was made in under two hours, as we had a good following wind. We had another touch of desert, and saw a few wild camels straying about. Later we passed over the Suez Canal, and on to Cairo, where we landed at 6 p.m. Cairo, to one who had not been there before, proved full of interest, fine streets, lined with beautiful trees, very good buildings, and evidence of law and order wherever you go.

We were up again early in the morning, and out at the aerodrome before we were properly awake. Without delay we climbed aboard *Hadrian*, and were soon on our way to Alexandria, where we landed at five o'clock. A short drive through the city brought us to the seaplane base, where we were given tea and biscuits. At six o'clock the *Scipio* was wheeled out, and looked like a huge albatross waddling down to the water. Once afloat she was a beautifully graceful thing, looking more like a seabird than ever. Luggage, mails and freight were immediately put aboard, and 16 passengers embarked. On schedule time the Bristol motors commenced to whine, and in a few seconds the four engines were things of life, and we were taxying out into open water. We had a run of about a mile before we stopped and turned into the wind, then suddenly the four engines were revved up and we absolutely leapt across the water. In a few seconds spray was flying past the windows, a few seconds more we were skimming the water at 60 miles an hour, and then into the air in an incredibly short space of time. Very rapidly we left land behind us, and were soon flying over the blue Mediterranean. For the next few hours there was nothing to do, so I got a book from the library. The *Scipio* beats anything one could imagine. The seats are luxurious (more comfortable than in most drawing-rooms), the cabin is so well sound-insulated that there is no need to raise one's voice, and there is practically no vibration.

We landed at Mirabella at 10.45 [and] left at 11.15, our next stop Athens. Before we reached there we had dinner on the 'plane. The meal was a classic – prawn patties, roast chicken and hot vegetables, strawberry flan and cream, and black coffee.

We arrived at Athens at about two o'clock and went ashore. Our cameras were taken away from us here and sealed in a bag. There are certain regulations about taking photographs over Brindisi, although there is really nothing interesting to take. We did not see much of Athens, just a distant view of the Acropolis and a general look at the city. On our way again half an hour later, and the trip to Corfu just a dream; hundreds of brilliant little islands sitting in the blue sea.

After Corfu we were flying over the sea, and at six o'clock we landed at Brindisi. There was no delay passing the Customs, and we were soon at the hotel; having dined at eight o'clock, the airways bus was ready to take us to the station, and we left by express at 8.30. It was not long before we were all in bed, and making up for a little lost sleep. The train was as comfortable as trains can be. I had a good night's rest, but it was noticeable that the noise and vibration was far greater than in the 'planes.

At seven o'clock the morning [of the day after] we were in Paris. A splendid breakfast, which only hungry passengers can thoroughly enjoy, was served at the hotel. We strolled to the Airways office, and at 8.30 left for Le Bourget. Soon we were in the air in one of the palatial Imperial Airways cross-Channel liners. We landed at Croydon right on schedule time.

The journey to Cape Town was as complicated: passengers transferred from Alexandria to Cairo, before setting off by landplane to Khartoum, where they joined a flying boat for the sector to Kisumu, on Lake Victoria; then it was by landplane via Nairobi to Cape Town. The flight to Cape Town took nine days, that to Singapore ten days, and to Australia twelve days.[12] The Dutch airline KLM, on the other hand, was able to fly its passengers in the same plane all the way from Amsterdam to Singapore and on to Batavia, at first with Fokkers, later with speedy Douglas DC-2s; in 1935 KLM was completing the journey in five and a half days.[13] By the mid-1930s, when French and Italian airlines found they in turn needed to cross large tracts of British territory to reach their colonies, their respective authorities began to relent and allow Imperial Airways overflight rights.

Imperial Airways might well have found itself facing new competition on the Empire route to India, had the airship R.101 not crashed into the hillside near Beauvais in France on its inaugural trip to Delhi in October 1930. After that the airship programme was abandoned and Imperials had the routes to itself, except for competition from pesky European airlines, especially KLM, which paralleled Imperials all the way to Singapore. As for its European routes, Imperials did not try very hard. Paris was important, as a major destination in its own right and also as the starting point for the long distance Empire routes, and was served luxuriously by the fabled Handley Page airliners; but the European network remained static, and much of the heavy lifting was done by the European carriers, Sabena, Deutsche Lufthansa, KLM, for whom Imperials acted as agent. The airline also built up a close if wary relationship with the four railway companies in Britain, whose agents, through the Railway Clearing House, were allowed to promote and sell Imperials and other European airlines' tickets. When the railway companies decided to launch their own internal air services, they turned to Imperials which provided them with operational assistance and aircrew. Indeed, Imperials had already tried its hand at operating domestic services, in 1930:

> From June to September, 1930, a thrice weekly service between London-Birmingham-Manchester and Liverpool was operated by Imperial Airways Limited with the assistance of small grants-in-aid from the municipal authorities concerned. The results were not sufficiently encouraging to justify the reopening of the service in the following year, when no internal services are recorded.[14]

At first the railways had been hostile to the newcomer. The Southern Railway in particular disliked having competition on its Paris route, and for a while refused to cooperate over matters like the carriage of excess baggage, but fearful of missing out on future transport possibilities – as had happened after the Great War with road transport – the four railway companies took out parliamentary powers in 1929 to permit airline operations; the Southern went further, and began secretly to buy shares in Imperials, hoping to gain overall control. Imperial Airways was nervous about the possible incursion of the railway companies into its arena, but in the clubby and rarefied atmosphere of British business between the wars, misunderstandings were resolved, fears allayed, and then nothing much happened. The situation changed after 1932 when a number of air services around the country were started, many of them by the proprietors of bus companies. The Great Western Railway (GWR) decided to join in too, stealing a march on the other railways by starting a regular air service on 12 April 1933 between Cardiff and Plymouth, with a stop at Haldon for Teignmouth and Torquay. The railway used a three-engine Westland Wessex, carrying six passengers and appropriately painted chocolate and cream, on loan from Imperial Airways, which also provided its top charter pilot, Captain Olley, to inaugurate the route. The service was suspended at the end of the summer, and resulted in a loss to the railway company of over £6,500, but to the Great Western goes the kudos and prestige of another innovation in its glorious history. By the following year, 1934, the railway companies had launched a joint airline, Railway Air Services (RAS), based at London's Croydon Airport, in which the four companies and Imperial Airways each held a 20 per cent share. Service was launched to Liverpool, Belfast and Glasgow; the London, Midland & Scottish Railway (LMS) was more enthusiastic about the project, with its favourable Irish Sea connection, than its neighbour, the London & North Eastern Railway (LNER), which saw little benefit. The GWR continued its Plymouth–Cardiff service, extended to Birmingham and Liverpool, and now using aircraft wearing the red and green colours of RAS. The Southern cooperated with an aircraft manufacturer turned airline operator, Spartan, and used its gangly products to fly between Croydon and the Isle of Wight.

If the railway companies had been ambivalent about the prospects for air travel, energetic bus operators were more easily persuaded. Road passenger transport had developed somewhat untidily after the Great War, although that did not prevent the emergence of territorial groupings of bus company owners or the development of municipally owned services. But the larger companies were vulnerable to low-cost competition from the hordes of small owner-operated companies that proliferated both in London and the provinces, often referred to as pirate operations. The railway companies, GWR especially, had played a pioneering role in developing early bus services, and by the end of the 1920s had begun investing in many of the larger bus groups, only to complain that unlicensed operators were having a serious impact on traffic. So the railways and the bus groups lobbied, pulled strings behind the scenes, and the government then took steps to regulate the road transport industry, requiring bus and coach companies to obtain route licences, and to meet much more stringent operating and safety standards (Road Traffic Act 1930); freight carriers came under similar discipline in 1933 (Road and Rail Traffic Act 1933). A start had been made to regulate public transport in London as early as 1924 (London Traffic Act) but that had not prevented the development of coach services into central London from the suburbs and home counties, which competed with the growing Underground system and suburban commuter trains. The government's eventual response was to nationalise all passenger services within the greater London area, with the exception of taxis and the railways, creating in 1933 the London Passenger Transport Board.

Because 'route licences' and 'licensing' appear throughout this book, bear with me if I seem to restate the obvious, and explain that in an unregulated, or deregulated, transport environment, operators can offer transport services to the public with little or no intervention from a regulatory authority; in other words a bus operator or an airline can simply state that it will be offering services between various points, when marketing and advertising the service, and on the appointed day or at the appointed hour, roll out the bus or plane. It is not quite as simple as that, of course, as the bus or plane has to be insured and driven or piloted by qualified personnel; there may also be police limitations as to where the bus may stop, and so on, but there is no adjudicator in the background, questioning whether the operator has done his sums right, is charging an economic fare, has determined that there is a reasonable demand for the service offered. Regulations, established by Act of Parliament, can also be introduced to impose a monopoly, as happened with London Transport; when monopolies prove hard to impose, regulations will establish a framework to allow adjudication between competing applications for services. In both road and air transport, the process was usually undertaken by a panel, sometimes chaired by a lawyer, which followed, to a greater or lesser extent, due judicial process, requiring lawyers, submission of evidence, serving of documents, examination of witnesses, all of which might lead to the award of a route licence to the successful applicant. Britain was a mercantilist country, by and large, and accepted the free-for-all of a robust market economy. But there was already *de facto* licensing in aviation, to the extent that Imperials was the chosen instrument and sole recipient of government subsidies for overseas services; as transport economics became more complex, as politics intruded, as competition emerged, more and more air services became regulated. 'Licences' and 'route licensing' appear with ever increasing regularity in this book.

Two coach operators, now denied their London services, turned to aviation with gusto. Ted Hillman, after launching a Romford–Clacton summer service in 1932, pioneered low-cost flights from Romford to Paris in 1933, undercutting Imperials' one way fare by over one pound sterling, and using his coaches to carry passengers from a London terminus near King's Cross to Romford. He was the first operator to use the twin-engine de Havilland DH.84 Dragon, a type which, with its successor the DH.89 Dragon Rapide, made feasible reliable air services. But this energetic and pugnacious man died suddenly on the last day of 1934, aged 45, and his airline, by then a public company, came under the influence of City interests, especially those of the financial house of Erlanger. The other London coach operator to take to the air was Walter Thurgood, former proprietor of People's Motor Services in Ware, who began flying de Havilland DH.84 Dragons and later four-engine DH.86 Expressliners to Jersey in the Channel Islands, landing on the public beach near St Helier as there was no airfield. Timetables had to be changed twice a month to allow for the tides, and using public beaches crammed with holiday-makers raised safety and operational issues. The islanders were pessimistic at first:

> The action of a company out for gain in encroaching on the rights of the public to the free use of the 'plages' of Jersey has already aroused feeling in the island and protests have appeared in the local press. Furthermore, as one Jersey paper points out, there is no pleasure for passengers in being dumped on a wind-swept beach on arriving or having to tramp along it to get to the aeroplane. Judging by these articles, Jersey Airways have not yet succeeded in becoming popular on the Island.[15]

But the islanders came round to the airline, building an airport for it, and resisting, albeit ineffectually, the British Government's decision to take over the airline after the war. In Scotland, John Sword sold his bus company, Midland Bus Services, a substantial undertaking with over 500 buses, to Scottish Motor Traction (SMT) and was retained as general manager of Western SMT. He also ventured into air transport, forming Midland & Scottish Air Ferries to launch services out of Glasgow, but after a year his employers told him to either concentrate on running the buses or quit, so he closed his airline down. It was left to three Englishmen, Captain Fresson, George Nicholson and Eric Gandar Dower, to overcome the geographical and climatic obstacles and develop services within Scotland, and to its many island communities in the Atlantic and North Sea, in the years before the war. In doing so, Captain Fresson's Highland Airways introduced a new source of revenue, the carriage of mail. The Maybury Committee's report acknowledged the innovation:

> (In 1934) Highland Airways Limited for the first time carried the internal mail under formal contract with the Postmaster-General between Inverness and the Orkney Islands without additional charge to the public for air transmission.
>
>   This experiment being successful, the Postmaster-General, in November, 1934, adopted the policy of sending first-class mail by any satisfactory service offering a material acceleration in delivery, subject to suitable terms being arranged with the operating companies. Internal air services have since been used regularly for mail conveyance between London, Belfast and Glasgow, to the Orkney and Shetland Islands and to the Isle of Man.[16]

In 1935 there were nineteen companies operating seventy-six services, and between them they carried around 136,000 passengers; as the decade passed, those companies pioneering services within the United Kingdom and to Europe fell increasingly under the thrall of two main groupings: either the railway companies, or the aviation interests of the Pearson family's Whitehall Securities, which controlled two airlines, United and Spartan, and was soon to take over Hillman's. The railway companies preferred to operate the main trunk routes themselves through RAS, but they also invested in local and regional airlines, serving the Isle of Man, the West Country and the Isle of Wight, many of them directed and part-owned by Captain Olley.

The railway companies could be quite nasty to those airlines that were not members of their club. Through their joint ownership of the Railway Clearing House and domination of travel agents up and down the country, they succeeded in making life difficult for outsiders, denying them access to travel agents and so stifling tickets sales. That included British Airways, formed in October 1935 (originally as Allied British Airways) following the amalgamation of all the airlines that Whitehall Securities now controlled: Hillman's, Spartan, and Blackpool-based United, together with United's two Scottish airlines, Highland, and Northern and Scottish. The Southern Railway, however, had a mutual interest with Whitehall Securities in both Spartan and Jersey Airways; this did not exempt the British Airways group from the ban, but it did mean that the issue was resolved more speedily. That still left a small number of independent airlines outside the net, five in all:

- Allied Airways (Gandar Dower) which had developed Aberdeen's Dyce airport, and flew service to the Orkneys and Shetlands;

- Lundy and Atlantic Coast Airlines, flying between Barnstaple and Lundy Island;

- North Eastern Airways, the only independent to try its luck flying trunk routes from London, to Doncaster, Leeds/Bradford, Newcastle and on to Perth in Scotland;

- Portsmouth, Southsea and Isle of Wight Aviation (PSIoWA) concentrating on its Portsmouth-Ryde services;

- Western Airways, which mainly flew high frequency services across the Severn between Cardiff and Weston-Super-Mare.

When it wanted to, the government could still get out of the way: 'I am aware,' replied the Minister of Transport, Oliver Stanley, in a written answer, 'that under the conditions of their appointment railway ticket agents are precluded from selling tickets for air services without the consent of the railway companies, and that such consent has been refused in the case of certain air services operated in competition with services provided by the railway companies. I see no reason to intervene in the matter.'[17] But British Airways knew how to pull strings, and quickly made itself indispensable to the government, undertaking to develop all those European services that Imperial Airways disdained. The government was amenable; it had just received an internal report by Sir Warren Fisher on this very question, recommending government support to more than one company on European services, and further, that each company should have its own 'de-limited' sphere of operation. Shucking off its domestic roots, British Airways persuaded the government to regard it as the second 'chosen instrument' with responsibility for air services north of the line between London and Berlin, and secured subsidies for those routes, to Holland, Germany, and Scandinavia; it also continued the unsubsidised Hillman's flights to Paris. British Airways took over British Continental Airways which had already pioneered services to northern Europe in 1935, but drew the short straw when it came to subsidies; its fleet of DH.86A Expressliner biplanes joined those of the former Hillman's in the British Airways fleet.

The Expressliners, however, with a cruising speed of around 140 mph, were just not express enough for the longer routes planned to northern Europe. The government seemed ambivalent about the value of higher speeds in air transport; passengers were looking for safety, comfort and regularity 'just as much as speed', claimed the Secretary of State for Air, the Marquess of Londonderry, as he went on to extol the success of Imperials' luxurious flights to Paris against the faster service provided by Air France, and to damn the Douglas DC-2s that KLM used with faint praise: 'The Douglas machine is undoubtedly a remarkably successful machine, which reflects the greatest credit on its designers and constructors. On the other hand, save for certain limited purposes, it is quite unsuitable for standard use on our Imperial Airways service.'[18] But for the Scandinavian routes, the government had stipulated aircraft with a cruising speed 'in the neighbourhood of 200 miles per hour'[19] so it was forced to acquiesce in British Airways' decision to buy the American built Lockheed 10A Electra, a twin engine ten-seat monoplane which cruised at 190 mph, and Lord Londonderry's Under Secretary, Sir Philip Sassoon, had to squirm a little when asked to explain this lapse from established practice:

> The agreement under which the service is operated and of which a summary was contained in the White Paper (Cmd. 5203) laid before the House last June, provides that except with the consent of the Secretary of State for Air all aircraft used by the company shall be of British design and manufacture. The agreement contemplated the use of the type of aircraft known as D.H. 86A for the operation of the night air mail service, and aircraft of this type were in fact purchased by the company. They were subsequently found, however, to be unsuitable for the night service and were withdrawn. In the situation which thus arose, no suitable civil aircraft of British design and manufacture being immediately available or in early prospect and the demands of Air Force expansion making it impossible to make available to the company suitable military machines, there was no alternative, if the night air mail service were not to be abandoned, but to resort to the power under the agreement to approve the use of foreign aircraft in exceptional circumstances. Consequently, when the company sought permission for the employment of foreign aircraft, my Noble Friend (Lord Londonderry) was reluctantly obliged to …consider the proposal to use the American Lockheed Electra 10A type when deliveries can be obtained. The use of these foreign machines is an unfortunate expedient necessary to maintain the night service with its important European connections. The day passenger and mail service between this country and Sweden is not affected; it is only in regard to the night air mail service to Hanover that the question of the use by British Airways of foreign aircraft has arisen.[20]

'To approve the use of foreign aircraft in exceptional circumstances' became a leitmotif in British aviation policy. If he genuinely thought that British Airways would accept this limitation, Lord Londonderry was quickly disabused; the Lockheeds turned up everywhere, competing against Imperial Airways on the route to Paris, helping to train the RAF in night-flying techniques on the long night mail services to Berlin, and famously, transporting Prime Minister Chamberlain to and from Germany for his meetings with Hitler in 1938. And European airlines bought Douglas DC-2s and its more famous successor, the DC-3 Dakota, by the score.

British Airways was soon able to resolve that unfortunate business of the railway booking ban, facilitated by the appointment of its chairman, the Hon. Clive Pearson, as a director of the Southern Railway in 1936. Sir Philip Sassoon could assure the House that he was 'informed that favourable progress has been made in the negotiations which have been taking place in regard to the use by British Airways, Limited, of the booking facilities of travel agencies, and I understand that agreement has been reached with the railway companies by which British Airways will be given the use of the booking agencies for their Continental services.'[21] One down, and five more to go. The Whitehall Securities group went on to collaborate further with the railway companies, transferring to them the Isle of Man and Isle of Wight services, and sharing with them ownership of Scottish Airways, so called after its two Scottish subsidiaries were reorganized in 1937; it sold its share in Channel Island Airways, formerly Jersey and Guernsey Airways, to the railways in 1943. By the end of the war – with one notable exception, Allied Airways (Gandar Dower) – the railways controlled, and substantially owned, all the domestic airlines flying within the United Kingdom.

If the Postmaster-General could see his way to carrying airmail without surcharge in the British Isles, why not within the Empire and Commonwealth too? Its announcement was surprisingly low-key, a short statement by Sir Philip Sassoon on 20 December 1934:

> The scheme contains three main features. In the first place, there is to be a very material improvement on present time schedules between the several parts of the Empire concerned; secondly, there is to be a substantial increase in the frequency of services; and, thirdly, all first-class mail to the Empire countries covered by the projected services is in future to be carried by air. As regards schedules, the scheme as suggested to the other Governments concerned envisages a schedule of just over two days to India, two and a-half days to East Africa, four days to the Cape, four days to Singapore, and seven days to Australia. As regards frequencies, provision is made for four, or possibly five, services a week to India, three services a week to Singapore and to East Africa, and two to South Africa and Australia respectively. With regard to the letter rate proposed, I can as yet say nothing definite, but we hope that, in so far as concerns letters posted in the United Kingdom for Empire destinations, subject to the successful outcome of our negotiations with the Governments concerned, it may be in the region of the present Empire rate of 1½d, but this will apply per half-ounce instead of to the first ounce as at present. I may say that correspondence covering at least eight sides of special light paper can be sent within the half-ounce limit. It will, of course, be for the other participating Governments to fix their own postal charges.[22]

Imperials ordered a new fleet of flying boats and landplanes expressly designed for the service with large mail compartments, and able at last to compete with the nimbler offerings of its European competitors, but in true Imperials style, more comfortably. The landplanes, Armstrong Whitworth Ensigns, were intended for European services and the route to Karachi, but in the event were much delayed entering into service, and were only used on flights within Europe until the outbreak of war. So the burden of Empire flying fell on the new Short C Class Empire flying boats. They had a maximum speed of 200 mph, and cruised at 164 mph; they were able to carry up to twenty-four passengers, although in practice the flying boats usually carried no more than fifteen or sixteen passengers, allowing the forward cabin to be given over to the carriage of mail, in which configuration one and a half tons of mail was carried. Although bunks were provided, the airline continued its practice of night-stopping passengers and crew along the route, including at Southampton the night before departure, to allow for a 6 a.m. take-off. Now that both the French and Italians had conceded overflights, the airline was able to fly directly from the marine base at Southampton; with accelerated timings, Singapore was reached in 5 days 2 hours, Durban in 4 days 10 hours. The 'Empires' were allowed to transit India, continue down to Singapore, and on to Brisbane and Sydney. There had to be some modifications on the African routeings. The flying boats flew from Alexandria down the Nile, and then over to Mombasa to continue down the African coast as far as Durban, leaving both North and South Rhodesia, Nairobi, and Johannesburg without direct service; instead feeder services were provided by local airlines. In 1938 a correspondent in *The Aeroplane* praised the slickness of the Imperials operation on a flight from London to Sydney:

> Too much cannot be said in praise of the organisation of Imperial Airways which has made this flight across half the World as comfortable as it is. Literally the passenger does not have to think; all he has to do is enjoy himself.

His every care is seen to. His comfort at hotels, stopping places, and refuelling stops, the bugbear of customs, passports, and money-changing…that is not his concern, but the worry of the Imperial Airways representatives at all stops.

The comfort of the hotels at the overnight stops, the fast, streamlined launches that connect the flying-boat with the land, and the refuelling arrangement, where everything is done by the local labour at the various ports, are a few of the features of the flight. Three years of flying on the London–Singapore section have made all employees of the company most proficient.[23]

The main routes were flown on a twice-weekly basis, later increased to three times a week. Extra sectors over part of the route system were operated by locally based aircraft. The flying boats, with their limited passenger capacity, might fleetingly splash through Egypt and Iraq on their way to Karachi and points east, but much of the local traffic was still carried by Armstrong Whitworth Atalanta and Handley Page HP.42 landplanes between Alexandria, Basra and Calcutta.

The government did not want to invest in upgraded airfields along the routes, essential if bigger aircraft with their higher loadings were to be used, and there was an assumption that it was less expensive to use marine facilities than upgrade existing airfields. Of course the British government wanted to upgrade the air mail service as cheaply as possible, and put some effort into persuading its imperial partners to help foot the bill, both through subsidies and meeting infrastructure costs. In Africa landplane operations were at the mercy of the rainy season, and a cheaper alternative to building all-weather airfields was to land on the rivers and lakes with which Africa is so liberally endowed.

The Atalantas had necessarily to be capable of operating on the African as well as the Asian routes and were designed to take off safely from the small, hot, humid, high-level airfields of the Cape route, most of which had not been much enlarged since the early days and all of which were frequently unfit for traffic; indeed, it was said that in the rainy season the airfield at Juba was more suitable for flying-boats than landplanes and what the Atalanta really needed was a planing bottom.[24]

Besides, Imperials had great faith in the Short Brothers who had already built many fine flying boats for the airline; the ability to fly along its routes without a change of aircraft was a benefit; and flying boats could operate across India to Singapore and Australia as well as on the African routes. The Shorts flying boats achieved some modest export success when they were sold to the Australians and New Zealanders, unlike most other products tailor-made for Imperial Airways by Britain's aircraft manufacturers.

Elsewhere, airfields were being enlarged and strengthened as a matter of course; the Swedes built the first paved runway in Europe at Stockholm's Bromma airport in 1936, and the war accelerated the building of airfields with longer and paved runways. The development of the flying boat was leading to a technological dead-end, yet it was a fine call; many countries, including the United States and France, built flying boats during this era for their long-haul services. But the operation of flying boats turned out to be more expensive than anticipated, as Brian Cassidy observes:

Unfortunately, [Imperial Airways] discovered to their cost that the initial assumptions made in favour of the flying boats were not all valid when the 'boats came into service. The handling of passengers, mail and freight on water, in the increased volume generated by the new service, proved more difficult than on dry land. Southampton was initially the only port with a pontoon for loading and discharging the 'boats…. At most of the other ports, all servicing had to be done on the open water by surface craft. Carrying out essential maintenance and minor repairs was more difficult on water than on land. Early morning and late evening fogs and mists, often associated with stretches of water, could also interfere with services.[25]

Those were not the only difficulties Imperials faced. There were a number of accidents, leading to a more or less permanent shortage of flying boats. Cassidy goes on to comment:

Accidents resulted in three 'boats written off in 1937, one in 1938 and five in 1939 … leaving a fleet of thirty at the end of 1939. The high attrition rate had shaken confidence in IAL's operating abilities and resulted in a shortage of aircraft. Ten crew and seven passengers had been killed and four crew and twelve passengers injured. One crew member of a refuelling barge had died in hospital and one had been seriously injured. Although forty-two Empire 'boats were completed, the year-end totals of the Empire 'boat fleet never exceeded thirty-one aircraft in service and that was at the end of 1940.[26]

Operations, pioneering as they were, could be difficult. Unfortunately for Imperials many of its passengers were people of influence, a wealthy and entitled elite who could afford to travel by air and who were not reticent about voicing their displeasure when things went wrong; they also tended to be heard in the right places, leading to a crescendo of unfavourable comment about the airline. The following extract from a speech that Lord Milford gave in the House of Lords on 15 April 1943 contrasts with *The Aeroplane*'s account above: the noble lord absolutely disparages the performance of Imperials, even though the airline was no longer in existence:

I have said that I consider that before the war our civil aviation was the laughing-stock of the world. Let me give you three personal examples of what I mean after all, example is better than precept. In 1935–36 we started by going to Croydon. There was a little mist, and we were told 'There is no aeroplane this morning; it has not arrived from Paris. There is a fog in the Channel.' Finally we were sent back to Victoria and put on a train. One reason why I prefer to fly is that I loathe the sea, but I had to endure the Channel crossing. Eventually we reached Paris, and were told that the plane for Brindisi had already left. We had to go back to the station and take the train through Switzerland and Italy to Brindisi. Finally, we got a plane at Brindisi and spent the second night at Athens.

The next morning we started off for Crete and Alexandria, but an engine seized up on the way to Crete, and so we turned round and went back to Athens. We spent two nights in Athens waiting for an engine, and then finally we were able to fly to South Africa. On our way home on the same trip we could not go to Athens because of some political trouble. So we were sent to Benghazi, and we spent a night there. Next morning we started for Malta, but there was bad weather in Malta and so we turned back and spent another night in Benghazi. Next day we did get as far as Brindisi, and we were then told that the plane we wanted to catch had gone, so that again, although we wanted to fly, we had to take the train to Paris.

Next year I decided in June that we wanted three berths to fly to Australia in December. We could not book them. This monopoly could not, in June, promise us berths in December. They said: 'We may have a lot of Christmas mail, and not be able to take you.' We had therefore to travel by the K.L.M., the Dutch line. Everything was beautifully done. It so happened that we started off on the same morning as the Imperial Airways machine, but we spent three days and nights in Java before the Imperial Airways machine turned up. That sort of thing does not encourage one to travel British, does it?[27]

And maybe the numbers were not quite as good as implied by the enthusiastic comments from government and Imperial Airways alike? Imperials was reluctant to release passenger figures by sector for the routes to the Far East and Africa, preferring to use passenger mileage numbers, which of course are more impressive, involving many more noughts. In 1937, Imperials performed 23,099,000 passenger miles, but carried only 4,340 passengers, on its Empire services to Africa and the Far East:[28] KLM, which operated to the Far East, managed 3,912 passengers in the same year.[29] Readers should note that passenger numbers refer to sector, rather than end-to-end, traffic; Gordon Pirie argues convincingly that most of Imperials' passengers were carried on the Cairo–Karachi–Singapore sectors, confirming Churchill was correct in his belt-and-buckle analogy.[30] Those 4,340 passengers comprised a very small percentage of the 244,396 passengers carried by British airlines that year, which might have been reason enough not to brag about them. Unlike the carriage of mail: 'It is difficult for those without experience of air transport to realize what in fact is being achieved by this [Empire Air Mail] Scheme. On an average, 19 tons of mails are normally transported each week on the Empire Air Services from the United Kingdom alone.'[31] A year later, in the House of Commons, the new Secretary of State for Air, Sir Kingsley Wood, continued the trend:

> Six years ago, also, 170 tons of air mail were carried in a year by British commercial aviation. Last year over 2,000 tons were carried in this way, and nearly 600 tons of letter mail were carried on the internal air services, nearly 750 tons on European sendees, nearly 850 tons on Empire services, and a small tonnage on other extra-European services. The British Empire continues to rank foremost as regards the length of route operated by regular air services, and at the end of 1938 the route mileage for the Empire as a whole was about 88,000 miles. The importance of civil aviation to the British Empire needs no emphasis.[32]

Certainly for the carriage of air mail: the mail and its accompanying subsidies enabled the dynamic thrust of the Imperial air routes to be realised. Despite the sumptuous passenger service provided by Imperial Airways and for which it was recognised, the airline evolved into a mail carrier. Mail, regular, reliable, uncomplaining mail, was more lucrative and subtly, Imperial Airways accommodated the change. By the end of its existence, Imperials was giving precedence to the Empire Air Mail scheme and rationing the seats available for passengers.

Nevertheless, Imperials' exploits still captured the headlines. A West African extension was grafted on to the main African route with connection at Khartoum. Hong Kong was joined to the Imperial network by a connection at Penang, and later at Bangkok, using DH.86 Expressliners. The latter service was not without its excitements, as on two occasions the aircraft were fired on by Imperial Japanese forces, but nevertheless continued until October 1940. Robin Higham elegantly commends the airline and the aircraft used: 'It is noticeable, and a tribute to the De Havilland Company, that the service operated over a most difficult terrain, particularly in the monsoon season, with no forced landings and with becoming regularity.'[33] Most ambitious of all was the attempt to conquer the Atlantic. The British struggled to build aircraft with sufficient range; extra tankage was added to some of the 'Empires'; they experimented with a composite aircraft, a small mailplane attached to a mothership which was then released in flight; and enterprisingly Imperials pioneered in-flight refuelling. But the British were left behind by other countries in the trans-Atlantic race; both the Americans and French built flying boats with sufficient range, and the Germans even built a landplane, the Focke-Wulf Condor, which in 1938 flew non-stop from Berlin to New York in 25 hours. Later, the Americans introduced the big Boeing 314 flying boat which was able to fly to Lisbon with a refuelling stop in the Azores; the British also bought Boeing 314s, and worked out a route across the Atlantic, via Foynes in Ireland and Gander in Newfoundland, which allowed it to use the extended range 'Empires' to show the flag, accompanied by minimal amounts of mail, on several occasions in 1939 and 1940.

There were also some notable omissions in the Imperials network: the West Indies; West Africa; and, despite substantial British interests there, South America. Services to the West Indies were seen as just too difficult: 'The West Indies present particular difficulties of approach as the Atlantic has first to be spanned.'[34]

An interim solution was found by allowing Pan American rights, but that only facilitated air services between Miami in the United States and Britain's colonies in the Caribbean as part of the airline's extensive Caribbean flying-boat operations. Imperials launched its own flying boat services between Bermuda and New York, but declined to venture further south. Enterprisingly the Dutch, who faced similar challenges with regard to their Caribbean possessions, bought Lockheeds which then remained in the western hemisphere and allowed KLM to develop a network of services linking Curaçao, Aruba and Dutch Guiana to Venezuela, Trinidad and Barbados. It was left to a New Zealander, Lowell Yerex, to establish the first British airline in the West Indies, British West Indian Airways, which started flying between Trinidad, Tobago and Barbados in 1940. As for West Africa, it had been hoped to extend the service from Khartoum through Nigeria to the Gold Coast, Sierra Leone and Gambia, but the service was proving expensive to operate, and would require substantial increase in funding to upgrade it to full Empire Air Mail standards; a shorter, and less expensive, alternative would be to route mail through Lisbon and down the west coast of Africa. That might also meet the third objective, of providing air service to South America, as Gambia was an established departure point for South Atlantic flights by European airlines: the British Post Office paid these airlines handsomely to carry its airmail to South America. But when the government invited tenders for the proposed service to West Africa and South America, none of the contenders for the 'chosen instrument' were deemed acceptable; indeed, only British Airways had any airline operating experience at all, and all the tenders were too high, which is another way of saying that the Treasury was not putting up enough money. British Airways proposed a landplane service as a less expensive alternative to the Shorts flying boats, but even that was 'substantially in excess of the "rockbottom" figure which, according to Air Ministry calculations, would be appropriate for such a service.'[35] So the government had to cut its cloth accordingly, and opted for a reduced service requirement, to Lisbon and Bathurst in Gambia, selecting British Airways as the chosen instrument; South America would be dealt with later. But first the Secretary of State had to have a word with the chairman of British Airways: 'I explained to Mr. Pearson that the selection of British Airways was based on the combined factors of the company's practical experience and their financial position, and that I must have a reasonable assurance that their air activities particularly on the Scandinavian route would not be materially curtailed.' Pearson was more than willing to give such an assurance, but there was just one small matter that the government could help his airline over. 'At the same time he stated very frankly the extent of the losses which the company had made, and said that their Continental position would be difficult unless they could also have an arrangement to carry the German mail to Cologne or Hanover, which would fit in well with their existing services and give them additional revenue.' The Secretary of State then explained to his Cabinet colleagues: 'The earlier intention was that Imperial Airways should carry this mail, but as they state that they cannot make the necessary arrangements before 1938, I think it is clear that we should adopt the alternative of adding this mail to the Scandinavian mail already carried to Hanover by British Airways.'[36] A fine example of wheeling and dealing by British Airways' savvy chairman, who not only got an enhanced European mail contract but further subventions to carry out route proving flights to Lisbon and Bathurst: for its part the government was able to add to its score of impending Imperial and transatlantic destinations.

Both Imperials and British Airways were pioneers, but for all their achievements, somehow, it was still not enough. Britain's prestige, an important issue in its politics, was at stake. Imperials, which did fly British built aircraft, incurred the wrath of its detractors because they were not perceived as modern enough. But British Airways also annoyed them because although it flew the most modern aircraft, they were not built in Britain. Both airlines aroused suspicion because they received government subsidies. As for the railways, which were losing their own money on their investment in air transportation, they received abuse because of their anti-competitive practices. It was a continuing muddle.

The first Armstrong Whitworth Ensign built, G-ADSR entered service with Imperial Airways in October 1938. Designed for the landplane route to India, and commodiously outfitted for twenty-seven passengers, this aircraft was instead used on the short Croydon to Paris Le Bourget route up to the outbreak of war. (*MAP*)

CHAPTER 2

1936 to 1939
Ominous Skies

'During the past year the various problems involved in the planning of our internal routes have been somewhat overshadowed by the magnificence of the Empire and Transatlantic projects.'[1] *Flight's* plaintive comment in its 21 May 1936 issue reminds us that other factions had an interest in the progress of civil aviation, or as seemed to be the case, its setbacks.

> I come to particulars of our own local air routes at home. Those of us who have viewed the advances which have been made in this direction cannot be satisfied with them up to date…Whether the buying up of air services or the assistance given to air communications by the railway companies means that they really intend to put their backs into the work or whether they intend to stifle those companies which are in competition with them, is a matter the development of which we shall await with interest.[2]

Churchill must have been absent from the Chamber, as surely he would have cringed at a fellow Harrovian, Sir Lindsay Everard, expressing himself in a manner 'up with which I will not put.'

Allowing for mergers and take-overs, there were three fewer airlines in 1936 over 1935, less route mileage, and fewer services operated. Certainly the domestic airlines were not making money. They would admit later that load factors were 'considerably less than 50 per cent', in aircraft with six to eight seats; regularity of operation was a challenge; and with no night flying, annual utilisation barely approached 600 hours, about half of what was needed to cover overheads. Peter Masefield blithely states that:

> The private companies (other than Imperial Airways) which operated between 1924 and 1939 flew some 24,600,000 capacity ton-miles and achieved about 8,540,000 revenue-load ton-miles in approximately 265,000 flying hours. They earned a revenue of some £1,722,000 and incurred an expenditure estimated at £3,231,000. Thus their operating costs worked out at some 3s.5d. per c.t.m. and their loss at £1,509,000.[3]

As a senior civil servant after the war at the Ministry of Civil Aviation, he undoubtedly had access to information to which the press and others were not privy, and there is no reason to disbelieve him.

Nor were problems limited to the profit and loss account; railway operating procedures did not always meet the expectations of those gallant gentlemen in their flying machines. Writing about the RAS winter schedule from Croydon to Glasgow via Birmingham and Belfast in 1937, *The Aeroplane's* correspondent noted:

> In the Winter there is one North-bound and one South-bound service a day. The first leaves Airways Terminus, Victoria Station, at 08.45 hours. R.A.S. passengers do not go to Croydon in the Imperial Airways

coach, but in a Daimler, or two, or more if necessary. Weighing in and details of that sort are all done at the Airways Terminus so at Croydon there is only a glance at the tickets and the ushering of passengers to their seats. The good ship *Venus* (a D.H. 86B) was waiting on the apron and within three minutes of getting out of the Daimler the machine and its passengers were air-borne for Birmingham…

At Castle Bromwich (for Birmingham), where we had to land a passenger and, we thought, take two aboard, there was no sign of the expected smart uniform and step-ladder. After a long and by no means patient wait, the Captain took off 35 minutes late, still without having seen the local official. I heard later that the change-over from Summer to Winter services on that day was the main cause of the misunderstanding. The clerk ought to have been there to deal with the load-sheet and the incoming passenger, and the fact that he was not caused rather an upheaval by the very rarity of such incidents.

There is rather a tendency, when things like this happen, for the Railway personnel to accuse the flying people of peculiar ideas on transport matters, and for the crews to complain that railway folk know nothing about flying.[4]

Aside from the lack of liaison over ground handling, just consider the airport connection, by Daimler limousine, and three minute ground to air transfer! Total journey time between London and Glasgow, with all the intermediate stops, was over five hours, including the transfer by road at each end, unlikely to challenge the speed and comfort of the crack railway expresses which made the journey in six and a half hours; and for that reason, the roundabout routing was probably intentional.

But it was clearly time for another review, and another committee, this one under the chairmanship of General Sir Henry Maybury, to make recommendations for the 'promotion of civil aviation in the United Kingdom….The committee is to take into account the requirements of the Post Office for air mails and the relation between aviation and other forms of transport.' General Maybury presented his report 18 months later, in January 1937.[5] The government accepted and indeed acted on its two main recommendations: to pay for air traffic control and radio facilities to facilitate en route flying; and to license airlines on specific routes, as 'it is a pre-requisite that cut-throat competition must be eliminated and that some measure of restriction must be applied to avoid indiscriminate multiplication of services.' (para 125) Although that particularly evocative description was frequently cried in aid by later governments, I believe that in this particular circumstance General Maybury was referring to the methods used by the railway companies. The committee was exercised by the issue of competition with the railways – 'Any state of affairs in which the various parties conducted their enterprises on the principle of the longest purse winning would prove expensive to them and inimical to the future of civil aviation' (para 106) – and the report is laced with references to the need for coordination, and the dangers of anti-competitive behaviour. The report commented naively: 'Any such attempt is perhaps unlikely and certainly we see no signs of it.' (para 31) This, as the railways continued to implement their booking ban. As for competition between airlines, there is no reference to 'cut-throat' competition; rather, the report goes on to say: 'We think that a system of licensing of all regular passenger services should be introduced with a view to ensuring the most effective service to the public, while avoiding uneconomical overlapping. We do not think, however, that such licences should necessarily be exclusive over these routes provided that satisfactory service and co-ordination were secured.' (para 135) Nor did the general think that air travel would necessarily divert demand from other transport modes: 'There is some evidence to show that increased and improved facilities for travel in themselves create fresh custom, which, linked with the growing habit of mobility on the part of the population, may well give a marked impetus to aviation in the years ahead.' (para 89)

The report's most innovative recommendation, one which predated the airline hubs of the later twentieth century, was the Junction Aerodrome System, which would have linked the main cities of

Belfast, Glasgow-Edinburgh, Newcastle, London, Southampton-Portsmouth and Bristol, through a junction airport located somewhere in the Manchester-Liverpool area. No doubt the committee was influenced by the recently inaugurated Associated Motorways, an association of six coach companies which coordinated their long distance services through the coach station at Cheltenham. The report points out that if all the cities had direct connections, the route mileage would amount to over 2,900 miles; using the hub and spoke, mileage would be reduced to 960, and four roundtrips a day would be feasible. Because the war intervened nothing came of the Maybury Junction, and just as the arrival of motorways eventually killed off the Cheltenham coach hub, so the increased range of aircraft would have rendered the relatively short sectors of the hub operation redundant, at least within the United Kingdom. Still, in later years, the Royal Mail developed its own hub and spoke system at Liverpool successfully. Government responsibility for the provision of air traffic services continued until the establishment of the Civil Aviation Authority and the later privatisation of the National Air Traffic Services; despite Maybury's advice to the contrary, the government also took over the ownership and control of a number of airports. On the other hand the government quickly established an air transport licensing authority which would go on to award domestic licences in 1939.

The Maybury report is now largely overlooked – 'Opinion of it deteriorated gradually'[6] – and was overshadowed by the Cadman report, which was to have much more serious consequences for British aviation, and which came out only a year later. The government's apparent indifference to the Maybury report may well have been because it had other things on its mind in those dark pre-war years, but there was a general irritability about Britain's lack of progress and muddle in civil aviation, and as a topic it would not go away. One should not be unduly influenced by the outspoken views of C. G. Gray, editor of *The Aeroplane*, but some of his criticisms were to the point. Here he is on moral hazard:

> The fact that the government has a big shareholding in Imperial Airways and has guaranteed subsidies to British Airways naturally makes the proposition more tempting to a financier, because he knows that whatever happens the Government dare not let down an air-transport company which it has agreed to subsidise and in which it has a capital investment.

On the influence of the railways:

> Many of us are naturally anxious when we saw the railways beginning to dabble in air transport, because it suggested that railways would either try to kill air competition by cutting prices, or that with their vast financial resources they would collar existing air lines and make them so inefficient, not necessarily purposely, but possibly through congenital idiocy, that the progress of air transport would be held up.[7]

So much for the golden age of railways. His colleague, F. D. Bradbrooke, was just as damning:

> The situation in flying equipment is dismal…The accessories to modern transport flying have shown no striking advance, at least on this side of the Atlantic…The airport front is not cheering in retrospect or prospect. Gatwick, which started auspiciously the previous year, got wet last year, with serious effects on its prospects… To top off a year in which Britain seemed determined to surpass itself in muddling every possible airport prospect.[8]

This was more than just grumbling, and it was all too much for one MP, Robert Perkins, who launched a sensational and devastating attack on the government and its civil aviation policy in a speech in the

House of Commons on 17 November 1937, dramatically declaiming that he was asking 'the House to-day to give me the head of the Secretary of State for Air in a charger.'[9] Some of Perkins's accusations were serious enough, at least to a later audience, involving issues of pilot fatigue, competition, and a very British distrust of subsidies. Perkins, who represented the newly formed Air Line Pilots Association, claimed that its members were unjustly discriminated against by Imperial Airways, a crusade he took up with gusto. He also highlighted one aspect of flight safety, sleep deprivation:

> We are also opposing them on certain abuses which are becoming very common. There was an air liner called the "Hanno" which forced-landed somewhere near Bahrein some time ago. I have good reason for suspecting that the pilot had flown all night and in fact had been employed continuously for 18 hours on end without sleep. I am also informed that this is quite a normal occurrence for pilots east of Cairo.

Imperial Airways received a prolonged tongue lashing over, amongst others, its dividends, its directors' pay, its pilots' pay, its safety record, its aircraft, and the problems of winter flying. He also disliked the apparent anomaly of two subsidised British airlines competing against each other on the Paris route, even though he acknowledged neither airline received a subsidy for that particular route; and for good measure he raised the railways' booking ban.

The pundits tended to be dismissive of his speech: 'These sensational accusations owed more to their presentation by Mr. Robert Perkins, MP, than to their fundamental seriousness.'[10] Labour MP Frederick Montague was more balanced:

> I cannot help feeling that the hon. Members who moved and seconded the Amendment took a great amount of time on somewhat irrelevant matters. That is a pity, because the questions that have been raised are of a very serious description. I agree with one speaker that the speech of the hon. Member for Stroud (Mr. Perkins) was a masterpiece. I could not help being intrigued by the hon. Member's suggestion that conditions in civil aviation in this country are of such a character as to make him, a Conservative—there is no doubt about his political and economic convictions—feel favourable to the idea of nationalisation of air transport services. If conditions are as serious as he said, I think a case has definitely been made out for an inquiry into the present position.[11]

The consequences of the debate were serious. The government conceded a departmental inquiry, a victory of sorts for Perkins and a pleasing reminder of the virtues of parliamentary democracy, and promised the results would be published – 'If that is not actually the head of the Secretary of State on a charger, I hope the hon. Member for Stroud will be satisfied that it is the scalp.' Lord Cadman, a former chairman of Anglo-Persian Oil, was appointed to lead it. Though unintended, the debate allowed another issue, the nationalisation of privately owned firms, to crawl out of the woodwork. Frederick Montague, again:

> Speaking personally and also for the party I represent, I believe the case for nationalisation of air transport services is overwhelming, and that case has been abundantly supported by the two speeches which began the Debate. The amount of confusion and the quantity of material that have been presented, suggesting that things are not all that they ought to be in regard to air services, and particularly that long list of competing air companies, with their own problems and difficulties, together with the difficulties between themselves, suggest that the time has come, indeed it came long ago, for air transport to be regarded as a public service. That is important from the point of view of what has been said about monopoly. There must be monopoly in

the air; you cannot help it. Even if you try to destroy that monopoly it remains monopolist in character, and because of that and the fact that the air is a service of the character that it is, without boundaries, without any question of private property in the air—all these things make out a case for a public air service.[12]

Unlike General Maybury, who took his time over releasing his report, Lord Cadman acted quickly: much too quickly. His hasty report blighted British civil aviation for decades; indeed, the damage he did continued up until the Edwards Report of 1969, over thirty years later. Having only been appointed on 30 November 1937, the government published the report, and its own comments on it, on 8 March 1938.[13] It is important for a proper understanding of the Cadman Report to realise that it concerned itself almost exclusively with air services within Europe, never Imperials' strongest suit, but one that was nevertheless being addressed through the development of British Airways:

> The report of the Cadman Committee deals mainly with the Continental services of Imperial Airways, and that is possibly unfortunate, because, as has been stated in this House to-day, probably 90 per cent. of Imperial Airways' flying time is done on the Empire services.[14]

Empire routes, Imperials' raison d'être, are only mentioned in passing. Domestic services also get short shrift. Referring to the Maybury Report, the Cadman Report comments bleakly: 'The picture remains virtually as black as they painted it.' (para 8)

In Europe, everything seemed to be a problem. Cadman promoted the wretched muddle over aircraft design, manufacture and operation, as well as the bizarre consanguinity of military and civil aviation:

> Aircraft operation and construction seem in the past to have been treated as separate and distinct questions, not as related elements of a single problem. (para 16)

> In our view the problem of the air is one—two sides of a single coin—and the military aspect of aviation cannot fundamentally be separated from the civil aspect. (para 19)

> The restoration of British prestige in civil aviation and the promotion of the aircraft industry are among the prime reasons for subsidising air services in Europe. (para 60)

Clearly much more money was going to be needed, as prestige and support of the aircraft manufacturing industry were inherently more expensive than the commercial operation of airliners:

> We emphasise that British civil aviation cannot compete with subsidised foreign aviation unless it is comparably subsidised. (para 35)

> We feel that, if our national prestige is to be maintained, our external air services must be concentrated in a small number of well-founded and substantial organisations, rather than dissipated among a large number of competing companies of indifferent stability. Subsidised foreign lines will provide all the competition necessary to stimulate improvement in services and equipment. (para 36)

> We consider that the same external route should not be operated by more than one British company, and that, as recommended by the Maybury Committee in the case of internal air services, some measure of restriction should be applied to avoid indiscriminate competition. (para 37)

Awkwardness over the London–Paris route, a bone of contention with Perkins who claimed that two subsidised companies were competing with each other, was overcome by this clumsy formula: London–Paris should be 'amalgamated under a single company with pro-rata shareholding....[to] avoid the position which invoked justifiable comment in the debate, that two subsidised companies were operating the same route.' (para 41) One idly wonders, if followed logically to its absurd conclusion, would there not have been a host of different joint venture companies operating between each city pair in Europe? Apparently not: the committee agreed that British Airways, suitably beefed up, should operate European services, but then could not agree to Imperial Airways divesting itself of its existing European operations, so the flying boat services to France, Italy and Greece remained. Not that it mattered: 'We conceive this Company (British Airways) as a counterpart to Imperial Airways in carrying out British civil aviation policy, and there must be close co-operation between the two companies.' (para 48) Other airlines, including those already operating international services such as Allied Airways (Gandar Dower) and North Eastern, did not get a mention in the Report, possibly because the Committee was unaware of their existence, more probably because the Air Ministry wanted it that way: 'The internal airline companies have never been invited to attend any conferences, or to meet Air Ministry officials to investigate how their organisations can be used for the benefit and progress of British Civil Aviation'[15] complained Lord Grimthorpe, Chairman of North Eastern.

Cadman is proud to point out the differences between his approach and that of the Hambling Committee of 1923, quoting Hambling:

> In the first place, we desire to make it clear that we do not recommend the creation of a Corporation or Company administered under Government control, but of a commercial organisation run entirely on business lines with a privileged position with regard to air transport subsidies, on terms and conditions to be defined later ... The Government should not exercise any direct control over the activities of the Company, other than by the appointment of Directors, except for the purpose of such checking as may be necessary to determine the amount of subsidy payable and except for such control as may from time to time be exercised by the Government through the Civil Aviation Department over all civil flying in the country.

Cadman remarks frostily: 'These recommendations were adopted, and have, we understand, governed the relations between the Department and the Company since its inception.' (para 44) The Air Ministry came in for some criticism – 'There must be much more virility in the initiation of policy and in forward planning.' (para 21) – but it is debatable if Cadman condemned 'the Air Ministry in the strongest possible terms for its mis-management of air transport', as claimed in *Air Transport & Civil Aviation 1944-1945*. For all the bluster, Cadman's recommendations did not go much beyond shuffling people around in the Air Ministry, and increasing the amount of subsidy. But he did go on to batter Imperial Airways, whilst grudgingly acknowledging that it met its prime goal with 'considerable efficiency':

> Although the carriage of air passengers in safety and comfort, and the conveyance of mails and freight, have been achieved by Imperial Airways with considerable efficiency, we cannot avoid the conclusion that the management of Imperial Airways has been defective in other respects. In particular, not only has it failed to co-operate fully with the Air Ministry, but it has been intolerant of suggestion and unyielding in negotiation. Internally its attitude in staff matters has left much to be desired. (para 46)

And there was worse. Fingers were pointed, names named, there were recommendations for dismissal:

It appears to us that the Managing Director of the Company—presumably with the acquiescence of the Board—has taken a commercial view of his responsibilities that was too narrow, and has failed to give to the Government Departments with which he has been concerned the co-operation we should have expected from a Company heavily subsidised and having such important international and Imperial contacts.

There should, in our opinion, be an immediate improvement in these respects, and this may well involve some change in directing personnel. (para 46)

Other matters, like the question of icing, blind landing equipment, Imperials' safety record, and more familiar topics, like the railways and the booking ban, were dealt with summarily and compliantly. There are, however, some excellent appendices which offer an authoritative historical review and much statistical information.

'We have, in fact, accepted practically everything of importance in the report,'[16] claimed the Prime Minister, Neville Chamberlain, but for all that, the report's main recommendations were never fully implemented; and then the war intervened. The government duly shuffled departments around, and Chamberlain dispensed with the services of the Secretary of State for Air, Viscount Swinton, admitting: 'I think my Noble Friend has, perhaps, suffered from the fact that he is not here to defend himself.'[17] The annual subsidy was doubled, to £3 million, albeit with significant strings attached. There were changes at the top at Imperial Airways, and the general manager, George Woods Humphery, was sacked. British Airways was able to launch more services to European points, using American-built aircraft, but plans to fly to South America never got further than proving flights to Lisbon, and a single survey flight to Bathurst in British Gambia. The question of dividends became moot when the government took over the two airlines. The suggestions about the aircraft manufacturing industry and the role it had to play remained little more than that, and it was to be two decades before the government of the day agreed a formula to provide launch aid for civil aircraft projects.

But the consequences of the report were much more serious and far-reaching. It changed the nature of government participation, from hands-off to hands-on. Gone was the breezy self–assurance of Churchill's advice: 'The first thing the Government have got to do is to get out of the way.' From now on, government bureaucrats would involve themselves in the minutest detail of airline operations, from choosing the aircraft to deciding which routes they would fly. The Imperial model would be discarded. What did that mean? Imperials was a commercial organisation, driven by the need to make profits and pay dividends. It was commercial in its outlook, careful in its investment. The airline could place substantial aircraft orders when needed, the Shorts Empire flying boats being a case in point, but at other times was let down by the British manufacturers, some of whom were not really up to the task. The Armstrong Whitworth Ensign, which was ordered at the same time as the Empire flying boats and was an important element in the airline's modernisation plans, was delivered late, overweight, and seriously underpowered; not until it was fitted with American engines did this aircraft begin to deliver on the promise of its original design, by which time it was outdated. The Handley Page HP.42s, with their unblemished safety record on European routes, were old-fashioned, but their quaint appearance did not seem to prevent Imperials from gaining the major share of the London to Paris market. C. H. Barnes commends their attributes: 'Each of these eight gentle giants had logged over 12,000 hours at a fraction of the operating cost of their successors and contemporary rivals.'[18] Of far greater significance is that this was achieved profitably; the cost to the taxpayer, through the mail and other subsidies, was significantly lower than those of its other European counterparts, especially the French and German airlines. No European airline could match the standards set by KLM, but given the inherent muddle in the British way of doing things, a hard-nosed commercial approach to making money by flying airliners is a good second best. It also seems to reflect Britain's mercantilist approach to doing business; before the war most people did not even know how to pronounce bureaucracy, let alone spell it.

Now that was to change: there was to be a new Fashion. Condemned by Cadman's harsh criticism, Imperials' approach was to be ground-looped. The pursuit of British prestige was the new goal, money was to be thrown at the 'problem', aircraft manufacturers would be told to build bigger and better planes, and so on. The analogy with public utilities was carried through by Cadman, who thought that Imperials' dividends should be on a par with those of other utilities, rather than reflect the much greater risk of pioneering world-wide air services. For the next forty years, Britain's chosen instruments, the eventual successors to Imperial Airways, would be hosed down with money: yet to little effect. And the issue did not end there: the requirement for ever closer cooperation between Imperials and British Airways, as well as the views already expressed by Labour members of Parliament during the debates, set the government to considering the future status of the two airlines.

The Cadman Report was debated briefly, on 16 March 1938, continuing on 28 March. Robert Perkins received many plaudits for having successfully brought his concerns to the House. The Prime Minister introduced the debate, but had little of substance to say: 'We sincerely wish to see British prestige in civil aviation raised to the highest point that is conceivable.' Clement Attlee, in opposition, explained his party's priorities: 'It is much more important that we should have a great civil aircraft industry in this country than that we should have a profit-making concern running for private profit.'[19] Lest it should be thought that it was currently accepted wisdom that commercial organisations should not be run for profit, a concept that seemed to disgust the Labour Party, at least one MP, Major Hills, had the decency to defend Imperial Airways' approach to business:

> At any rate, the committee accuse Imperial Airways of taking a too commercial view. I would remind the House that Imperial Airways were told to take that view by the Hambling Committee, which called for a commercial organisation run entirely on business lines. Moreover, if hon. Members will turn to paragraph 6 of the Preface to the Cadman Committee's Report, they will see that it is stated that: The aim was to help civil aviation to become self-supporting, so that in the course of time it might 'fly by itself.' Imperial Airways were directed so to organise their business and so to forecast their operations that at some future date the service might 'fly by itself.' That entailed certain grave disadvantages. It entailed a descending scale of subsidies, it entailed strict economy of management, and, above all, it necessitated a different view from that held by some hon. Members, who want a service that is run independently of commercial possibilities. These facts cut through a good deal of the criticism in the report, and I think it is wrong to blame the company in this respect. They were told to do certain things, and now that the Government have changed their mind, it is rather hard if it is said to the company, 'Why did you not act in the way we now want you to act 14 years ago?' …With regard to the charge that Imperial Airways' machines are obsolete, four years ago an order was placed for new machines, the first delivery to be in September, 1936, but not one machine has been received up to date. That is true, but although many of the machines are obsolete, the company run a service which is a very safe one and a popular one, and the committee say that they are not dissatisfied with the proportion of cross-Channel traffic carried by Imperial Airways.[20]

The government now had to consider how to implement the Cadman Report. Firing Woods Humphery was the easy part, but now it had to find his replacement, and a full-time chairman, as well as concoct the strange London–Paris joint-venture airline. Parliament was asked to approve the doubling of the subsidy, to £3 million a year. The government also made it clear that although only the two chosen instruments would benefit from subsidies on international routes, it would pledge to divert £100,000 of the extra subsidies to support internal air services, contrary to Cadman's advice.

Most of that money would go to the railway owned companies, strange reward for their bad behaviour. For the controversy over the railway booking ban still rumbled on. The matter had been taken up robustly by Colonel Moore-Brabazon during the 'Perkins' debate of 17 November 1937; he had seconded Perkins' 'head in a charger' motion. Moore-Brabazon, a noted sportsman, related the plight of North Eastern Airways, an airline at the time gamely trying to fly between Croydon, Doncaster, Yeadon, Newcastle and Perth:

This question of not being allowed booking facilities still exists, and I want to bring to the notice of the House the question of North Eastern Airways, a recognised company which has been admitted to membership of the International Air Traffic Association as conforming in all respects to the international code, and members of the International Association, in fact recognised as on a par with Imperial Airways, British Airways, and other national air lines. I know nothing about it. I do not know any of the directors, except Lord Grimthorpe, and I only know him because he has always been a rival of mine, in riding the Cresta. This company appointed a firm in Perth, called Central Garages, to sell their tickets. They started very well, because they were well situated and conducted their business well and with people who might well use air services. All went well, and then North Eastern Airways received this letter: We regret to have to inform you that we have been informed by Messrs. W. Alexander and Sons, of Falkirk (a firm that runs motor coach tours) that, owing to an agreement which they have with the railway companies, we cannot be allowed to continue as agents for them as well as to be agents for you. They have asked us either to relinquish the agencies with the airways companies or relinquish our agency with them. Seeing that for the moment Messrs. Alexander's agency is more worth while for us, it would appear that we shall have to relinquish the agency you were good enough to give us.

Consequently they have to give up selling tickets for North Eastern Airways. It would not be so bad if this was just competition, but it is not, because there is no air service operating on the East Coast of England, and consequently it is pure restraint of trade. It cannot do any good to anybody at all, and when the Government permit this sort of thing, soon pilots will be refused licences because they do not fly on approved routes. The Government have encouraged local authorities to build aerodromes, but how could they justify them putting down these aerodromes when at the same time they allow this kind of thing to go on? I think that sort of difficulty calls for an inquiry. If that sort of thing is going to be allowed, it is obvious that the state of civil aviation, anyhow in this country, is far from happy. We also have to remember that the Maybury Committee's recommendation has been with us now for a long time. They themselves suggested that there should be a licensing authority set up to co-ordinate and organise internal air lines, but if the Government do not hurry up, there will be no internal air lines at all except those run by the railway companies, and I think that will be a great pity.[21]

North Eastern Airways received further attention later in the debate, from Geoffrey Mander, a Liberal MP:

A good deal has been said about the difficulties of booking. This is a very serious handicap. Here is one example. Of the services that are run from this country in the summer to Le Zoute in Belgium, one is run by North Eastern Airways with no subsidy and no booking facilities, and the other is run by Imperial Airways, with subsidy and booking facilities, but not by British machines but by the Belgian Sabena Company, which is put in front of North Eastern Airways and given preferential treatment against this British company, flying British machines with British pilots.

But not only did the railway companies refuse to lift the booking ban, they defended it vigorously. In a letter to *The Times*,[22] Sir Josiah Stamp saw the ban as legitimate commercial practice, asserting that the national interest was not served by duplication on routes which, he claimed, provided scarcely traffic enough for one company. This opinion was contrary to the Maybury Committee's findings, but the powerful chairman of the LMS railway clearly understood that he could interpret the 'national interest' his way. Even after the railways had lifted the booking ban on North Eastern in 1938, Perkins was less than enthusiastic:

> First of all, there is the question of this booking ban imposed by the railway companies on various services. I heard the Under-Secretary's answer, but I am not satisfied with the position as it now is. He based his case solely on the fact that progress is now being made, that we are getting along slowly but surely, and that the ban on North-Eastern Airways has been lifted. I remember when this matter was first raised on the Floor of this House nearly three years ago, and during the last three years we have had promise after promise from various Under-Secretaries and various Ministers that something would be done, but at the end of three years the Under-Secretary has announced to the House that the booking ban on one company has been raised. But there are five others, and if we are to proceed at this steady rate of progress, it will be 15 years before the last booking ban has been raised. I, for one, am not satisfied with that, and I intend to go on to the best of my ability embarrassing the railway companies by every method in my power until the matter is put right.[23]

His colleague, Colonel Ropner, was more effective, managing to squeeze in a threat as the debate on 28 March 1938 was ending:

> I do not want to delay the House for more than two minutes, but I want to make a suggestion which I feel will be supported by hon. Members. If the Government are not prepared to act in connection with the ban which railway companies make on the booking of tickets for air travel, then private Members in this House might take action. From time to time the railway companies promote private Bills in this House. While I understand that it would be beyond the Rules of Order for hon. Members to give reasons why they vote against those Bills, it is possible for us to vote against them in the Lobbies. I hope that hon. Members will combine and vote against them in this House until the ban is removed.

The threat worked. With the inauguration of the licensing process for domestic routes, and following continued questioning over progress in the House of Commons, the Under Secretary of State was finally able to confirm on 14 December 1938, in response to yet another question from Perkins: 'Booking facilities at railway agencies are now available for all existing air services.'[24]

But if one dragon had been slain, another was emerging from its lair. C. G. Grey would refer to the beast as the BOA Constrictor, but it was better known as BOAC, British Overseas Airways Corporation. All those noises about nationalisation, especially from the Labour front benches, had at first produced some vigorous denials. 'The proper function of the Government is not to own or manage the air services but to make regulations in the interest of the safety of those who use those services,' was the view of Major Procter in the debate of 18 May 1938. Captain Balfour, a flying ace in the Great War, a former director of Whitehall Securities and British Airways, who was now the new Under Secretary of State had to agree:

In the first place, the Government have decided that private enterprise, controlled and limited by Statute, shall be the principle of the development of civil aviation during the period in which the present agreements are to run. I think the case for nationalisation depends on the view taken of the functions of Government. It may be said that Imperial Airways, which is, in essence, a public utility company, controlled by contracts with the Government, in consideration of the subsidies granted to it, is in a better position to function successfully in the commercial world than a Government Department under the present form of Constitutional control, by Treasury and Parliament...But we have to decide on a policy now, and the policy of the control of private enterprise, with profits limited by Statute, is, I am sure, the soundest course for us to follow at the present time.[25]

The 'present time' was to be embarrassingly short. Just over six months later, the government performed a complete about-turn, when the Secretary of State for Air, Sir Kingsley Wood, had to announce on 11 November:

[In] the light of the opinions expressed by the Cadman Committee that dividends of subsidised air transport companies should be restricted to public utility rates and of the Government agreement in principle that public money should not be used for raising dividends to undue levels, it appears desirable to take steps to ensure that the large additional capital needed for development should be raised on terms which would not prove unduly expensive to the Exchequer. The rapid expansion of overseas services coupled with the great technical advances which are being made in this sphere moreover call under present circumstances for the pooling of resources and the strengthening of administrative and operating organisations to the fullest possible extent.

In these circumstances the Government are of opinion that the most satisfactory instrument for the development of overseas civil aviation would be provided by the association of the two chosen instruments—Imperial Airways, Limited, and British Airways, Limited—in a single public corporation. The Government, therefore, propose to recommend to Parliament legislation setting up a Public Corporation which will acquire the existing undertakings of Imperial Airways and British Airways....It is proposed that the new Public Corporation should obtain the funds for the purchase of the two existing undertakings and for its further capital requirements by the issue of fixed interest stocks guaranteed by the Government.[26]

So what happened to cause civil aviation to veer off in yet another direction? Why yet another new Fashion? In a word: Reith. A friend of Woods Humphery, Sir John Reith was persuaded to take over the chairmanship of Imperial Airways after the Cadman affair. It was not a position he sought, but the government could offer few other candidates to the board and shareholders of Imperial Airways. And Reith was inclined to favour state ownership. Nervous about boardroom politics in the newly established British Broadcasting Company, of which he was managing director, he encouraged the government to nationalise it, and became the first director general of the British Broadcasting Corporation (BBC). Reith had wanted to retain the chairmanship of the BBC, but Cadman, who appeared to misunderstand the role of chairman in a company – he maintained the chairman should 'personally control the management of the company' – had insisted that the new chairman of Imperials be a full time appointment, so Reith had to relinquish the BBC. Reith brought with him his preference for public ownership, demanding a restructuring of the two main airlines and their take-over by the state. Nationalisation had worked well for him at the BBC, and during his long incumbency there he had successfully set limits for government interference. He saw no reason why the same formula could not work for Britain's airlines. In retrospect he would have found it difficult to achieve the same measure of financial independence with BOAC that the BBC's licensing fees had allowed him with the latter corporation, but at least one wily BOAC chairman successfully coerced the government into paying its bills while remaining independent and aloof, and Reith certainly had the experience and know-how to do it.

He was pushing on an open door. Stung by the criticism it had received over the granting of subsidies to a publicly traded company, the government was inclined to roll up the issue by nationalising Imperial Airways and, as a fall-out from the absurd Cadman joint-venture proposal on the London–Paris route, British Airways too. Negotiations on the London–Paris project gave Reith the excuse to demand its expansion into full amalgamation of the two airlines under government ownership. Britain had given itself a fright over the Sudetenland Crisis in 1938; the realisation had dawned that war with Germany was by no means avoidable, and rearmament became a priority. At that time the Royal Air Force had little in the way of a transport organisation, and the government realised it would need to call on the resources of the airline companies to maintain most of the military's air transport functions.

The domestic airlines, meanwhile, also had to face a brave new world. The recommendations of the Maybury Committee for establishing an Air Transport Licensing Authority were implemented, and by late 1938 the first applications for route licences had been heard. As the railway companies controlled so much of domestic flying, instances of competition were rare, but the usual suspects, like Allied Airways (Gandar Dower) and North Eastern, could be relied on to buck the trend. A complicating factor, especially in Scotland, was ownership and operation of the airports. Allied Airways (Gandar Dower) owned and operated Dyce at Aberdeen, and was not prepared to allow a competitor to use it; Scottish Airways operated Sumburgh in the Shetland Islands, the only really usable bit of flat land in that rocky landscape, and was annoyed when it was forced to share it, and the Orkney–Shetland route, with Allied Airways (Gandar Dower), a curious case of competition on one of the routes least able to sustain it. The Authority granted forty-seven licences all told, to fourteen airlines. The pioneers were rewarded with seven-year licences for their original routes, all of which involve water crossings:

- Allied Airways (Gandar Dower), between Thurso and Stromness (Orkney);

- Great Western and Southern (jointly owned by Olley and the railway companies), between (1) London and the Isle of Wight, and (2) Penzance and the Isles of Scilly;

- Isle of Man Air Services (jointly owned by Olley, the railway companies and Isle of Man Steam Packet), between Isle of Man, Blackpool, Liverpool and Manchester;

- Jersey Airways (now owned by the railway companies and Whitehall Securities), between Jersey, Southampton, Portsmouth and London;

- Lundy and Atlantic Coasts Air Lines, between Barnstaple and Lundy Island;

- Portsmouth, Southsea & Isle of Wight Aviation, between Portsmouth and the Isle of Wight;

- Scottish Airways (jointly owned by British Airways, LMS and David McBrayne), between (1) Kirkwall and Wick, and (2) within the Orkney Islands;

- Western Airways, between Weston and Cardiff;

- Western Isles Airways (a subsidiary of Scottish Airways), between (1) Glasgow and the inner Hebrides, and (2) Glasgow and the outer Hebrides.

Notably absent from the list are the main trunk routes of Railway Air Services, and indeed both it and North Eastern were only granted short-term licences as the two airlines began to negotiate on longer term cooperation – now that North Eastern enjoyed some legitimacy – planning to resubmit amended and mutually acceptable applications; if you can't beat them, join them. RAS solved the problem by buying the goodwill of North Eastern, which was grounded at the outbreak of war. Not listed, because it only flew international services to Dublin in Ireland, was West Coast Air Services, another joint venture between Olley and the railway companies.

The impending war provided a grim backcloth to the more optimistic attitudes now prevailing. The airlines introduced new and better aircraft into service, and even the lowly internal airlines started to receive some modest subsidy. Imperial Airways now flew the DH.91 Albatross as well as the Ensign on its services to Paris, and both it and British Airways ordered promising new long-range designs from British manufacturers, respectively Short Brothers and Fairey. Jersey Airways used the first of a new de Havilland design, the DH.95 Flamingo, an all-metal twin engine seventeen-seat airliner, during the summer of 1939, and the type was also ordered by Captain Olley. Meanwhile the men from the Ministry had to consider how best to utilise the resources available in the event of war, and so they drew up elaborate, and on the whole effective, plans to disperse the airline fleets away from the obvious targets of London's various airports, and to use the fleets of airliners in support of the military. The charter airlines were already flying army cooperation sorties and were used as 'targets' to train the army's searchlight operators at night: ominous skies, indeed.

Civil aviation continued to fascinate the members of the House of Commons. The next item on their agenda was the forthcoming nationalisation of Imperials and British Airways, with MPs exercised over the compensation to be paid to their respective shareholders; Imperials' were to receive 32s 9d per £1 share, whereas British Airways' were offered a measly 15s 9d for their £1 shares. British Airways was happy enough with its offer, as the government also undertook to repay the £311,000 that the shareholders had advanced to British Airways, but it allowed Perkins one more opportunity to excoriate Imperial Airways, the airline he had done so much to destroy, as he happily kicked it about after it was down during the debate on the establishment of British Overseas Airways on 10 July 1939:

> There is this very thorny question of the price of the shares. It seems absolutely monstrous that one company, which has been controlled in the past by an incompetent board of directors, un-progressive, lacking in imagination and initiative, a company which has been receiving large subsidies, far larger subsidies than this House realises, because many of them have been concealed subsidies, and when out of those subsidies the company has paid dividends as high as 9 per cent; when it has equipped its services with obsolete machines and obsolete equipment and has succeeded in bringing British prestige in Europe down to zero, such a company is to get 32s 6d. The other company has had a live board of directors, progressive, full of initiative, full of imagination, receiving little or no subsidies until the last two years, equipping its fleet with modern machines and equipment, and it has succeeded in upholding British prestige in Europe. It is to get only 15s 9d. Surely it is obvious to anyone that such a differentiation is unfair and indefensible.[27]

The Secretary of State, meanwhile, continued his steady retreat from the line that the Hambling Committee had drawn sixteen years previously as he outlined the new corporation's goals in the debate, which emphasised other matters rather than profit:

To secure the fullest development consistent with economy of efficient overseas air transport services. A much wider interpretation of its objects than that, for instance, which is given to Imperial Airways, which is: 'To use its best endeavours to make its service self-supporting at the earliest possible moment.' I suggest that with increased funds and always with the aim before it of securing the fullest development of air transport, there is little doubt that the corporation can secure important advances in civil aviation, and at the same time provide reasonable charges to the public. I have observed what I suggest has been legitimate criticism of past policy. We have, perhaps of necessity, put the emphasis on cheap flying rather than on real aeronautical progress.[28]

Colonel Moore-Brabazon's comments were more fey:

There are one or two things which I should like to say about this Bill. My first point is the dreadful name which has been given to it. I know that a rose will smell as sweet by any other name, but the Government need not have saddled the corporation with the name of a serpent. B.O.A. is really too much —a boa constrictor corporation. Really, initials do mean a lot in these days. My right hon. Friend set up an important committee which is now known as the C.A.D. Committee. Initials do count for something…To me, this is a day of regret and also a day of great pleasure. I feel relieved that from now on we shall see that thing happening for which I have been hoping all my life, the divergence between military aviation and civil aviation. The Government, the House of Commons and the country have hitherto always looked upon civil aviation in the same way as a cow looks at a passing train — 'very wonderful, but nothing to do with us.' … I hate the word 'prestige,' but I like to bring it in, for the reason that every English aircraft which travels from one side of the world to the other is a little bit of England. England will be judged by that little bit by those for whom that is the only thing they know of England. Wherever they go, English aircraft must be the best and the finest in the world.[29]

One MP, Sir Hugh Seely, questioned the cure, the panacea: 'I was staggered at this idea, which is now put forward on behalf of the Government, that everything is right when you get nationalisation. Personally, I do not believe in it.' The debate ended with Perkins rounding on another favourite target, the railway companies:

Then there is the question of the very near future of civil aviation at home. At the moment, I believe the greatest enemy civil aviation has got is the railway companies in this country. The House will remember how those companies did everything they could, with the railway booking ban, to drive people to the railways, and prevent them from flying. When the House decided that that must stop, they changed their tactics. They adopted a much cleverer course of trying to buy up all the internal air lines and slowly strangling them. I have here the timetable of railway air services to Glasgow. There are two services a day. I imagine that the more convenient is in the afternoon. This leaves Victoria at 2.45, and, after three stops, arrives in Glasgow at 8.30. That is practically six hours traveling —roughly the same time as a train. Those are the internal air lines run by the London Midland and Scottish Railway. The railways are out, by any method, fair or foul, to strangle aviation in this country.[30]

The British Overseas Airways Act, 1939, to nationalise Imperials and British Airways, received the Royal Assent on 4 August 1939, but that did not prevent the latter from placing an order for nine Douglas DC-5s on 30 August 1939, 'after comparative analyses of the potential of the de Havilland (DH.95) Flamingo and the DC-5 on the London–Berlin route had been prepared during the spring of

1939.'[31] By that time the two airlines were coordinating their operations, and British Airways was flying services for Imperial Airways. The Paris services were under Imperials' direction, and talks to pool the services with those of Air France were at an advanced stage. Imperials' route to Brussels and Frankfurt were handed over to British Airways, and even though Imperials resumed service to Switzerland in April, many of these flights were flown by the Lockheeds of British Airways. Robin Higham points out:

> The war…caught Britain's overseas airlines in a critical transitional period. Imperial Airways had never really caught its breath since 1934. The new landplanes had not been delivered in time, and of these, the Ensigns were not fully serviceable in 1939, when they were already three years late. British Airways was operating almost exclusively with American aircraft while new British aircraft on order were only just coming off the stocks, or were still on the drawing-boards.[32]

However beguiling the future prospect of the new corporation may have seemed, the reality was six years as a surrogate transport service for the Royal Air Force; the new found optimism that had prevailed throughout the civil airline and aircraft manufacturing industry expired the day after British Airways' order for the Douglas DC-5 was signed, when Germany invaded Poland.

On 3 September the Prime Minister announced that the country was at war with Germany. During the short parliamentary session that followed the statement, Chamberlain was in anguish: 'Everything that I have worked for, everything that I have hoped for, everything that I have believed in during my public life, has crashed into ruins.' His despair is in marked contrast to the resolution of the man who would succeed him, Churchill:

> We are fighting to save the whole world from the pestilence of Nazi tyranny and in defence of all that is most sacred to man. This is no war for domination or imperial aggrandisement or material gain; no war to shut any country out of its sunlight and means of progress. It is a war, viewed in its inherent quality, to establish, on impregnable rocks, the rights of the individual, and it is a war to establish and revive the stature of man.[33]

Five Avro Yorks were allocated to BOAC during the War. G-AGJA shows its hybrid civilian markings imposed on the camouflage colours. (*MAP*)

CHAPTER 3

1939 to 1945
Civilians in Wartime

I wish I could say more about civil aviation. I have been very disappointed that the war has meant such a blow to the plans which we had made so carefully during the last few months before war broke out. It has been a tremendous disappointment to me and to members of my Department, but, anxious as I am about what the position may be at the end of the war, I do feel that it is my duty to put first things first and to put every ounce that we can into our military effort. After all, everything depends upon that, for if that goes civil aviation and everything else goes too.[1]

In the days immediately following Chamberlain's declaration of war, domestic air services were suspended, as were international flights. Imperials' and British Airways' aircraft were moved to Whitchurch, near Bristol, the flying boats transferred to Poole. But internal 'cross-water' services, in Scotland, to the Channel Islands, the Isle of Man and the Scillies were soon resumed, as were European flights from neutral states, Belgium, Denmark and Holland, and the Paris flights of Air France. Because Croydon was now given over to the RAF, these services used Shoreham on the south coast. The government suspended the Empire Air Mail Scheme, but Imperials continued to operate its Southern and Eastern routes, and also completed a successful weekly operation of eight flights between Southampton and New York in August and September, refuelled in flight by converted Harrow bombers based at Shannon in Ireland and Botwood in Newfoundland. Imperial Airways passed into history on 1 April 1940 when BOAC was vested; the British Airways name was revived in the 1970s. The government also revoked the recently awarded domestic licences and, as the RAF lacked transport aircraft in Britain, all the remaining airlines were gathered up into the National Air Communications scheme to fly at the government's direction, mainly helping move RAF squadrons to France.

BOAC entered a hostile new world without the guidance of Sir John Reith, who joined the War Cabinet as Minister of Information in January 1940, and without the benefit of the top echelons of Imperials' former managers either. Reith's replacement was the Hon. Clive Pearson, who was joined on the board by Gerard d'Erlanger; they were both from the British Airways camp, as was Major McCrindle, the new Deputy Director-General in charge of western routes. Operations were complicated. After Italy's entry into the war, and following the fall of France, BOAC's operations were dispersed; the maintenance function was transferred to Durban in South Africa, and another major base was established at Cairo. Flying boat services within the Empire and Commonwealth continued in the southern hemisphere, starting in Durban and progressing to Egypt and the Middle East, through India and Malaya to Australia and New Zealand, the so-called Horseshoe Route. Air connections across Africa and within the Middle East, where Britain had extensive economic and political interests to defend, became extremely important; BOAC deployed a fleet of Lockheeds on the routes linking the Gold Coast and Nigeria in West Africa with Khartoum in the Sudan, and onwards to Cairo. From Cairo, with the help of Egyptian airline Misrair, landplane services supplemented the Horseshoe Route, flying to Turkey, Teheran, Aden and Asmara (another important engineering base). The Belgian airline Sabena was co-opted, bringing much needed aircraft and crews as well as adding valuable connections to the Belgian Congo. After President Roosevelt agreed to provide equipment to the British under Lend-Lease in 1941, Pan American took over many of the ground arrangements on the Trans-Africa route in order to facilitate the delivery of military aircraft to the Middle East and India, and also provided an air service between Khartoum and Bathurst which connected with transatlantic flights to New York. To the consternation of some members of Parliament:

> Why did the Air Ministry make an agreement with a selected, privately owned, commercial firm in America whose president, Juan Trippe, has been publicly acknowledged in the United States to be using the war as a golden opportunity of winning concessions and of obtaining a long lead over his future competitors?[2]

Once again, as it had been in the early 1930s, the missing link was with the United Kingdom: British aircraft could no longer fly across Europe or within the Mediterranean area. BOAC already had a small number of extended-range Empire flying boats, and these were used out of Poole on occasional transatlantic services in 1940, before being transferred to maintain the vital link with West Africa, which operated via Lisbon in neutral Portugal; BOAC also chartered DC-3 Dakotas from KLM to run the England–Lisbon service, an arrangement which lasted throughout the war and at its peak involved seven flights a week. Help came when the British government bought three of the mighty Boeing 314 flying boats from Pan American in 1941; later two more extended-range Empires became available as well as a Catalina flying boat. The Boeings were of limited use on the West Africa service, however, as they had to return to Baltimore in the USA for servicing after 120 hours flying, but at least that allowed the corporation to resume transatlantic flying, via Foynes in Ireland. So did the Return Ferry Service. For this operation BOAC used converted Liberator bombers to fly the RAF crews of Ferry Command between Prestwick in Scotland and Montreal; the aircrew were needed to deliver by air to the United Kingdom the new aircraft that were now coming on line in the USA and Canada.

Travel from London to Egypt was by a circuitous route, down through Lisbon to West Africa, across to the Sudan, and up to Cairo. Late in 1941 BOAC began flying to Malta from Gibraltar and Cairo, through an active war zone, often landing at night in Malta during its many air-raids; but even that had to stop in mid-1942 as the Germans under Rommel's command advanced towards Egypt. The corporation flew over 200 flights from Cairo in support of British forces in the Western Desert during the last six weeks of 1942, and another 270 such flights during the first half of 1943. The Air Ministry's record, *Merchant Airmen*, describes the conditions under which BOAC's crews operated:

> The flying in the forward area all had to be done at only a few feet from the ground, to minimise the risk of enemy fighter interception, and of enemy anti-aircraft fire when the route led over one or other of the strongly held pockets behind the main advance. Few pilots went on the Western Desert run without finding themselves, at some time or another, sharing the sky with enemy fighters, or crouching behind the nearest stone while enemy strafed the landing-ground.
>
> By mid-December the western terminal of the desert run had moved on to Bu Amud, near Tobruk. It was from there that they started the night-mail back to Cairo, in order that important despatches might be available to Middle East headquarters first thing in the morning, and that the troops' mail, that important item in any campaign, might get started on its homeward journey with the greatest possible speed.[3]

Flying to the relief of Malta and in the Western Desert campaign were not the only operations that BOAC undertook in hostile conditions. In 1941 flights were resumed between Scotland and Stockholm in neutral Sweden, albeit on an irregular basis. The service continued intermittently throughout the war. Lockheeds were used, four of them crewed and supplied by the Norwegian government; the Swedish airline ABA flew Douglas DC-3 Dakotas over the route. During the long summer nights, BOAC used converted high-speed de Havilland Mosquito bombers which could outfly most hostile aircraft. The German Air Force shot down one ABA aircraft, and attacked another which was subsequently able to land safely. The British had one Lockheed forced down in Sweden, and both BOAC and the Norwegians lost aircraft in accidents. The Germans shot down a KLM DC-3 Dakota over the Bay of Biscay in 1943, and closer to home, in June 1941 Great Western & Southern lost DH.84 Dragon G-ACPY on a flight from the Scillies to Land's End, believed destroyed by a German raider.

After America's entry into the war, Pan American was taken off the trans-African service and replaced by the United States Army Air Force, which concentrated on routeing war supplies to its own forces in India and the Far East, as well as to its allies in China and Russia. BOAC introduced larger aircraft on the Takoradi (Gold Coast)–Khartoum route, Dakotas and the former Imperial Ensigns. A more direct routeing from the United Kingdom to Cairo was possible after the Eighth Army successfully halted and, after the battle of El Alamein, forced Rommel's Afrika Korps into retreat; BOAC resumed flights via Lisbon and Algiers to Cairo early in 1943, using Liberators. The Empire flying boats still maintained the Horseshoe Route, but following the fall of Singapore it was terminated at Calcutta or in Ceylon. Instead Australian pilots flew a direct non-stop service across the Indian Ocean, using PBY Catalinas, from Ceylon to Perth in Western Australia, a 27-hour flight.

Before the war, the government had contributed almost nothing in the way of subsidies to the domestic airlines. Now, having gained operational control of the seventeen internal airlines under its National Air Communications, the government found that it had to pay to keep these companies in business, by its estimate around three-quarters of a million pounds a year. *Flight* magazine commented coyly: 'The Air Ministry came to the conclusion that it was not fair to the taxpayer to spend so much for so little result.'[4] So the government adopted another Fashion and did some pruning early in 1940, sparing those airlines which were deemed essential, and requisitioning the aircraft of those that were not. By a curious coincidence the essential airlines, which maintained cross-water services of 'national importance', proved to be those owned by the railway companies, with the sole exception of Allied Airways (Gandar Dower), which flew from its Aberdeen base to Wick, Kirkwall in Orkney, and Sumburgh in the Shetlands. Perkins was instantly suspicious, asking the Secretary of State for Air on 30 April 1940: 'How many of the internal air-lines now operating are entirely free from any influence of the railway companies?' Captain Balfour had to admit, 'I understand that of the five companies now operating internal air services four have some connection with railway interests.'[5]

The remaining privately owned airlines were closed down, but even after they had been grounded many continued to contribute to the war effort through the operation of Civil Repair Organisations. The railway companies banded together to form the Associated Airways Joint Committee (AAJC), based in Liverpool, taking over the flying operations from Imperials; later in the war they also bought out the remaining significant shareholders, Whitehall Securities and Olley's backers, British and Foreign Aviation. The various airlines in the group still continued to operate as separate entities, and they were all called upon to assist in the evacuation of British forces and civilians from France:

On (15 June 1940) all AAJC services were suspended and the aircraft sent to Exeter for evacuation duties. RAS DH.86Bs G-AEFH Neptune and G-AEWR Venus, together with Dragon Rapides G-AEPF of Air

Commerce and G-AEBW belonging to Isle of Man Air Services, had to be abandoned by their crews at Bordeaux on 18 June, their crews returning by sea. One of Scottish Airways' Dragon Rapides was nearly lost to the enemy when engine trouble forced it to land in Jersey but brilliant work by its crew had the troublesome engine removed and replaced with one from an abandoned Jersey Airways aircraft.[6]

For the rest of the war internal cross-water routes were flown by the members of AAJC and Allied Airways (Gandar Dower), using DH.89 Rapides and DH.86Bs, painted in dark green and brown camouflage with red, white and blue nationality markings; the passenger windows were 'blacked-out', albeit with white paint! Most of the traffic was within Scotland, to the strategically important Western and Northern Isles; Scottish Airways, based in Glasgow and Inverness, and Allied Airways (Gandar Dower) accounted for 41 per cent, around 180,000, of the 430,000 passengers carried during the six years 1940 to 1945, and 64 per cent of the mail and freight. Railway Air Services flew just under 100,000 passengers in the same period on its Liverpool–Belfast–Glasgow service.[7] From Liverpool Isle of Man Air Services maintained the air link with its namesake island; Great Western & Southern Air Lines flew between Land's End and the Scilly Isles. Jersey & Guernsey Airways lost their raison d'être after the Germans occupied the Channel Islands in June 1940, but the surviving DH.86Bs were impressed and continued to fly as a communications unit for the Fleet Air Arm. Both RAS and West Coast Air Services, which together with the Irish airline Aer Lingus flew between Liverpool and Dublin, were affected when a total ban on travel was imposed to and from Ireland in 1944. There were no air services in the London area. Radio stations were maintained to allow civil operations, although radiotelephony was prohibited, and pilots and radio operators had to cope with censorship, secret codes and recognition signals, not always successfully. Captain Fresson, pioneer and now managing director of the northern division of Scottish Airways, recounts how he had a narrow escape early in the war when carrying Labour leader Clement Attlee:

> Passing over the southern shoreline of the Pentland Firth, a large battle cruiser appeared ahead, dead on our track. Standing naval orders said 'Aircraft were not to fly directly over warships' so I commenced to veer off course to the east. Suddenly, signal lights commenced blinking away frantically on the cruiser. I had no signalling light installed on my aircraft to reply with, even if I had understood the flashes, which I didn't. We had nearly got abreast of the cruiser when she suddenly started shooting us up with her anti-aircraft guns. Suddenly, we were surrounded with white bursts which rocked the Rapide aircraft severely. I called to Mr Attlee and told him we were being fired on and to hold on tight as I was about to put the plane into a steep dive.[8]

Fresson was able to avoid the aerial artillery, the culprit an Australian cruiser, but he thought: 'Their aircraft recognition should have been better … I accepted [the incident] along with the many other risks our pilots and myself took operating in war-time air communications.' One of his pilots, Henry Vallance, had an encounter with a German Junkers Ju 88 shortly after leaving Inverness, but by sticking to the German's tail, he was able to avoid being shot down, and returned safely to Inverness; somewhat shaken, he rested for half an hour before gallantly setting off again. Fresson later observes that he and his other pilots were flying the maximum number of hours permitted, 120 per month.

By the time civil aviation came to be debated again, in March 1941, the tone was serious. 'Internal air-lines in this country have suffered the most severe restriction, for none but those which are essential to our war effort can be retained. No nation involved in total war can afford to maintain in civil aviation a single aircraft which is not directly helping to win the war.'[9] But by now the members of the House were more concerned about the troop-carrying capabilities of the army and air force, having witnessed the use to which the Germans put their transport aircraft:

> We are told that the Germans are able to transport four fully-equipped infantry divisions, and not only transport them but supply them from the air by dropping the necessary supplies on parachutes until landing grounds have been taken over. After that they can land supplies…. What have we done comparable with that? I would not, even if the House was in Secret Session, dare to ask my right hon. Friend whether the number of troops which we can transport can be counted in hundreds or in thousands with our existing potential of civil carrying machines…. The Army is very short indeed of aircraft both for carrying troops and for supplying them.[10]

Lord Apsley had reason to be concerned. Aside from the impressed civilian aircraft that were used for communications around the United Kingdom and in the French campaign, the RAF's meagre fleet of transports were mostly to be found in the Middle East, eked out by BOAC aircraft. Perkins was rather rude about the state of BOAC's fleet:

> British Overseas Airways have a considerable number of aircraft. It is probably not in the public interest that I should divulge the exact number, but at this moment they are using daily 13 different types, and in the near future they will be using 17 different types. As far as engines are concerned, they are now using 14 different types. This mixed assortment of aircraft consists partly of old crocks, five, six, seven years old, many of them ripe for the scrap-heap. It consists partly of R.A.F. throw-outs, crumbs from the rich man's table, machines which the R.A.F. do not want, and partly, owing to the generosity of our American friends, modern American machines.[11]

In fact the twin-engine fleet comprised twelve unsuitable Armstrong Whitworth Whitley bombers, four equally unsuitable Wellingtons, twenty-nine Lockheeds, including eleven on loan from the RAF and four provided by the Norwegian government, six de Havilland Flamingos, one Mosquito and the prototype Curtiss-Wright Commando. Larger four-engine transports were sparse: fourteen Liberators, nine Ensigns and the remaining three de Havilland Albatrosses, the latter used for the connection between Ireland and Britain. There were just twenty-two flying boats, the three big Boeings, sixteen Empires and four PBY Catalinas. Perkins wisely refrained from commenting on the RAF transport component. A handful of Vickers Victorias and Valentias, biplanes whose design dated back to 1920, flew on under the desert sun, supported by fewer than fifty Bristol Bombays: it was not enough. The Germans, with admittedly different strategic aims, built 2,804 of their tough, three-engine Junkers Ju 52/3m transports between 1939 and 1944.[12]

Not until the delivery of the first Douglas Dakotas in 1942 did the RAF begin to acquire a worthwhile transport capability, eventually receiving 1,928 Dakotas, many of which were then passed on to other Commonwealth and Allied air forces.[13] To accompany the new arrivals the RAF was also gaining greater expertise in the operation of regular air services; the service had recruited a number of the former managers at Imperial Airways, and RAF pilots were delivering more and more aircraft across the Atlantic; they returned to North America by BOAC's Return Ferry Service which operated under the direction of the commander-in-chief RAF Ferry Command. As more transports became available, the RAF, active in Europe, Africa, the Middle and Far East, decided it needed to broaden the scope of Ferry Command into a specialist Air Transport Command, rather than relying on the expertise, equipment and crews of BOAC. Although the Return Ferry Service functioned efficiently, the RAF had been disappointed at the failure of other cooperative ventures, in particular the so-called Tedder Plan which had envisaged a comprehensive hub-and-spoke network based on Cairo, which Air Marshal Tedder planned BOAC should operate in support of the military. But as the Air Ministry later conceded: 'B.O.A.C. had to conclude that they could not take over the whole of the air line operations of Middle East Command, but could continue to operate only the fleet of 40 aircraft already flying on routes side by side with an R.A.F. Transport group.'[14] Captain Balfour was unsympathetic, if not antagonistic, towards his former colleagues: 'The Board of B.O.A.C. were objecting to the degree of authority and control we felt it necessary to impose on the Corporation. Air Marshal Tedder pressed B.O.A.C. to start a service between Cairo and Malta. He offered the loan of men and aircraft. B.O.A.C. claimed their lack of expert operational personnel prevented this.' Tedder himself went on to criticise the management of B.O.A.C. as 'hopelessly defeatist' and added: 'Future of British Civil Aviation is not my concern but I suggest its prospects of winning the peace are in direct proportion to the value of its contribution towards winning the war.' Balfour agreed: 'Those words expressed exactly my policy and sentiments.'[15] Doubtless Balfour was irritated at having failed to coerce his civilian charges at BOAC to do the air marshals' bidding, and maybe his own military background made him more ready to accept orders from on high; his uneasy relationship with former colleagues at British Airways, now in charge at BOAC, made communication between them starchy. His harsh riposte is at variance with other official views: 'Despite the manifold difficulties of regular airline operation in war-time, of which the chief has been the lack of aircraft designed for transport work, the Corporation have done a fine war job in many parts of the world and their performance augurs well for the future.'[16] The corporation continued under the full glare of parliamentary scrutiny and interference. As Lord Londonderry started off yet another interrogation, he would remark: 'This is the seventh occasion on which I have raised this subject in your Lordships' House in practically identical terms.'[17] For the meantime, Perkins continued to set the agenda:

> Surely the first thing to do is to take civil aviation away from the Air Ministry and hand it over to some other Department. Secondly, are we really wise in concentrating after the war on one chosen instrument? Would it not be better, in view of what is going to happen after the war, to have at least two or, if possible, three chosen instruments? Thirdly, would it not be possible to set up a Committee now with instructions to publish a report to the Government not less than three months hence to consider civil aviation in all its aspects?[18]

The government was indeed beginning to think about the future of civil aviation, and had been minded to do so since the publication of the Cadman Report:

> The Air Ministry should form an advisory panel comprising representatives of operators, constructors and the Ministry itself. With the collaboration of this panel and in the light of information regarding the probable requirements, two years ahead, of aircraft in Europe and the Dominions, the Air Ministry should specify broadly the requirements of a limited range of types of suitable air transport aircraft, and should ascertain which constructors would be interested in the production of these types. (para 55)

The former Secretary of State for Air, Sir Kingsley Wood, had made reference to establishing such a committee in his infrequent utterances on civil aviation, and in 1942, the Minister of Aircraft Production, Colonel Llewellin, asked Colonel Moore-Brabazon, now Lord Brabazon, to 'inquire and advise in regard to the question of the development of types of aeroplanes for civil aviation'. Even Balfour acknowledged the changing circumstances:

> Hitherto we have had to concentrate our manufacturing resources on combat types of aircraft, and it is only now, for the first time since this huge struggle in the air started, that we can commence to lift our eyes from the immediate requirements of combat aircraft to supplying some part of the needs of our war effort in terms of British transport aircraft.[19]

Brabazon formed a small committee from the Air Ministry and Ministry of Aircraft Production, somehow omitting to include anyone from BOAC, and went to work. Within weeks it had reported back, recommending that with varying degrees of modification four existing aircraft types would be suitable for civil use, and recommending the design of five new types. A second committee was then established in May 1943, still under Lord Brabazon's chairmanship, and with a bigger membership – this time including BOAC – which was instructed to look at the design proposals for the new aircraft in more detail.

If the government was at last thinking about the supply side of civil aviation, it was also receiving lots of advice as to the future development of its airlines. There was a craving for internationalisation, a united nations of the sky, even for just one global airline, a World Airways Ltd or an International Aviation Ltd, and if not that, then maybe an Empire corporation, a joint British Commonwealth airline. Competition would be eliminated; air transport should be used for the good of mankind.

> I cannot close without again emphasising that our policy is to develop civil aviation as a service of mankind. I believe it is vitally necessary for the economic and political security of the world that air transport shall be developed on the basis of international co-operation. There must be no return to the pre-war system of unbridled competition leading to political rivalry between the nations.[20]

So declared Clement Attlee, Deputy Prime Minister, in the House of Commons on 1 June 1943, echoing the sentiments of a Labour colleague, Wilfred Burke, in an earlier debate: 'We ought to get away from the competitive notions of the 19th century and look upon civil aviation, not as a profit-making concern, but as something of service to our own people and to mankind as a whole.'[21] Civil aviation was marked out as something different, to which normal rules of trade did not apply. To an extent that is still true; most sovereign states will not allow foreign majority ownership of their airlines, and only recently have developments in Europe bucked that trend. But nevertheless hoping that there would no longer be competition on international routes, especially given the strength of the American airline and aircraft manufacturing industry, was politics in a bubble. It was left to a Tory MP, Arthur Tree, to point this out, and note that it was having an adverse effect on discussion of the industry's future:

> From time to time the Secretary of State for Air, the Minister without Portfolio, and other Ministers get up and say that they intend that after this war we shall have an air service second to none. They also tell us that they are working very hard to bring that about. Yet nothing seems to happen. What is it that is retarding and hampering the Government in this matter? Personally, I have no means of knowing, but I cannot help thinking that they are becoming bogged down on the subject of internationalisation, and that in some quarters, not confined to the Air Ministry, there are people who are pursuing this hare and intend to pursue it to its death. In this vast field of endeavour which is civil aviation I and my friends have found more misunderstanding and more differences of opinion on the question of the meaning of the

word 'internationalisation' than on anything else. If by internationalisation is meant the setting-up of an international body analogous to the Board of Aeronautics in Washington or to the Air Registration Board here, having as its duty the co-ordination and making as uniform as possible such matters as airworthiness of craft, rates, pilots' certificates and so on, I am quite sure we can get full agreement on that. If by facilities for planes of every nation, with obvious restrictions of cabotage, and so on, I hope we can get agreement upon that as well. But if by internationalisation is meant a world-operating company having a board on which there are members of all the countries in the world, flying planes of all different sizes and makes, piloted by pilots of every nationality under the sun, then I believe that, however fine it may be as an ideal, it is pursuing the impossible. Not only that, but it is going against the well-established principles on which the United States have built up the finest civil air service in the world, and I am perfectly certain that they would not and do not intend to relinquish those principles.[22]

Alarmed by these developments as BOAC peered dimly into the future, its chairman had sought assurances from the government in February 1943:

The Corporation, as it appears to us, if they can be given full information regarding the intentions of and requirements of the Government, can in the light of such information, make their plans and be responsible for putting them into execution. Alternatively, the Corporation can be given the limited responsibility of carrying out specific orders.

We feel that we are not in either of the above positions and that as your appointed members we are in an anomalous situation.[23]

The Secretary of State suggested a meeting, at which he told the board about the proposal to establish the RAF Transport Command. Now the board of BOAC scented real danger; the corporation might not just be forced to fly services and aircraft not of its choosing, but more importantly would always rank below the RAF. Both sides rapidly became entrenched in their respective positions, the government determined to keep air transport services under its direction, BOAC anxious about its future status. John Longhurst describes what happened next:

On March 10, 1943, the Under-Secretary of State for Air, Capt. Balfour, found himself in the unpleasant position of having to ring up his former co-director and chairman of British Airways Ltd., Clive Pearson, and tell him that the view of the Board of the Corporation made further discussions very difficult because it seemed to suggest that the settlement must be one extreme, namely the complete independence of B.O.A.C. and its direct responsibility to the Secretary of State for Air as envisaged in the B.O.A.C. Act, or the other extreme of being completely subservient to Transport Command.[24]

Four of the five members of the board of BOAC then resigned; d'Erlanger was the only board member not to do so, but had in any case not played an active role as he was busy running the Air Transport Auxiliary, the organisation which delivered newly built aircraft from the factories to the operating squadrons. BOAC's staff, demoralised by the decimation of its senior management, asked for the return of Lord Reith, which annoyed the Air Minister. Instead, he appointed the governor of Bermuda, Lord Knollys, as chairman, and Air Commodore Critchley as the new director general. Critchley, like many of his colleagues a veteran of the Great War, but one who had been promoted general by the time he was 27, was anxious to enhance the prestige of the corporation in view of the perceived threat to its independence. He reorganised the airline into new departments, losing many experienced personnel along the way, and recruiting in their place a 'steady flow of Marquesses, Group-Captains and Wing Commanders and first-class golfers.'[25] However Critchley made sure that BOAC received the aircraft it needed, Dakotas, Sunderland flying boats (converted to carry twenty passengers), and the first five Avro Yorks, a workmanlike adaptation of the famous Avro Lancaster bomber with a capacious, boxy fuselage which entered service in 1944. By the end of 1944, BOAC had forty-four flying boats and 111 landplanes in service, including fifty-two Dakotas and twenty-two Sunderlands.[26] A milestone in 1944 was the completion on 7 September of the 1,000th crossing performed by the Return Ferry Service, the first regular transatlantic service. The corporation had to extend its operations as the main theatres of war switched from North Africa to continental Europe and the Far East. Services to Africa declined; those within the Middle East and beyond increased. The Horseshoe flying boat service still operated twice weekly between Durban and Calcutta, but was now supplemented by additional direct Sunderland services to India from Poole in Dorset; the Armstrong-Whitworth Ensigns flew between Cairo and Calcutta rather than west to Nigeria and the Gold Coast. Like its predecessor Imperial Airways, BOAC preferred long-haul routes; many of the more immediate transport tasks in Europe were taken up by the RAF. After the invasion of Normandy CATOR (Combined Air Transport Operations Room), a joint Allied operation, initially carried supplies and members of the armed forces to join the advance on Germany, often returning with the wounded; No. 110 Group of RAF Transport Command was later established to provide regular services to formerly occupied countries, and began operations in September 1944 to Brussels, Paris and Lyon.

Perkins had also asked: 'Are we really wise in concentrating after the war on one chosen instrument?' Creating BOAC as the state-owned international flag carrier had seemed a good idea at the time and it had certainly facilitated government control of the major air transport provider in wartime, but was that formula apt in times of peace? There were many interested parties pressing their alternative claims. The shipping companies had suffered extraordinary losses during the war and now claimed they needed some short-cuts to restore profitability, among them the right to operate air services. Shipping lines like Cunard saw transatlantic airline services as complementary to their own liners serving the North Atlantic routes; its forceful chairman Sir Percy Bates wanted to offer enhanced first class passage by air to its clients, and had previously tried to interest Imperials in working together. He was not alone. A consortium of shipping companies with interests in South America took up where the pre-war attempts to launch air services had left off, and even registered an airline, British-Latin American Air Lines, to exploit that previously neglected market. Coastal and continental shipping companies also organised an embryo airline, Shipping Air Lines; four of them already had an interest in joint airline ventures with the railway companies, Coast Lines, MacBrayne's, Isle of Man Steamship, and the North Company. The railway companies, with a near monopoly of internal air services, believed they should continue to play a part in post-war civil aviation, and in 1944 proposed a major expansion of post-war services, to cover not just the British Isles but most of Europe as well, sweetening the proposition with the claim that no subsidies would be needed; they also turned their attention to their existing services, and in November resumed air services from Croydon, flying to Liverpool and on to Belfast. After many years of silence, the demands from business interests old and new were strident.

Viscount Swinton found himself about to resume his old career. He had previously served as Secretary of State for Air until dismissed following the ruckus over the Cadman Report, and had spent most of the war as Resident Minister in West Africa. Now the government decided to accept another of Perkins's recommendations, and began the lengthy process of prying civil aviation away from the Air Ministry. A first step was to announce in October the formation of the Ministry of Civil Aviation, headed by a minister with cabinet rank. In a straight swap, Balfour was consigned to West Africa, and Swinton recalled. His appointment was not greeted with much enthusiasm: 'Now, through the continual drip of these debates upon the stony hard Government, there emerges Lord Swinton,' Lord Brabazon acknowledged. 'That is fine. Lord Swinton is an ex-Secretary of State for Air. I do not know whether Lord Beaverbrook's description of him as "unsurpassed" will go with a swing among some of his fellow Ministers, but still Lord Swinton has a good many very good acts to his credit in the past as Secretary of State.'[27]

One of Swinton's first tasks was to represent Britain at the forthcoming international aviation conference in Chicago. Although the government in its White Paper *International Air Transport* [28] stood by its proposals for internationalism in the air –'some form of international collaboration will be essential if the air is to be developed in the interests of mankind as a whole' – it was having difficulty even getting the Commonwealth to agree – Australia and New Zealand were supportive, but Canada was not – so adopted a more protectionist stance as back-up. The British still professed support for the freedoms of the air, which in a rather British way they insisted on referring to as privileges, but only if they were regulated by an International Air Authority. 'Uneconomic competition' had to be eliminated, so frequencies on defined international air routes would be distributed between the countries concerned, and rates, that is fares, would be 'fixed'. The Americans, with almost a monopoly of civil aircraft production, had no interest in fettering their air carriers and wanted universal adoption of the so-called 'five freedoms of the air', which would give their airlines unlimited access both to international markets to and from the United States, and also to any other markets they might choose to enter. The freedoms of the air can be summarised thus:

First Freedom: the right to overfly another country without landing;

Second Freedom: the right to land in another country for non-traffic purposes, for example, to refuel;

Third Freedom: the right to disembark passengers, mail and freight from the country of origin of the aircraft in another state; for example, a British airline may carry passengers from London and disembark them in Paris;

Fourth Freedom; the right to embark passengers, mail and freight for the country of origin of the aircraft from another state; thus, a British airline may pick up passengers in Paris and fly them to London;

Fifth Freedom: the right to pick up and set down traffic to and from destinations neither of which is in the country of origin of the aircraft. A much wider ranging privilege, and more contentious; a British airline, for example, might embark passengers in Paris for Madrid, or in this context, an American airline might pick up passengers in London to fly them to Paris.

At the conference, the British were unable to get the Americans to agree to their more restrictive agenda, the Russians did not attend, the Commonwealth was divided on the issue, and the best the Convention on International Civil Aviation, otherwise known as the Chicago Convention of 1944, could achieve was an agreement to formulate non-contentious, that is non-commercial, requirements, such as those relating to air navigation, airworthiness, aircraft registration, radio and meteorology, under United Nations auspices. As for the freedoms of the air, the Chicago Convention, signed on 1 December 1944, accepted just the first two, those that permit overflight, and landing for technical purposes only. States would remain firmly in control of their airspace, their air routes and by extension, their airlines; any commercial services would be subject to bilateral agreement, just as had been the case before the war. The United States went its own way after that and indeed had some success in persuading other nations to accept its more liberal interpretation of the five freedoms on services to and from America. Britain, the Commonwealth and Europe tended to favour the more restrictive sharing of international routes between their respective national carriers.

At the same time as Swinton was undergoing his initiation under fire in Chicago, his colleague Sir Stafford Cripps at the Ministry of Aircraft Production was pondering the future of the British aircraft industry. The aircraft manufacturing teams were further along in their planning, with Lord Brabazon gamely drawing up his wish-lists for future aircraft projects which by now had expanded way beyond the original five aircraft types, and included sub-types, additional types, interim types, conversions, and even some purely commercial offerings, anything, really, to try and keep Britain's twenty-seven aircraft manufacturers and 1,700,000 aircraft production workers in employment after the war was over. By contrast, Swinton only had two substantive players, BOAC and the railway companies' Associated Airways Joint Committee. He and his Tory colleagues thought two was not enough: the Labour Party thought it was one too many. Cripps, a socialist, wanted to delegate 'the technical side of flying' to just one organisation, BOAC, leaving it to other organisations, including BOAC, to 'provide the transport service'.

> A single central organisation (e.g. B.O.A.C.) to be responsible for all the technical matters…while private enterprise can provide all the initiative as regards (providing a transport service). This can be done by making B.O.A.C. an owning corporation, i.e. to own all aircraft and a servicing body, i.e. to do all training and employment of pilots and crews. The B.O.A.C. would then charter to private companies such planes as they desired from time to time, providing the crews with planes.[29]

Edgar Granville MP, an air transport expert, thought everybody had got it wrong:

> Whenever civil aviation has got going in this country some enthusiastic amateur has come along, backed very often by the Treasury, and the result has always been to put back the clock. I was one of those who opposed the idea behind the 1939 Act, of lumping together British Airways and Imperial Airways. Unfortunately nobody knew how to resist the ideas of Lord Reith, and disastrously, Lord Reith knew nothing about civil aviation. The British Overseas Airways Corporation was never set up by informed opinion in the House of Commons: the House of Commons was actually presented with a *fait accompli*. It was the child of Treasury mandarins, backed up by the Air Marshals and the Air Ministry. In my judgment, having had some experience on this matter, the development of the British Overseas Airways Corporation has been a failure.[30]

Perkins had come out in favour of five organisations: three corporations – one would be solely committed to flying the mail – and two privately owned airlines, for South America and Europe. Swinton was less sure about the numbers, he just wanted the management to be inclusive:

> Civil aviation is first and foremost a Transport business. To make it efficient…we must have the best brains and experience in transport. If we refuse the partnership of shipping, motor transport, railways, we deprive ourselves of the best and most varied experience in traffic management…There is much to be said for having the competitive experience of several large British undertakings. This does not mean competition on the same routes.[31]

I am not sure what it does mean, but Swinton then goes on to suggest that the underpinning of all these ventures would still be BOAC. 'If we decide to have several chosen instruments for civil aviation, it might well be desirable to give B.O.A.C. an interest in each company. This would ensure a day-to-day pooling of experience and ideas.'

Swinton had settled for three chosen instruments when he came to announce his proposals in March 1945,[32] at the dawn of his new ministry. Except chosen instrument was a misnomer: Heath Robinson contraption might have been more apt. True, three corporations would now be assigned different parts of the globe to exploit: BOAC, the existing corporation, would retain the North American and Empire routes, and would gain services to the Far East; British-Latin American Air Lines would be given exclusive rights to South America; and European and domestic routes would fall under the purview of a new British European Corporation. But any shipping line with an interest in any of BOAC's routes 'shall be afforded the opportunity of becoming associated with B.O.A.C. in the operation of these routes to which they can make a useful contribution. It will probably be convenient, in any case, for B.O.A.C. to operate certain of these routes through subsidiary companies.' So there would be a spider's web of associated companies, with different managements, different marketing teams and sales outlets, pursuing their differing aims. It was all too reminiscent of the silly European joint ventures that Cadman had proposed between Imperials and British Airways before the war. The South American venture was more clearly defined, except that the minister thought BOAC should participate in that too, 'in order to make B.O.A.C. technique and experience available to the new Corporation.' As for the European and domestic services, the new corporation, which might or might not be an extension of the railway companies' present monopoly, would operate an 'agreed schedule' of assigned routes; it was assumed that these would be lucrative, so in order to cross-subsidise 'some of the Commonwealth routes' BOAC would be allowed a substantial interest in that new corporation as well, joining a diffuse and unlikely collection of fellow participants, railway companies, short sea shipping lines, travel agencies and pre-war airline operators (including those which had been shut down at the termination of the National Air Communication scheme), all of whom would be allowed to join in the fun too. Nor were foreign carriers ruled out: 'It may be found wise in routes shared with other countries to run those routes through a joint mixed subsidiary company.' Longhurst pointed out, it was the 'most peculiar hotchpotch of public and private control and finance.'[33]

Swinton's plans were met with bafflement. Lord Rothermere saw the sign of the Holy Trinity: three in one, and one in three. Not everyone understood why BOAC had to be involved in all segments of civil air transport, nor indeed why it had to be protected from the horrors of competition. 'If we can have a thousand-bomber raid over Cologne, over one single city, why are you afraid to have more than one air line on any single route?' asked Hore-Belisha in the subsequent debate on 20 March 1945. Part of the reason for the muddle lay in its presentation. Swinton, speaking in the House of Lords, was as yet without a functioning ministry, and his place in the House of Commons was taken by the Minister of Aircraft Production, Cripps, a Socialist, clearly uncomfortable in promoting a policy with which he did not agree. He was especially vague on the subject of subsidies and losses, claiming that the two new corporations would have to bear any loss, and when that became unsustainable, would '… have to give up the service and somebody will take it on.' It was difficult to understand who that somebody might be.

Later, in June, just days before the first post-war election, when the subject came up for debate again, Swinton had a new parliamentary undersecretary to speak for him, none other than Robert Perkins, on whom fell the responsibility of trying to clarify matters; instead he contrived to muddle the issues further, adding to the general confusion by allowing yet more runners to approach the starting line.

Some internal airlines would now be allowed to resume their pre-war operations, he said, provided they met the necessary licensing criteria, so there would have to be a new licensing tribunal as well; newcomers would be allowed to apply for routes that had not been assigned; and in Scotland, well, there the three new corporations would actually be denied some international routes, as these would be handed over to a Scottish airline. As the plum route appeared to be from Prestwick to Copenhagen, I cannot help thinking that this sop to Scottish nationalism, noticeably on the increase after the war, was some kind of Sassenach joke. The government was criticised for being inconsistent. Having gone to all the trouble to nationalise the major airlines before the war, why was the government unpicking it?

> It is astonishing to me to find that, whereas in 1939 that admirable Conservative, the late Sir Kingsley Wood, came forward with the policy of B.O.A.C., and all the proposals that go with it which we have never had an opportunity of putting into operation and trying out in practice in any way, the Government should come along now and say that the matter should revert, to a very large extent indeed, to private enterprise. I do not understand it; it seems inconsistent with the way things were marching in this country. We go in the direction of what is regarded as progress; we do not, as a rule, step backwards. Here, there is a definite step backwards from the high water mark of Conservative policy just before the war.[34]

Over the whole plan loomed the spectre of the Future of the British Aircraft Industry.

> Finally I come to what is to me a most important part of the whole matter, the provision of adequate and suitable British aircraft for these British transport services. There is not the slightest doubt in my mind that, if we are ever to do any good in the field of civil aviation, or in our aircraft industries, we must fly British. Unfortunately, as the House knows the war has very seriously interfered with the development of British transport aircraft.[35]

Brabazon's committees were churning out suggestions for new designs, but it was going to be months, indeed years, before some of the more ambitious aircraft took to the air. Manufacturers began promoting their own projects. Bristol may have been awarded the plum project for its ambitiously huge transatlantic design, the Type 1, better known as the Bristol Brabazon, but laid off its bets by designing and building the Bristol Freighter, a more down to earth freight and people carrier which came to epitomise the post-war cross-channel car ferry services. De Havilland had an interest in three of the Brabazon Types: the Type 4, the revolutionary jet powered mail carrier that evolved into the Comet; the Type 5 feederliners, of which there were two subtypes – de Havilland built the eight seat twin-engine feederliner known as the Dove, Miles the larger four-engine Marathon; and in the Type 2, the elusive Dakota replacement, which was also divided into two subtypes, the twin piston-engine Ambassador built by Airspeed, now owned by de Havilland, which faced off against Vickers's ambitious Viscount, powered by four gas turbine engines. Armstrong Whitworth, a major supplier to Imperial Airways before the war, produced a sleek four turbine-engine Type 2 design, the Apollo, but its Armstrong Siddeley Mamba engines were no match for the Rolls-Royce Darts used on the Viscount and the design never got beyond the prototype stage. As for Vickers, it already had a Dakota replacement in the Viking, a so-called Brabazon interim design, that is, a development rather than a modification of an existing wartime airframe, in this case the Wellington bomber. Flying boats continued to play an important role in the immediate post-war era, as Shorts developed successful conversions of the Sunderland to produce larger and more powerful boats. Even more ambitious was the huge Princess flying boat proposed by Saunders-Roe, which was to rival Bristol's Brabazon landplane in size and range. Mention of Roe brings one to his former company, A. V. Roe, better known as Avro, builders of the Lancaster and Lincoln bomber, which became truly and appallingly mired in the debacle that surrounded the last of the Brabazon projects, the Type 3, a medium sized transport for Empire, Commonwealth and transatlantic routes.

This was an important aircraft, a competitor for the long-range, four-engine transports that the Americans were already producing in increasing numbers, an aircraft lying somewhere between the extravagance of the Bristol Brabazon and the ingenuity of the Comet; it is telling that Brabazon's committee had at least three stabs at the transatlantic requirement, and none of them made the grade. The Type 3 should have been the workhorse of BOAC's routes; instead it was never built. The project was entrusted to Avro, but Avro was already committed to the design and construction of a stopgap design, the Avro Tudor. Approval for the Avro Tudor was pushed through the Cabinet by Lord Beaverbrook, anxious to have something in the air quickly, and certainly sooner than the six year horizon for the Type 3.

> We need aircraft now, suitable for carrying passengers, mail and cargo on the Atlantic range, and over the mainline routes of Empire. We must parallel the American Douglas C-54A and the C-54B [Skymaster] … I therefore recommend that design and construction of the Tudor be undertaken forthwith … The York will not suit our necessities. It cannot make an Atlantic flight against high winds, and fuselage tanks installed to give extra tankage will damage the payload, reducing it to 4,000 lb. That is less than half of the load carried by the C-54B.
>
> The choice that must now be made should be understood. It is between having or abandoning British Civil Aviation after the War. On this we must take our decision. If we cannot provide the machines, we cannot establish the services.[36]

Avro had already contributed to the wartime development of transport aircraft, producing the York in increasing numbers, and its Canadian subsidiary had developed the first Lancastrian, a Lancaster modified for passenger use, without the turrets and bomb-bays. In between building Yorks and Lancastrians, adapting its little Anson twin-engine light trainer as a feederliner, and trying to freeze the design of its Type 3 proposals, the company was now committed to producing the Tudor, which married a new pressurised fuselage to the wings and Rolls-Royce Merlin engines of the Avro Lincoln, itself derived from the Lancaster. The Tudor I would have carried twelve passengers across the Atlantic, the larger Tudor II was designed to carry more passengers, up to sixty; intended for African and Australian services, the Tudor II did not have the range for transatlantic services, but together with flying boats, it was seen as an important interim aircraft for the Empire routes. Engagingly, the aircraft were referred to respectively as 'the thin and the fat Tudors'. There was scepticism from the outset, especially about the Tudor's economics. Even Brabazon was diffident about it: 'It would do the job as stop-gap machine fairly well, even though not very economically.'[37] Perkins was also resigned: 'We shall have to make do with makeshift machines like the Tudor. They will be fast and probably faster than the American machines, and they will be safe, but the cost of running them will be prohibitive and enormous subsidies will be needed to get them into the air.'[38] Note Perkins's breezy assurance that the Tudor would be safe. The development of the Tudor was unexpectedly protracted, however, and any advantages the type would have had as a stopgap diminished as its entry into service became delayed. Britain's long term future lay in leapfrogging existing American aircraft and producing innovative designs that would give the country's industry a technological lead, but much energy and money was to be squandered on the infill.

The end of the war in Europe, and the victory of the Labour Party in the 26 July election, did not immediately bring about the changes that an economically debilitated country hoped for. The Labour Party had made no secret of its desire to nationalise the remaining major elements of Britain's transport industry; it was just that in the sphere of aviation there was not much that needed to be nationalised, given the status of BOAC. Perhaps the resumption of air services from Croydon to the Channel Islands by Jersey & Guernsey Airways on 21 June reminded the lawmakers that not all air services were under state ownership.

There were other signs of a return to peacetime conditions. Railway Air Services had resumed Croydon–Liverpool–Glasgow services in April (initially operated for them by Scottish Airways) and in June BOAC transferred the Stockholm service from Leuchars to an increasingly congested Croydon, which it had to share with the RAF's No. 110 Transport Wing, now deploying its Dakotas across more and more of Europe; BOAC's European route network at this stage was merely an extension of its wartime services to neutral countries, Ireland, Portugal, Sweden and latterly Spain. The *Aeroplane* observed: 'Transport Command has the "monopoly" of British air services between this country and Europe.'[39] Indeed by September No. 110 Wing flew four times a day to Paris, three times a day to Brussels, and twice daily to Naples; there were also daily services to The Hague, Hamburg, Berlin, Frankfurt, Copenhagen, Oslo, Prague and the Channel Islands; and weekly frequencies to Marseilles, Rome and Athens. Considerable mail and air freight was flown from nearby Blackbushe. The RAF faced some 'competition', though, as European airlines began to resume services; by November, Air France, Sabena the Belgian airline and Swissair had all started flying into Croydon.

The Labour victory at the polls cut short Perkins's new career; he lost his seat too, which meant he was no longer able to skewer ministers in the House of Commons. It also meant that the White Paper, the Swinton Plan, was in limbo; one of the first priorities for the new Minister of Civil Aviation, Lord Winster, was to make an early announcement of the Labour government's plans. 'However much Ministers may have felt obliged to compromise in the production of the White Paper for the sake of national unity, there is national unity no longer,' bragged Francis Bowles, who had entered the House as a Labour MP in 1942. 'The party fight is now on; we are the Government.' But Winster was content to stay with the National Government's plans, with some adjustments. He discarded the notion of associated companies participating with BOAC on Commonwealth and North Atlantic routes, ditched the Scottish airline proposal, and by the same token, the rights of the pre-war privately owned domestic airlines to resume their operations, and he wanted BOAC to be the majority shareholder in the South American airline venture. But he was happy to see private interests continue in the South American airline as well as in the European Corporation, up to 40 per cent in the case of the latter – 'The participants would be B.O.A.C., the railways, the travel agencies and the short-sea shipping lines. I do not propose to find a place for the independent pre-war operators as I do not consider that they have a useful contribution to make.'[40] Charter airlines would not be controlled, merely 'watched to ensure they did not encroach on the field of scheduled flying.'[41]

Winster came up against the parliamentary Labour party, however. Some of them still clung fervently to their belief in the internationalisation of air transport, maybe watered down to a single instrument, a unique Commonwealth air corporation, but as for allowing 'sectional interests' to participate, the outrage was palpable. 'It is of cardinal importance that [the government's plans] should provide for fully socialised ownership, operation and control, as…any compromise with sectional interests would jeopardise the efficient and virile development of the new Civil Air Transport service.'[42] With only days to go before the government's announcement of its intentions, the Cabinet still argued that private enterprise had a role to play: 'We believe the [Parliamentary Labour Party] have underestimated the important contribution which can be made, particularly in the near future, by surface transport interests and of the vital need for rapid progress.'[43]

But even that minor concession was denied. Lord Addison, the Dominions Secretary, talked the rest of the Cabinet round, and whatever the 'important contribution' might have been, it was buried under the need for 'socialised ownership'. When Winster came to announce his plans in the House of Lords, on 1 November 1945,[44] he even sounded aggressive in the pursuit of a socialist dream:

The Government have given to this matter the full and careful consideration which its importance deserves. They have decided that public ownership shall be the overruling principle in air transport, and that there shall be no financial participation by existing surface transport interests in the arrangements contemplated.

So the three corporations remained, but they would all be wholly owned by the government. There were some pot-shots at entrepreneurs:

Pending legislation and following the lifting of the ban on civil flying, during that interim period, it is the case that any air transport operator will be legally free to run air services without specific permission. In the circumstances it is only right for me to mention that such an operator should bear in mind that legislation will be coming along, and that, when it does, no claim for compensation in respect of services so started will be entertained.

Wearily, he observed:

We have to develop an important new form of transport. Mistakes will inevitably be made in the course of doing so, because at the present time, in civil aviation, almost everything is in an empirical state. But at least we are not going to make the old mistakes. Railways the world over developed amid a wild frenzy of speculation which has handicapped them ever since. All over the world Mercantile Marine services were built up amid a scramble for profits which inflicted inhuman misery and cruelty upon fine seamen who were treated like beasts. That may be old history, but speculation and greed rear their ugly heads very quickly if given half a chance.

He was taken to task by his fellow peers for his intemperate language: 'No one has suggested that companies engaged in civil aviation should under-pay, ill-treat or sweat their labour in order to provide paying services. I do not see, therefore, why that peroration was brought into a statement of policy regarding this change of front.' Lord Balfour, formerly Captain Balfour, agreed with Lord Rennell: 'In my view the least accurate and, if I may say so, the most deplorable part of the noble Lord's speech on the last occasion was when he virtually sneered at the railways and the Mercantile Marine in order to create political prejudice.'

Lord Balfour came under some fire himself, especially from Lord Reith, the first chairman of BOAC, who accused him of not having done enough to stimulate civil aviation during the war years. After Balfour complained that he had 'been the stalking horse or whipping boy warding off attacks made on the late Government in another place, having to defend the fact that civil aviation had to go to the wall in the greater interests of the war', Lord Reith remarked sternly:

I do not feel that he was either stalked or whipped sufficiently frequently or sufficiently energetically. Why go to the wall? "Civil aviation had to go to the wall." Go to the wall, my Lords! Second place, yes, a distant second, if you like; and that it was permitted to go to the wall by the noble Lord... is the explanation of the unfortunate position in which this country finds itself today.[45]

And he went on to remind the Lords of the proper relationship between the government and the industries that it had taken into ownership through nationalisation:

The chief characteristics of the public corporation system is that it is established and owned by the State, but not—repeat not—managed by the State ... [L]et us be clear that ownership is not management, and must not be management; that the employees are not civil servants, and that there is no public interference in management.

Now that he had staked out his claim, Winster had to come to grips with the practicalities. British-Latin American Air Lines was already constituted, had begun recruiting staff, appointed Air Vice-Marshall Bennett, a former Imperial Airways captain and wartime Pathfinder bomber pilot, as general manager, and was taking delivery of Avro Lancastrians. Winster did not want to lose the organisation and staff, so the government agreed that BOAC should buy out its backers, but that otherwise the new corporation would stand alone. The AAJC was allowed to fly on until the new European corporation could take over its operations. There were, however, two airlines outside the Joint Committee, Channel Islands Airways (the former Jersey & Guernsey Airways) and Allied Airways (Gandar Dower), both of them flying scheduled services, which would have to be dealt with too; to make matters more interesting, Eric Gandar Dower, the owner of Allied Airways (Gandar Dower), had just entered Parliament as Conservative MP for Caithness and Sunderland. Then there were problems regarding No. 110 Wing and integrating its activities into the future European corporation; most of its aircraft were lend-lease Dakotas which would need to be purchased from the Americans if the British government wanted to use them on domestic and other civilian services.

A White Paper came out in December 1945[46] outlining the general requirements and plans for implementing them. The government promised that the corporations should 'have the maximum freedom in the operation and management of the air services assigned to them'. The use of the word maximum already implied a limit to the government's tolerance of freedom, which was further exacerbated by the negative tone of the following sentence. 'In deciding to set up three Corporations, for the purpose of securing the advantages of flexibility and initiative in the approach to the problems of air line operation, His Majesty's Government do not desire to stultify this policy by imposing unnecessary limitations on freedom of management.' (para 15) Winster tried to bridge the gap: 'Civil aviation, which has so many international and economic reactions, can, under public ownership, be kept more easily in step with general policy by Parliament. That can be done without Parliament interfering vexatiously in management, but allowing the Corporations to be conducted as the great business organisations which they will be.'

When it came to debate the White Paper early next year, on 24 January 1946,[47] the House of Commons was low-key. Harold Macmillan, for the opposition, sidestepped any criticism that his party had already nationalised the two major air carriers before the war by claiming that his party had always believed that 'the best way to put British civil aviation on its feet would be to give full scope to private enterprise'. The Swinton plan would have encouraged private interests 'in addition to B.O.A.C. to stake their own capital in civil aviation'. Others were not so sure: 'I confess I cannot see any difference of substance between the scheme that was brought forward by the Coalition Government and the scheme in the White Paper, except possibly that the one would have been administered by

Lord Swinton, presumably, and the other would be administered by Lord Winster', was Lady Lloyd George's comment. She went on to 'regret that the freedom of the charter and taxi service has not been extended to the smaller companies, many of which have a record of success in the past which the great air lines could not claim.' The debate was chiefly notable for no less than five maiden speeches, but the government emerged undented, to such an extent that in summing up, the deputy prime minister, Herbert Morrison, was able to congratulate himself on the 'good and useful debate and discussion', adding he had been 'charmed to hear' the maiden speakers.

But the minister, Lord Winster, was more uncomfortable defending a policy not of his choosing, as he pushed through the new legislation during the first half of 1946 in the House of Lords. His counterpart, Lord Swinton, was equally uncomfortable attacking a policy that so closely resembled his own. It all made for bad-tempered exchanges in both Houses of Parliament, leading to a general air of gloom which was admirably summed up by Sir Wavell Wakefield MP, an important figure in civil aviation in later years:

> This is a sad and depressing day for the future air development of our country in this great air age. As I listened to the funeral oration pronounced by the Lord President of the Council, I thought of the other funerals which we have had during this Parliamentary Session and are apparently to have so long as this Parliament lasts—funerals of initiative, of responsibility, of enterprise. I could not help being reminded of the story of a village funeral at which there was an incident, thus reported by the local Press: "As the undertaker was lowering the coffin into the grave, he fell dead. This incident cast a gloom over the whole proceedings." That is what I felt when I heard the Lord President of the Council expound the reasons why we should have this Bill setting up a State monopoly.[48]

There was dismay over the size of subsidy that the corporations would need over the next ten years: 'The sum of £84 million is a lot of money. Even if one says it quickly, it still is a considerable sum of money.' Indeed it was, at just under £10 billion in 2010 values; £20 million were set aside for the first two years, and £8 million a year for the remaining eight years up to 1956. There was much tussling over the rights of charter airlines. Charter airlines had flourished in the years up to the war, mainly flying small aircraft as air taxis, useful for people in a hurry, or in more specialised roles, delivering films around the country, or taking photographers up for news stories. Obviously they could not fly any scheduled services as these were to be the monopolies of the state corporations. But the government was reluctant to state what flights they could perform, and consequently got into difficulties when writing the legislation which would reserve scheduled services for the corporations. Its first attempt was to declare that a scheduled flight was one for which an 'announcement calculated to give information as to the time when, or the place to which, the journey is to be made.'[49] So anything that was advertised as a flight was a scheduled service, and therefore reserved for the corporations. Except for this important proviso:

> Provided that for the purposes of any proceedings for contravention of this section a journey shall not be deemed to be a scheduled journey by virtue of any such announcement if the defendant proves that the announcement was solicited in the course of negotiations for the making of such a contract as aforesaid.

And no, I do not think Lord Winster understood what it meant either.

'It is admittedly difficult to define legally what is a "scheduled air service", but it is an expression commonly used and well understood,' Winster explained, but was called to order by Lord Fairfax:

The words "scheduled journeys" are ill-defined. It is not purely to be pedantic that I am moving this Amendment, but because I think that to start these Corporations without a clear idea of what "scheduled journeys" really are, bodes extremely ill for the future, both for the Corporations and for all those connected with them. [50]

In the end the government rewrote the relevant clause, number 23 (2) in the Civil Aviation Act: '"Scheduled journey" means one of a series of journeys which are undertaken between the same two places and which together amount to a systematic service operated in such a manner that the benefits thereof are available to members of the public from time to time seeking to take advantage of it.' As for charter flights, Lord Cranborne came up with a succinct and accurate definition of charter flying, clearly based on his own experiences:

To my mind, a chartered service is a service where an aeroplane is chartered by somebody, in the same way as one takes a special train, or whatever other form of transport it may be. An ordinary scheduled service is a service which runs regularly in any case. Now suppose someone representing the Workers' Educational Association, or the Y.M.C.A. or some organization of that sort, were to go to a flying concern and say: "I should like to charter a plane to send some of my members on the 1st of January, the 1st of March and the 1st of June, on a round trip to the Continent and back." That, to my mind, would be charter service, and it does not make a ha'porth of difference whether those people charter from a Corporation or from some private company. It is still a charter service. [51]

But Winster would not concede that point; any service that operated to a regular schedule was, in his opinion, a scheduled service, no matter what the commercial arrangements. However, the Lords did force the government to permit charter airlines to carry passengers on inclusive tour holidays, provided that a round trip involving three flights was involved. What the Lords understood by this was something akin to an aerial coach tour, starting from somewhere in the United Kingdom, flying to a city in Europe, spending one or two nights there, then flying to a second city and so on, before returning to the original point of departure, 'organized as a tour for the common enjoyment of those passengers', the latter observation sounding the only happy note in the whole proceedings. Of course over time tour operators and charter airlines were able to interpret the requirement for three trips quite flexibly; they also put a spin on the meaning of 'systematic service' and 'members of the public' that was far from the government's intention. I think Lord Winster realised all this, and did not greatly care: 'I am quite clear…that the original Amendment is open to exploitation by astute persons in such a way as to enable scheduled services to be operated under the guise of chartered services.' [52]

As for the aircraft that the corporations would use? The initial proposal had been to prohibit them from buying foreign aircraft, except with the special permission of the Minister. Labour policy was to subordinate airline operations to the manufacture of the airliners themselves. The British airline corporations were to showcase the best that Britain could offer, and in the interests of the common good were expected to lose money in the process; the important thing was to build aircraft which would maintain Britain's prestige abroad and, it was hoped, earn foreign exchange through export sales. That position was riddled with anomalies. For one thing, the state owned airlines would be saddled with many of the development costs of the new aircraft. BOAC already had to endure the wretched performance of existing designs, and by now had developed a dangerously cavalier attitude towards the general principles of airline economics and the accretion of overheads: its deficit in 1945 of over £5 million was merely a foretaste of what was to come. For another, the state owned airlines were expected to support the privately owned aircraft industry by buying its products, transferring taxpayers' cash to the private sector. There were twenty-seven aircraft manufacturers in business after the war; to keep them all happy, investment and resources had to be spread thinly, and it made for a bewildering choice of new products. Furthermore, the products were either not right, as in the case of the Tudor, nor yet in existence, as was the case with most of the Brabazon types, so BOAC, which was the most affected by the post-war aircraft production debacles, happily continued buying American aircraft in order to remain in operation, unlike its gallant predecessor, Imperial Airways. It is incorrect, in this general context, to claim that BOAC was 'forced' to buy American products; there is nothing to indicate that the corporation did anything other than bound down that path with unalloyed pleasure.

The new government's prognostications about the future of the British aircraft industry continued gloomy. 'At a time when the United States is starting operations all over the world our own progress reports on civil aircraft production are a melancholy story of delays, disappointments and retardations.'[53] The aircraft programmes had by this time taken on a life of their own, with government seemingly unable to stop them. Here is a telling extract from the Cabinet meeting held a few months later on 18 March 1946 regarding the Bristol Brabazon (Type) I:

> The total cost of the project, including the construction of airframes and engines, would be £7,535,250. The first aircraft to be produced (the Mark I) would be powered with Centaurus reciprocating engines, and would be followed by three Mark II aircraft with Proteus gas turbines. B.O.A.C. were prepared to give orders for the Mark II aircraft, but they did not regard the Mark I type as a satisfactory aircraft for its intended purpose; and the [Civil Aviation] Committee had formed the impression that the Ministry of Civil Aviation did not regard either type of the Brabazon I with great enthusiasm. If, therefore, the matter had to be determined solely on the operator's opinion, the Committee would have had some hesitation in recommending that the project should proceed. They had felt, however, that, in view of the great experience in aeronautical knowledge which would be gained from the development of the Brabazon I aircraft, in the field of both civil and military aviation, the project should be carried out.[54]

Of course the workers at Bristol benefited from the Keynesian outlay, but it still sounds like grown-ups playing with Monopoly money. Both the Board of Trade and the Foreign Office objected to the prohibition on the use of foreign aircraft, pointing out that it would make it more difficult to sell British manufactured products like ships and locomotives abroad. So, instead reliance was to be placed on the power of the Minister to give directions 'which the Minister thinks necessary in the public interest'.

Such were the defining issues governing British air transport policy over the next thirty or so years: the acquisition of aircraft by the corporations; the staggering financial losses inflicted on taxpayers by the corporations, BOAC in particular; and the extent to which the privately owned charter airlines could push the boundaries of what they thought they could get away with. The government found itself in the middle on all three counts. In the next chapter we look at how these developments played out in the real world.

CHAPTER 4

1946 to 1948
Meddle and Muddle

The first day of January 1946 was a busy day: wartime restrictions on civil flying were revoked, with at least two charter airlines gleefully taking to the air, Cambrian Air Services and Hunting Air Travel; Air Vice-Marshall Bennett left Heathrow in command of a British South American Airways (BSAA) Lancastrian on the first of six proving flights to South America; Marshall's Flying School at Cambridge reopened for business; and the British European Airways Division of BOAC was formally constituted, but had to wait until 4 February before it could take over the European services of No. 110 Wing, 46 Group RAF Transport Command, and thus end the RAF's 'monopoly'. Two BOAC directors, Sir Harold Hartley and Gerard d'Erlanger, were put in charge of the European Division; Hartley had up until then been chairman of Railway Air Services, and d'Erlanger has already appeared on these pages. On his way out was Air Commodore Critchley, unsympathetic to the new government, and who disliked the break-up of BOAC into three corporations. The AAJC, comprising RAS and its affiliates, continued to fly domestic services under contract with the European Division, and acquired Anson XIX airliners and Dakotas; RAS finally inaugurated a direct Croydon–Glasgow service, taking just 2 hours and 45 minutes in an Anson. The Weston–Cardiff shuttle was resumed, now flown by the railways' Great Western & Southern Air Lines; this AAJC participant also owned Channel Islands Airways. The latter was registered in the Channel Islands; it had used a Bristol Wayfarer during the summer of 1946 to boost capacity, but its future was a matter of some concern to the islanders, who feared their airline was about to be nationalised along with the other airlines. RAS remained at Croydon, but BOAC's European Division started flying out of Northolt, a RAF station to the west of London. BSAA inaugurated the first British scheduled service to South America on 15 March, flying its Lancastrian out of Heathrow to Buenos Aires; BOAC remained at Hurn for the time being, and its flying boats continued to use the nearby Poole base. One could fly to Australia speedily by Lancastrian in 60 hours, or in the greater comfort of a Sunderland flying boat which took 5½ days to get to Sydney. By the middle of June 1946 BOAC had switched its landplane services to Heathrow, just in time to start its New York flights with new Constellations, on 1 July.

The new services had been facilitated by the air service agreement that Britain had just signed with the United States in February 1946 on the island of Bermuda. Post-war air-links had been surrounded by controversy, indeed some American flights had had to divert to Shannon in Ireland when permission to land in the UK had not been forthcoming, and the Americans had been forced to accept an upper limit of 500 passengers per week. All these issues should have been sorted out at the Chicago Convention, but as we have seen the conference was unable to agree anything substantive in the matter of traffic rights, that is, the right to carry passenger, freight and mail between two or more countries. The talks which took place in Bermuda during January and February 1946 were more narrowly focused. The British government no longer had to concern itself with internationalism, but the British still held weak negotiating cards; they needed to buy more US built transport aircraft, and to negotiate a large dollar loan from the Americans. Lord Keynes, in Washington, DC at the time, was anxious that the British negotiators did nothing to queer his pitch. The British wanted an 'equitable division of traffic', pre-determined frequencies, strict capacity sharing, high fares, no disorderly competition; the Americans wanted almost the opposite, 'equality of opportunity', maximum competition, no capacity limitations, and low air fares. In the end the British did well enough in achieving a deal which offered 'fair and equal opportunity', signing up to an agreement which restricted the routes airlines could fly, which they favoured, but not the number of flights they could operate – that was conceded to the Americans. That meant there were only a limited number of routes that British and US carriers could operate, but no limitations on frequencies and size of aircraft. The British also gave the Americans fifth freedom rights out of London to a number of European destinations. In return the Americans accepted restrictions on fares; fares would be set by the airlines themselves through their cartel, the International Air Transport Association (IATA). The Americans also accepted that only designated carriers, a limited number from each side, were allowed on each route. They were also going through their own upheavals. Wartime operations had eventually broken the overseas monopoly of Pan American, so some unfamiliar names had been appearing at British airports. Transatlantic routes were shared, with some overlap, between three US airlines, hence the need for 'equality of opportunity': Pan American; Transcontinental and Western Air (TWA), later known as Trans World Airlines; and American Export Airlines, which in turn was taken over by American Airlines and renamed American Overseas Airlines. The British fielded just BOAC; BSAA was confined to the Caribbean and South America, and would, over the next two years, take over both Bahamas Airways and British West Indian Airways (BWIA), Britain's belated acknowledgment of its colonial responsibilities in that area.

Elsewhere, there were continuing signs of muddle; decisions by the government affecting one sector of industry undermined decisions made by the same government in another. The government had deliberately crafted the air transport industry so that there would always be two ministries battling for influence and funding from the Treasury: the Ministry of Civil Aviation, in the airlines' corner; and the Ministry of Supply – successor to the Ministry of Aircraft Production – which owed allegiance to the aircraft manufacturers. The most obvious anomaly was the decision taken early in 1946 to allow BOAC to buy Lockheed Constellations to replace the Boeing flying boats and converted Liberator bombers which still flew the transatlantic routes. The decision favoured the airlines, and was a victory for the Ministry of Civil Aviation. But however sensible, it ran counter to the stated aim of bringing into service the Tudor as a transatlantic stopgap, and was therefore a blow to the Ministry of Supply. Winster's parliamentary secretary, Ivor Thomas, fudged the issue when he claimed during a debate on the government's White Paper in the House of Commons:

> Their purchase will do no harm to British industry, because we shall be able to take every machine that British manufacturers can produce in the next few years. The combination of Constellations and Tudors will provide a well balanced service across the North Atlantic, capable of meeting the needs of all travellers.[1]

Avro was rightly concerned by the announcement as BOAC's diminishing interest in the Tudor I now evaporated. The first Tudor should have entered service the following October but there were problems with directional and longitudinal stability to be sorted out, so a much larger fin, rudder and tailplanes had to be fitted. Testing continued, with endless tweaking of aerodynamics, before BOAC in March 'called for no fewer than 343 changes in layout and décor, even though the whole production programme was already in serious disorder after two years of ever-changing decisions.'[2] It has long been fashionable to criticise BOAC at least in part for the overlong and ultimately unsuccessful development of the Tudor, but even so stern a critic of the corporations as John Longhurst had to point out that this was unfair:

> It was not a very pleasant experience the other day to be present at a news conference organized by the Minister of Supply at which we were told a very disappointing story about the development troubles in the Tudor I, only discovered, apparently, 18 months after the prototype first flew.
>
> But what was much more unpleasant was the air pervading the whole meeting, and not discouraged by any of those officials representing the Ministry of Supply and the constructors, implying, as it seemed to us, that it was the unfortunate operators, B.O.A.C., who were to blame for the trouble. Great emphasis was laid on B.O.A.C.'s decision to carry 12 sleeping passengers instead of 24 sitting passengers on the Atlantic service to be operated by the Tudor Is. This commercial decision had nothing to do with the subject of the conference which concerned swing at take-off, tail buffeting and a high fuel consumption. Great play was made of the weight of B.O.A.C.'s furnishing requirements, but little or nothing was said of the empty weight of the aircraft itself.
>
> There seems to us to be no need to make a mystery of these difficulties. The plain fact is, as is now revealed after 18 months of flight testing and trials since the Tudor I first flew, that the adaptation of a new and fatter fuselage to the Lincoln wing and undercarriage has not succeeded as it was hoped it might.
>
> It is not playing the game to indulge in buck-passing at this stage, using the operators as a convenient scapegoat. When the Brabazon committee decisions were taken the civil operators had much less say than anyone on the question of types and designs to be constructed. We have mentioned in this journal before that B.O.A.C. originally asked for an aircraft of 60-70 tons to be built for the Atlantic and Empire routes, powered by four Centaurus 2,500 h.p. engines. The military people ruled otherwise, and the folly of their view is now revealed.[3]

By mid-1946 BOAC had decided that the Tudor I, short on range and restricted to only twelve passengers, was unsuitable for the New York service, and asked to be allowed to order Boeing Stratocruisers, able to carry sixty-four passengers across the Atlantic. Maybe the Tudors would be used on the Montreal service, BOAC hinted. The outlook was not good for the Tudor II, either. The aircraft was growing fatter, longer and heavier, as Avro accommodated the many design and configuration changes asked for by BOAC, and airfields on African and Far Eastern routes would need to be lengthened for the bigger aircraft. The Constellations were not the only airliners obtained from abroad. The government decided to use some captured Junkers Ju-52/3m transports on internal services, ostensibly as replacements for the war-weary Dragon Rapides, and bought seventy-two lend-lease Dakotas outright for BOAC and the new European Corporation to use without restriction; over 100 Vickers Vikings were also ordered to replace the Dakotas. Both Dragon Rapides and Dakotas long outlasted their successors in corporation service.

Lord Winster had his brief moment of glory when the Civil Aviation Bill received Royal Assent on 1 August 1946; the Act established the British European Airways Corporation (BEA) and the British South American Airways Corporation (BSAA). BEA immediately took over the European services, but RAS continued to fly domestic services, now under contract to BEA. Hartley was appointed BEA chairman and d'Erlanger was its managing director. BSAA retained Bennett as its chief executive. The arguments over the passing of the Bill continued right down to the wire, with the Lords holding out for more concessions for Scotland. Winster was prepared to accommodate his fellow peers, even conceding a separate Scottish corporation, to operate alongside the other three, but this was rejected by the Commons. The Lords did not stop trying. Their next proposal was for a Scottish airline to operate as an 'associate' of BEA, but again this was rejected by the House of Commons. In order to placate the Lords, and just one day before the Bill was due to be signed into law by the King, Winster told the Lords that there would be a Scottish Division of BEA, and a Scottish Advisory Committee with a Scotsman chairing it; that was the best he could do, and of course the Lords were not going to make a constitutional issue of it, so pragmatically they let it go. Shortly afterwards Winster himself moved on, appointed the new Governor of Cyprus, and was replaced by Lord Nathan. Almost the first thing that the new Minister had to do was explain to the Lords exactly what BOAC was doing:

> There are services from the United Kingdom to South Africa four times weekly; to India, four times weekly; to Australia, three times weekly and three connected by trans-Tasman service to New Zealand; to Canada twice weekly. From the United Kingdom to the United States there is a service four times weekly; to Egypt 17 times weekly; to Malaya once weekly; to Hong Kong one service weekly; from Singapore to Hong Kong once weekly; from the United Kingdom to West Africa, three times weekly; Palestine and the Lebanon, once; South Africa, Egypt and India, twice weekly. I should say that this last-mentioned service will be withdrawn at the end of the present year.[4]

The passing of the Act should have ended any uncertainty as to what the charter airlines were allowed to do, since it was now legally established that these carriers were absolutely not allowed to operate scheduled services. But as *Flight* observed: 'The question of what a charter company can or cannot do seems almost impossible to answer,' before going on to conclude:

> With the best will in the world neither the Minister nor his legal advisers can satisfactorily sort out the situation, or re-word the Act in such a way that it is clear. No rules, regulations, good advice, or even goodwill can alter the fact that, from the moment when the Act becomes law, the Government is all-powerful. And the charter companies must operate from hand to mouth, depending finally on Government favours.[5]

There were already a number of these airlines in existence; it was clear, however, that their continued existence was barely tolerated, at least by the newly empowered bureaucracy that was one of the consequences of the war. 'The interior of the Ministry of Civil Aviation, which needs a coat of paint, is in keeping with the rather niggardly attitude of the Government to date.'[6] Indeed, much depended on the attitude of the civil servants – 'British aviation has for some time been controlled in detail, if not in the wider sweep of general policy, by a few civil servants,' complained Major Oliver, editor of *Aeronautics*[7] – so each charter flight became the subject of much haggling over the phone as operators sought clearance. 'These men are not enthusiasts for aviation,' Oliver continued, 'they regard aviation as an offshoot to procedure and to forms and the intricacies of departmental process. The power is passing from the doers to the politicians and the administrators.' Skyways, a new and well-connected charter airline, which had been established by Critchley and Sir Alan Cobham as a corporation-equivalent in the emerging arena, found itself thwarted by the ministry as soon as it prepared for its inaugural flight to Basra, at the start of a major contract it had gained from Anglo-Iranian Oil to support operations in Iran.

[S]ure enough, the crabbing has started already. Skyways, Ltd., has made an arrangement with B.O.A.C. that the latter should be its traffic-handling agents throughout the World. Therefore they sought to despatch the York from Northolt on May 14, Croydon being unsuitable for York operations with a full load. But, oh dear no, that would have made it far too easy for Skyways, and the Ministry of Civil Aviation said Skyways could not use Northolt, because it would mean letting all the other operators in as well, for which Northolt is not ready. "All right," said Skyways and its handling agent, B.O.A.C., "let us use Hurn." Another excuse was thought out to veto the use of Hurn, and the long and short of it was that, through the kind assistance of Hawkers, Skyways has to put passengers on board at Langley, B.O.A.C. traffic staff have to cart over there from Northolt to handle the departures and arrivals, then before departure from England the aircraft has to land again at Manston, a Customs aerodrome, to sign out for departure overseas.[8]

Skyways was just one of a number of new charter airlines with ambitions far beyond the limits of air taxi services and the ubiquitous Dragon Rapide. Both Hunting Air Travel and Airwork had been in existence before the war but did not start charter flying operations until 1946, both buying Vickers Vikings to supplement their smaller units; Airwork also used a Bristol Wayfarer to launch a special service contracted with the government of Anglo-Egyptian Sudan to take its officials on leave back to the United Kingdom. Scottish Aviation relied on its fleet of Liberators and Dakotas to undertake contract flying for a number of foreign airlines as well as BEA. The Ministry of Civil Aviation claimed there were eighty-five companies engaged in charter activities by the end of 1947. One company was Westminster Airways, established in 1946 by four MPs including Air Commodore Harvey, a Tory newcomer to the House of Commons, which assembled a small fleet of Dakotas and Airspeed Consuls and concentrated on passenger work. Others found opportunity in flying freight, either seizing the moment and carrying fresh fruit and vegetables from France and Italy, often to be sold at stalls on the streets of London, or emulating tramp steamers and carrying urgently needed goods worldwide.

BEA had ambitious plans. As well as strengthening its domestic trunk routes, it announced new 'cross-country' routes: Liverpool–Manchester–Bradford/Leeds–Doncaster–Hull–Grimsby was one example. Aficionados of Dan-Air's famous Link-City service will recognise another proposed new route: Newcastle–Bradford/Leeds–Manchester–Bristol. There were to be many seasonal, holiday routes: for example, Bristol–Bournemouth–Isle of Wight–Brighton. In Scotland all manner of services were to be introduced, or resumed. There would be numerous routes from points in the United Kingdom to the Channel Islands, Isle of Man, and the Isle of Wight. The route planning ran riot, possibly facilitated by someone Captain Fresson, managing director of Scottish Airways, encountered early in 1946:

[W]hen I was in Renfrew discussing the 1946 summer timetable with our traffic manager, I was introduced to an individual I had not seen in Renfrew before … It turned out that the stranger was attached to the new BEA traffic office in Northolt, and he opened up on me by saying that the intention was to provide three different types of aircraft for the Scottish runs. They all had different cruising speeds, which would make the aircraft non-interchangeable on a given route without hopelessly upsetting the timetable. On enquiry, he admitted they had little or no spares with which to service the aircraft, and more important, no engineers qualified for maintenance, and no maintenance equipment. Without any of the aforementioned prerequisites, the airline would be a shambles within a week.[9]

When BEA took over all the remaining services of the AAJC on 1 February 1947, the government having paid the railway companies £550,000 in compensation, the corporation maintained the trunk routes to Belfast and Glasgow, and continued to serve the Isle of Man and the Channel Islands, the latter after finally wresting the business of Channel Island Airways from the unwilling hands of the Channel Islanders on 1 April 1947; BEA had to wait until 12 April before it could take over the routes of the very last anti-nationalisation hold out, Allied Airways (Gandar Dower) at Aberdeen. Alas, the new corporation did not apparently listen to the advice of those professionals who had been flying Scotland's air routes since the 1930s:

> The flight from Renfrew [Glasgow] to Aberdeen is normally made in [Junkers] Ju-52s, but on the morning we were due to leave, after going through the usual actions before taking off one engine of the German aircraft was found to be misfiring and we made the return journey to the passenger hall. A last minute breakdown with any aircraft is understandable, but the inconvenience to passengers should be avoided. In this instance we were kept waiting for about an hour and a half before a Rapide replaced the original aircraft for that journey. Bad luck, perhaps, but we gathered that the Ju-52 has a reputation for unreliability, which surely calls for there being a standby aircraft always immediately available.[10]

The writer, Roy Pearl, had a wretched time of it as he flew around Britain's newly nationalised airways, complaining about the facilities at all the airports – 'The passengers' assembly hall is large and furnished with but one settee and two armchairs,' he noted at Liverpool. 'The whole presents a dismal picture except, of course, when a service is held up and passengers are kept waiting in the entrance hall without seating accommodation.'[11] – and being thwarted when the one flight he was looking forward to, from Edinburgh back to London, which was to have been operated under charter to BEA by Scottish Airlines whose 'Dakotas are more pleasantly decorated inside and are more comfortably equipped than the B.E.A. aircraft', was delayed overnight waiting for a replacement part. 'It would seem that more confidence would be gained by assuring regular service by providing standby aircraft than by attempting a frequency which is impossible to operate through unavoidable unserviceability.'[12]

With the arrival of the Viking, services to Europe began to improve, so that by August 1947 100 weekly services were scheduled, up from seventy a year before. The aircraft met with grudging approval, the service sometimes not:

> In the opinion of this correspondent, the Viking does provide reasonable comfort. The interior is finished in pleasant cream and brown. If the carpet is not as thick as the floor covering of a super cinema, it is most definitely a carpet. The chairs are restful, and one can see out of the windows with fair ease.…[L]unches certainly could be improved, but their standard is, of course, conditioned by the general lack of tasty things to eat that afflicts this country…each contained two paste sandwiches, two fish rolls, one apple, one small pie (contents indeterminate), one chocolate bar and some sweets.[13]

Whatever a fish roll might be, Air Commodore Harvey encountered an even scarier experience:

> When we crossed the Suffolk coast at Southwold the emergency door blew off its hinges and hit the tail plane. The air hostess was laid out by the wind that came in, there was a considerable to do and I had to go along and tell the pilot what had happened. I am only pointing out all this because I feel that we must not put aircraft into service before they have been proved. It will absolutely ruin our trade. The Viking is a perfectly good aeroplane but I am convinced that it went into service far too soon—perhaps six months too soon. It was laid up for four months with de-icing difficulties and now there are the incidents of yesterday.[14]

BEA seemed to be tempting fate as it struggled to find appropriate names beginning with V for its V-Class Vikings: *Valet*, *Varlet*, *Villain* and *Violent* must have been dredged up by a crossword enthusiast in its planning department.

Scarcity and *Paucity* might have been appropriate names for two of BOAC's aircraft; beset with conflicting demands and advice, starved of appropriate aircraft, the corporation was struggling to keep its route network in the air. The government had just announced that BOAC would be allowed to buy Boeing Stratocruisers for the North American routes, at the same time blandly confirming that Tudors were still being developed for corporation use, but otherwise BOAC had to rely for its services to Australia and West Africa on inadequate and uncomfortable bomber conversions, the Lancastrian and the Halifax: 'We are very tired of conversions which do not give the passenger the standard of comfort necessary for long-distance travel', complained a correspondent in *Air Transport*.[15] The workhorses of the fleet – Dakotas, Yorks and Sunderlands – dated back to 1944, despite the well-meaning efforts of the Brabazon Committee. At BOAC's own estimation, the York was twice as expensive to operate as a comparable modern aircraft like the Skymaster: the Sunderland, two and a half times. By the end of 1946 BOAC, disillusioned with the Tudors, was issuing its own recommendations for both a long-range and a medium-range type for the Empire and Commonwealth routes. The Ministry of Supply, dismayed by the slow progress in developing suitable aircraft for the Empire routes, suggested buying Constellations with Bristol Centaurus engines; maybe Bristol could build the aircraft under licence? For now, there was a lack of suitable aircraft and a lack of spares; Dakotas were kept flying by cannibalizing other aircraft; bases were widely dispersed in Canada, South Africa and Cairo, as well as four in the United Kingdom, none of them near London; and the dead mileage flown was estimated at 500,000 miles a year. The fleet stood at 169 units by the end of 1947, which included just five of the modern, pressurised, long range Constellations; some of the holes had to be filled by chartering aircraft from Skyways. BOAC still operated a network throughout the eastern Mediterranean, Africa and the Middle East from its hub at Cairo, a legacy of its wartime responsibilities, and had only just abandoned the remnants of the Horseshoe service, between South Africa and India, retiring the last of the Imperial Airways Empire flying boats. This last caused problems for two Australian mining companies, the Zinc Corporation and Imperial Smelting Corporation – the two companies merged in 1949 – which had mining operations in South Africa and Burma, and now needed to make alternative arrangements to fly their South African miners to other locations. The solution was to start their own airline, Silver City Airways, using Lancastrians and Dakotas operated for them by British Aviation Services, a recently formed company that specialised in ferrying aircraft worldwide for sale or conversion.

The government, or rather the Treasury, turned down the Bristol built and powered Constellation, but the corporation and Bristol kept on talking anyway, and dreamed up a specification for the aircraft that eventually became the turbo-prop Bristol 175 Britannia. The Ministry of Supply continued along its erratic course, and placed orders with Handley Page for the Hermes 4, a medium range, pressurised piston engine airliner that the company developed alongside the Hastings transport ordered for the RAF. The Hermes 4 had a nose wheel undercarriage, and Bristol Hercules engines, but did not look all that different from the Tudors, which type BOAC now suggested could perhaps be converted into a freighter? The Tudor had friends elsewhere, however, and found an enthusiastic operator in BSAA, which accepted six of the Tudor IV version, six feet longer than the Tudor I, and able to carry thirty-two passengers. Although this version undoubtedly made more economic sense, its range of 2,800 miles was somewhat less than that of BOAC's twelve-seat Tudor I.[16] Bennett experimented with in-flight refuelling as a way of closing the long 2,000 mile gap between the Azores and Bermuda, but it was difficult to reconcile the heavy extra costs of this operation with any appropriate financial returns, and indeed nothing came of it.

BOAC's Commonwealth partner airlines began to reequip their fleets with more modern aircraft. The Canadians, up until now loyally continuing to operate Lancastrians over the Atlantic, introduced in 1947 the Canadair C-4, a hybrid development of the Douglas DC-6 powered by Rolls Royce Merlin engines; it was not all that dissimilar in concept to the Bristol built Constellation proposal. Both Qantas and South African Airways lost interest in the Tudor and went their different ways too, Qantas buying Constellations, South African Douglas DC-4 Skymasters. BOAC was again in a difficult place with no competitive equipment on offer or in the pipeline; the Lancastrians were relegated to carrying freight and mail, and for the time being BOAC's passengers had perforce to content themselves with the slower flying boat service.

Its sister corporation, BEA, had different problems to contend with. As Britain plunged into a new economic crisis accompanied by vicious balance of payments difficulties, the government imposed travel restrictions on the long suffering travelling public, effectively banning any travel for private purposes to countries not in the sterling area from October 1947. BEA responded by reducing its international services, and cutting a number of domestic routes, including the link between Cardiff and Weston-super-Mare; BEA had been chagrined to find that 93 per cent of the revenue on this route just went to paying the airport landing fees.

All these issues were about to be submerged by an avalanche of bad news. Both corporations reported heavy losses in their respective reports to March 1947; BOAC came in for further criticism when a government appointed committee, chaired by Air Chief Marshal Sir Christopher Courtney, published its report on what had become the Tudor fiasco in January 1948; the Tudor itself caused further anguish when a few days later, on the night of 28 January, one of the new Tudor IVs of BSAA disappeared on a flight from the Azores to Bermuda, in circumstances which are still unexplained.

'We now have the reports and accounts for the year ended March 31, 1947, of all three of the Government air Corporations,' Lord Nathan confessed.

> Two of them present indeed a very gloomy picture. I doubt whether any of your Lordships expected to see great profits, but I do not suppose any of your Lordships expected to see such enormous and formidable losses. The B.O.A.C., whose accounts cover a full year, have lost no less than £8,000,000. The B.E.A., doing the European and the domestic services, whose accounts cover only eight months, have in that eight months lost over £2,000,000.[17]

BOAC was not especially apologetic: 'Heavy deficits will inevitably continue until the Corporation has the aircraft and facilities to make it financially self-supporting,' and continuing, 'with the present types of aircraft, even with a high low load factor, receipts barely cover direct operating costs. On many routes little or no contribution was made to indirect costs and overheads.'[18] Since they had risen by £2.75 millions, that was unfortunate. Nor was Lord Nathan any more bashful:

> Let me make it clear, in the first instance, that I have not come here to-day to offer apologies. Losses, substantial losses, have, of course, been incurred by two of those Corporations. I will show why these losses have been incurred, why indeed they were inevitable … My predecessor in my present office warned your Lordships that he could not be certain that the whole of the £10,000,000 would not be required in the first year. But this loss is part of the price we have to pay if the British aircraft industry is to have the chance to produce the new breed of aircraft which we are confident will lead the world.

A reminder of just how costly was the government's policy came later that year when one MP asked the new Secretary of State to compare the current losses of the nationalised British airways with the civil aviation subsidies during the period 1929–39: 'The subsidies and grants in the prewar period rose from £361,000 in 1929–30 to £1,339,000 in 1938–39. The total of the deficiency grant payable in respect of operations in 1946–47 amounted to about £10,320,000.'[19] Lindgren was too modest to do the arithmetic for the 10 years of pre-war subsidies, but it came to £6,521,576.[20] Longhurst fulminated:

> Money is being spent, losses are being accepted and effort is being wasted on a scale which even the most reckless private enterprise would not even contemplate. This profligacy is attributable solely to one cause; it is because public money is involved, and the people who are spending it have a feeling of unreality about money which comes from the Exchequer.[21]

But despite Longhurst's outburst, other commentators, like *The Aeroplane*, accepted this state of affairs:

> B.O.A.C. has to run its services with aircraft that were not originally intended to be used as air liners. As a result the nation has to foot a very large bill every year. If B.O.A.C. were equipped throughout with Constellations then no doubt the national air transport industry would be making a profit like Sabena or K.L.M. who do not have to worry about the future and prestige of their aircraft industries.[22]

Prestige: an overused word in post-war British politics. This air of resignation coloured the debates in both Houses which followed, which concerned themselves more with the state of the aircraft industry than the airlines. The Earl of Selkirk talked about millstones:

> We have heard much about the disadvantages that B.O.A.C. suffer, and it would be fair to recapitulate all its advantages. It is a statutory monopoly, with power to do almost anything it likes. The Minister took ample powers under the Act. He collected what he thought was the cream of civil aviation traffic, and if he has failed to produce what he wants it is not because he lacks power but because he lacks the capacity to use those powers effectively. The Corporations are not pioneers of these routes. They were more or less pioneered not only before the war but also by the Air Forces during the war. A great volume of development took place at the public expense during the war, although some of it was not entirely what was wanted and changes have had to be made. It was basically, however, of tremendous value to our airfields. The number of trained personnel, although admittedly they require conversion, is considerable. The impression one gains from these advantages is that there must be some very heavy millstones hanging round the necks of the Corporations.
>
> The first is the supply of British aircraft. That is a terrible thing to say, but that is one millstone. The second is the manner in which they are assisted by the Ministry. I say that with regret.
>
> I am not one for defending B.O.A.C. generally, but in this particular they took the correct action in regard to an aircraft [Tudor] which could not have been used, except at considerable cost to the taxpayer of this country. It is stated that one reason why they ought to have used the Tudor I is for the manufacture. If I may say so, it is quite a different thing for the Government to order B.O.A.C. to use it, and for B.O.A.C. to accept it on their own responsibility.[23]

In the House of Commons on 26 February 1948, Sir Basil Neven-Spence (MP for Orkney & Shetland), who had witnessed the precipitous decline of air services in the north of Scotland, was able to pinpoint correctly one of the main factors behind the corporations' deficits:

It is becoming clearer and clearer that "Great Expectations," a novel in three volumes by the Socialist planners, has now been withdrawn from circulation and replaced by "Bleak House," a true tale in two volumes, published by B.O.A.C. and B.E.A.C. … It seems to take, under the present set-up, about three times the number of staff to operate the concern that it used to take before the war, when everything was as efficient as the present organisation.[24]

Alan Lennox-Boyd pointed out the disadvantages of the government's present policy:

We are in the parlous situation that British civil aviation is one of the very few commercial undertakings where increased business means increased loss. It is ironical, as was pointed out a day or two ago, that if everybody who travelled last year by B.O.A.C. had been paid £50 not to travel, financially the country would be far better off.[25]

Others were also sceptical as to the benefits to the United Kingdom of its airline industry:

The management of both American Overseas Airlines and Pan American World Airways, particularly the latter, are so impressed by the inefficiency and poor quality of operations of their British competitors (with the possible exception of BOAC's Constellation services in the North Atlantic) that they genuinely hope that the British airlines will be able to buy serviceable aircraft in order to afford some competition, and in order to prevent the British government from taking restrictive measures against more able airlines to enable its own to keep going.[26]

Crocodile tears, I feel sure, but indicative that it was not just the pursuit of prestige that was behind the corporations' failure to provide Britain's taxpayers with a decent level of service.

Only BSAA claimed to make a profit; it was also an enthusiast for British-built aircraft, Yorks, Lancastrians, Tudors, and now bought Vikings for its BWIA subsidiary. When the Courtney report[27] into the developing Tudor fiasco was published, the committee drew an unflattering comparison between BOAC and its young sibling: 'There was, on the part of B.O.A.C., a lack drive and determination to get the Tudor quickly into service.' The committee reserved almost all its criticism for BOAC – the aircraft manufacturer was gently chided for not having sought outside help soon enough when design flaws became apparent – on the grounds that all the participants were in this together and should have known what was expected of them, including the operation of uneconomic British built airliners; no doubt the tone of the report was set by its sponsor, the Ministry of Supply. Lord Brabazon, in his unpublished report commissioned by the Ministry of Civil Aviation, the rival ministry, and which was submitted one year later – it is discussed in greater detail in Appendix 4 – was much less charitable towards the aircraft manufacturer: 'It is considered that the general standard of workmanship is good…Nevertheless, there are patches in the assembly, repair and mod. section of the firm which, in our opinion, does not show that pride in workmanship we like to attribute to British manufacture.' He then went on to lambaste the poor design and construction methods:

The most severe criticism concerns the region under the floor of the centre section where the heating system resides together with a mass of controls and other machinery.…Unless men of unusual patience are employed, both on assembly and in maintenance, items will inevitably be skimped through sheer exasperation.

Lord Reading took the Courtney Report more or less at face value:

The Courtney Report seems to me to contain almost every ingredient which those who like bureaucratic control hoped would be avoidable and those who dislike it prophesied would be inevitable. It would be almost possible to reduce it to the terms of a recipe in the work of the late lamented and invaluable Mrs. Beeton: "Take two Departments, a Corporation and half a dozen Committees; rub well the wrong way until all are thoroughly sour; cut up responsibility into as many pieces as possible; add procrastination, hesitation, lack of co-ordination, lack of imagination, lack of control"—in fact almost every ingredient except ginger—"do not stir. Leave to simmer for several years and serve lukewarm."[28]

Unlike his colleagues at BOAC, Bennett at BSAA had a much clearer idea of what he wanted, and as a superb pilot himself, was more tolerant of the Tudor's shortcomings. The Courtney Report applauded the eagerness at both Avro and BSAA.

The workpeople were convinced that British South American Airways were determined to put the aircraft into service at the earliest possible moment. The effect was to create a spirit of enthusiasm amongst the workpeople, who were prepared to, and did in fact, work for long periods without a break in order to get the aircraft out quickly.

The good will was short lived. On the night of 29–30 January 1948, one of the new Tudor IVs disappeared without trace between the Azores and Bermuda. Lord Nathan immediately grounded the aircraft, and for his pains, was criticised by Bennett in a newspaper interview; Bennett was then fired by the board of BSAA. BSAA now became the target of malicious questions in the House of Commons:

Mr. Ward: To what does the hon. Gentleman attribute the fact that the accident rate of B.S.A.A.C. does not compare favourably with the other two Corporations? What action is he taking to reduce the accident rate of that Corporation?

Mr. Lindgren: I do not think that the high accident rate is unrelated to the fact that the operations of the Corporation were very near to the bone. I said earlier that my noble Friend had instituted an Air Safety Board inquiry into the general operational standards of the Corporation. The result of that inquiry has been submitted to the Board of the Corporation, which is acting upon it at the moment.

Mr. Lennox-Boyd: Can the hon. Gentleman say what he means by operations being "near to the bone"?

Mr. Lindgren: The inference has been made with some justification, I think, that training and maintenance standards were not as high as they should have been.[29]

BSAA continued to fly its Yorks and Lancastrians, and extended its influence in the Caribbean by buying out Bahamas Airways. When the Court of Inquiry published its report[30] on the loss of the Tudor, it contained criticism of BSAA's operational procedures, but offered no explanation for the aircraft's disappearance. The Court's recommendations, on training, flight planning, rest facilities, estimation of fuel reserves, had already been put into effect, claimed BSAA. As *Flight* commented: 'This would rather tend to show that the Corporation was aware that certain aspects of the operation of the route were open to improvement.'[31] In August the Tudor IVs were reinstated in service, but had to fly the long war round, via Gander in Newfoundland, to reach Bermuda, the Caribbean and South America.

Changes, and new challenges, were in the air in 1948. George Ward MP summed up BOAC's difficulties in the House of Commons on 26 February 1948:

It is now generally agreed that the Tudor I can never be economically operated. I believe that they are now being turned into Tudor IVs at even more expense. It is not by any means certain that the Tudor IVs will be an economic aircraft, and no one has yet decided how on earth we can use the Tudor IIs at all. Looking further ahead, there is the giant Saunders Roe flying boat, which is presumably to be used on the Empire routes as well as for the Atlantic. But one has only to turn to page 14 of the B.O.A.C. report to find these words: The indirect operating costs of the flying-boat services are particularly high. B.O.A.C. is the only major user of flying boats, and has had to provide its own marine air ports, whereas aerodromes and aerodrome facilities are normally provided by the Government concerned on payment of a landing fee. This situation involves the Corporation in the abnormal expense of providing marine craft, moorings and essential services and the duplication of staffs at stations where the Corporation also use land airports. Moreover, the provision of accommodation for passengers at night stops on the flying-boat services is costly and the night stops reduce the utilisation of the aircraft. While the flying-boat services are popular with the public because of their comfort, their use involves provision of marine airports and accommodation at a cost to the Corporation of roughly £1,150,000 per annum. In view of that statement, are we satisfied that this big flying boat will ever be an economic proposition? From that report, one would think the answer must be "No." Then there is the huge Brabazon I, which is costing millions of pounds to produce. We are told that it can operate only on three or four airfields in the world. It can be used only on the Atlantic route, for which we already have the Boeing Stratocruisers on order. Are we sure the Brabazon I is ever going to be an economic proposition, and that it will not be too big?

We cannot go on muddling through and making these colossally expensive mistakes.[32]

The suggestion now was that BOAC should use the Tudors, modified to Tudor IV standard, on the Empire routes, for which the larger Tudor II, the 'fat' Tudor, had been designed and also found wanting; never mind that the Ministry of Supply had just ordered the Handley Page Hermes for these Empire routes. And there was continuing dispute over the role of flying boats, which still had many defenders. The Sunderlands were gradually replaced by larger and more powerful Sandringhams and Solents, manufactured by Shorts, and the maritime base was switched from Poole to Southampton. The flying boats operated through Egypt, Kenya, the Victoria Falls and down to Vaaldam for Johannesburg in South Africa, replacing Yorks; and to the Far East via Karachi and Hong Kong. Roy Pearl, writing again for *Flight*, had a much better time of it on his leisurely four day flight to Johannesburg, calling it an air cruise and praising especially the ground arrangements, which included night stops at Luxor and at a rest camp in Uganda. At Victoria Falls he noted:

Passenger reception buildings have been built on the banks of the Zambesi by the government of Southern Rhodesia, and a road was cut through the bush in 6½ weeks from Victoria Falls to the hotel—a distance of 4 miles. Such co-operation from the government of Southern Rhodesia has saved B.O.A.C. considerable expense in opening and maintaining the base.[33]

Colonial governments were still doing their bit, even if the government at home was wobbly. The Ministry of Supply continued to fund the huge Saunders Roe Princess, although one of the ministers concerned seemed to rule out using flying boats on the North Atlantic: 'My information, from those who are supposed to know,' said Lindgren on 11 May 1948, 'is that on the North Atlantic in particular, the landplane is a much safer plane than the flying-boat.' *The Aeroplane* criticised 'the deplorable conflict of thought and policy among those who hold the final authority for deciding what British air liners are to be built. Britain is building flying boats and yet the responsible ministers are openly running them down.'[34] At least one new airline was prepared to stake its fortune on flying boats, when Aquila Airways bought two of the now redundant BOAC Sunderlands later that year.

There was some good news for BOAC. In order to hold its own with its pool partners, Qantas and newly formed Air India, both of which operated Constellations, BOAC was allowed to acquire more Constellations, buying five of them from the Irish airline Aerlinte, which accepted payment in sterling. Lancastrians were now used for fast mail and freight services; many of the wartime Cairo-based services were discontinued; and certain West African routes were taken over by a new BOAC subsidiary, West African Airways Corporation. Oil support flights to the Middle East were chartered out to Skyways and its Skymasters. Although 1948 was tumultuous for BOAC, and still accompanied by massive losses, it was nevertheless the year that the corporation turned itself round; it acquired a new deputy chairman, Sir Miles Thomas, a proper businessman with many years behind him working for Lord Nuffield's car manufacturing organisation. Thomas became chairman at the end of June 1949.

BEA plodded on, insouciantly racking up huge deficits, uselessly and endlessly reorganising itself – the latest had led to the firing of the luckless Captain Fresson – but its fortunes too were about to change. In the longer term, a change of management at the top would secure the corporation's future, but in the meantime, questions were being asked after the latest round of cost cutting and route paring. Sir Walter Smiles, a Northern Irish MP, made a positive suggestion during the debate on 26 February 1948:

> The first point I wish to raise is with regard to the B.E.A. and the continuance of the service between Liverpool, Manchester and London. It is a service by which I have often travelled, and it has been made use of in the past by a great many manufacturers in Belfast. The discontinuance of that service will be most inconvenient. I do not think that I will raise any political point or speak about the profit motive, but I would appeal to the Parliamentary Secretary not to be "dog in the manger" about this Liverpool and Manchester-London service. If B.E.A. are not able to run this service at a profit themselves, then an opportunity should be given to some air charter company to have a try. I do not say that they will be able to run it with the large Dakotas that were used before, but they should be able to continue the service with a much smaller plane, such as the Dove.[35]

He was articulating ideas that were doing the rounds – another example during the same debate was the steady drumbeat endorsing the possible purchase of the Canadian built Canadair C-4, to tide BOAC over until either the Tudor or the Hermes entered service – but both Lord Nathan and the charter airlines began to look again at the Civil Aviation Act and note that there was provision for them to operate scheduled routes as 'associates' of the corporations, provided of course that the corporations did not want to maintain the routes themselves. To an extent this had already happened the previous year, 1947. BOAC had organised two consecutive airlifts in Pakistan and India, following India's partition on independence, to transfer transport officials and personnel who were urgently needed to coordinate the much larger displacement of refugees between the two new dominions; although BOAC contributed Dakotas and technical support, the bulk of the flying was performed by British charter airlines, which provided twenty Dakotas and a Bristol Wayfarer. Now the demand for extra service was much closer to home, and the government, without fanfare, was about to shift the weight slightly from its left foot, and relax its hitherto unbending attitude towards the independents. The catalyst was the withdrawal of the Cardiff to Weston service, and the man who thought he could make it happen was Whitney Straight, a well-connected entrepreneur who had owned Western Airways, the operator of the route before the war. Now Straight was also managing director of BOAC and even better connected, but he still owned Western Airways in a private capacity. He proposed to Nathan that the two airlines with an interest in the route, his own and Cambrian, be allowed to take it over as 'associates', and for good measure persuaded the Ministry to cut the airport fees to a more realistic level. On 25 May 1948, the Cardiff–Weston ferry service was resumed, to general clucking all around:

> The new arrangement for independent operators to run some of the internal services that B.E.A. has wiped its hands of, is typical of the infinite capacity for compromise so many examples of which are part of this Island's story.
>
> A Bill is passed, backed by threats of a fine of £5,000 or two years' imprisonment to reserve regular air services to the Corporations. Within two years of the bill's becoming law, the chocks under the independent wheels are kicked away.
>
> It is a first-class example of British expertise for muddling through. And surely proof of this is the fact that B.E.A. was paying landing fees at the rate of £15 a day … while Western Airways and Cambrian Air Services will be paying £3 12*s*. a day for the same number of services.
>
> Could it happen in any other country in the World that the Government supporting a national company should inadvertently favour the private operator? And, incidentally, could any other country boast a Managing Director of its leading Corporation, Mr. Whitney Straight, as owner of the private company, Western Airways, which is setting out to show the other leading Corporation how to suck eggs.[36]

When the government announced details of the arrangement, it transpired that a number of other airlines had also been granted approval, under the counter, for 'associate agreements'. These were for holiday routes, to Jersey and the Isle of Man, but a number of international destinations were also included, mainly in Switzerland, for what we would now recognise as inclusive tours; establishment charter airlines like Airwork and Skyways benefited, as did some historic tour operators, Bath Travel, Polytechnic Touring Association, Sir Henry Lunn, Hotel Plan.

Like BOAC, BEA was also about to turn a corner, helped along by the appointment of Lord Pakenham, later to become Earl of Longford, as the new Minister of Civil Aviation on 1 June 1948. A convert to socialism, and all the more zealous for that – 'The noble Lord was a little sensitive about his Socialism, I thought, but no one will challenge his own enthusiasm as a convert to the political faith he now espouses', was Lord Swinton's rejoinder during Pakenham's first debate[37] on 21 July 1948 – he had been Chancellor of the Duchy of Lancaster with special responsibility for Germany, where he had got to know the military governor, Marshall of the Royal Air Force Lord Douglas, a pioneer aviator, now also with left-leaning tendencies. Pakenham took trouble over his brief, and by the time he addressed the Lords for the first time as Minister, he had already begun to face up to realities and started clearing the backlog. The first was what to do about BEA:

> I should like to say a few words on a special and very important topic—the internal services of B.E.A.C. During the year 1947–48, the direct operating loss of B.E.A.C. was close on £1,000,000. The striking fact is this: that the direct operating loss on the European services amounted to only a few thousand pounds— £24,000 on present calculations—while all the rest—between £900,000 and £1,000,000—was lost on the English and Scottish services, including the services to the Channel Islands, the Isle of Man and Northern Ireland.

These were services that had required no subsidies at all in the previous decade, apart from £100,000 belatedly allocated just before the outbreak of war. His solution, so he told the Lords, was to ask

Lord Douglas to look into the workings of the 'associate agreements' and report back to him. He continued:

> To avoid any possible misunderstanding, I may say that the very last thing I have in mind in asking my noble friend to undertake this inquiry is to retreat from the policy of the 1946 Act—the policy of treating the Corporations as the chosen instruments. I could never agree that a socialised corporation, properly organised, is incapable of successful pioneering.

Pakenham then turned to 'the aircraft issue', which really meant the various marks of Tudor and what to do about them. First of all, the Tudor II project would be abandoned: 'We must cut our losses on it; to persevere with it would simply be throwing good money after bad… The Tudor II is a disappointment.' BSAA, now under new management, was to become the dumping ground for the remaining unwanted Tudors of all marks, thus freeing BOAC of its obligations. He warned the House about getting the various marks of Tudor mixed up:

> I would emphasise that the two main varieties of the Tudor are the Tudor II, with its variant the Tudor V, designed to carry 44 passengers—the "fat" Tudor—and the Tudor IV, designed to carry 32 passengers—a development of the "thin" Tudor. I must ask the House to keep clearly in mind that distinction between the Tudor II and the Tudor IV: on no account must the "thin" Tudor IV suffer from being confused in the public mind, here and abroad, with the "fat" Tudor II.

He then got himself into a complete muddle and talked about converting Tudor IIs into Tudor IVs, or alternatively, using them for a new concept, 'pressurized freighting'. (His parliamentary secretary Lindgren had to explain later that what Pakenham had meant was that some of the completed Tudor IIs would be converted into unpressurised freighters.) BSAA was to be the repository of another new aircraft type, the huge Saunders Roe SR.45 flying boats, having apparently decided that was where the future of long distance flying lay. BOAC, meanwhile, was to get what it had asked for, twenty-two of the Canadair C-4s. Lord Selkirk wondered: 'That is an aircraft built in Canada, with a Rolls Royce engine from the United Kingdom. I do not see why we could not have followed that example.' Indeed. At this point, just five years after the Brabazon recommendations, BOAC's aircraft purchases had totally veered off course; its front line fleet, Constellations, Stratocruisers and the Canadair C-4s, was now wholly manufactured in North America. Still, there was some hope on the horizon for British manufacturers. Both the jet-powered de Havilland Comet and the long range Bristol 175 – not just a 'Constellation six years late' – showed promise; even the mediocre Handley Page Hermes would have a role to play, displacing the last of the flying boats to Africa. And BOAC could also find nice things to say about the Type 1 Brabazon as it subtly distanced itself from the project: 'Providing suitable financial arrangements were made, B.O.A.C. would be glad to operate the Brabazon I. It was to be regarded as a national experiment.'[38] If that sounds familiar, just substitute 'Concorde' for 'Brabazon'.

With the Tudor and its sibling, the aborted Brabazon Type 3 project, out of the way, and the Brabazon Types 1 and 4 (the Comet) accounted for, there remained for consideration two further Brabazon types, both with subtypes, the Type 2, ostensibly the DC-3 replacement, and the Type 5 feederliner. The Type 2 came in two varieties, one powered by two piston engines, the other more adventurously by gas turbines. Airspeed had flown its first Ambassador in July 1947, and was followed almost exactly a year later by Vickers with the turboprop Viscount. There was inevitably much dithering about which to order into production by the various ministries, but BEA was persuaded to order twenty forty-seven-seat Ambassadors in September 1948, hoping for first delivery in January 1951. The Vickers Viscount was perceived as being rather small, a riskier technological challenge, whose economics did not surpass those of the more conservative Ambassador. Vickers stuck to its guns, however, even after the Ambassador order, and encouraged by Rolls-Royce, which in turn managed to increase the power of the Dart turbine engines, was able to move on from the prototype to the larger V700 series Viscount, able to carry forty-seven passengers over longer distances and at higher speeds than the Ambassador. At this point the two aircraft types' development diverged. Airspeed's owner, de Havilland, engrossed by the Comet project, was unwilling to extend production of the Ambassador beyond the initial order for twenty, and consequently the design remained frozen. However, for Vickers and Rolls-Royce, the V700 Viscount was just the beginning; after BEA ordered the aircraft in 1950, the design was constantly improved, with an important contribution coming from Trans Canada Air Lines, an early buyer, to such an extent that the Viscount became a serious and successful competitor in the American market. But all that was in the future; for now BEA had to maintain its European services with twenty-seven-seat Vikings as other European airlines, KLM, Sabena, Swissair, upgraded to twin-engine forty-seat Convairs, a modern, pressurised nose-wheel design which scooped up any European orders that Airspeed might have been contemplating.

At the other end of the scale, a parallel story played out in the case of the Brabazon Type 5 designs. Here the differences were in scale, not power plants. Both designs, the Miles Marathon and de Havilland Dove, used de Havilland Gipsy Queens; the Marathon needed four, the Dove just two. The Marathon had a difficult development; the Miles Aircraft Company went bankrupt in 1947, but production of the Marathon was assumed by Handley Page, against orders from the Ministry of Supply for fifty aircraft, thirty for BEA and the rest for BOAC's associated companies that were beginning to proliferate around the world as the corporation concentrated on its long-haul business. Designed as a fourteen-seat monoplane with a high wing and retractable undercarriage, it was perhaps too sophisticated for the rugged role it would need to assume as a potential Rapide replacement, and was eventually spurned by BEA, leaving the Ministry of Supply with the problem of disposing of the unwanted aircraft; the long-suffering RAF took them on as navigation trainers. Nor was the Dove ideal as a Rapide replacement, even though it was closer in size, a twin-engine eight-seat low-wing monoplane, for it was much more expensive than the war-surplus Rapides and Airspeed Consuls that were in plentiful supply. The Dove was ordered in some numbers by air forces as training and liaison aircraft, and early versions were indeed sold as feederliners, but the aircraft found its true role as an executive transport; the type continued in production until 1967, by which time over 500 had been built. A stretched version, the de Havilland Heron, with four engines and a fixed undercarriage, was launched in 1950, and was much closer to the needs of the airline industry than the Marathon.

As Britain's airline industry, in all its manifestations, began to turn the corner, it was despite, rather than because of, the aircraft that British manufacturers offered to the market. Of greater significance, perhaps, is that for all their shortcomings in frontline service with the corporations, with the honourable exception of the Viscount, most Brabazon and post-Brabazon airliners had a much more fulfilling second career in the service of Britain's privately owned airlines. In socialist Britain, there was irony in that.

CHAPTER 5

1948 to 1951
Along the Corridor, Turning the Corner

For now, the independents did not yet enjoy the benefits of the corporations' cast-offs; instead they had to make do with the RAF's wartime surplus hand-me-downs. Charter airlines did order Doves in small numbers: Cambrian began using them on their 'associate agreement' services; Captain Olley – yes, still around and in a slightly anomalous position now as he was 'owned' by the nationalised British Railways, but his Olley Air Service, a charter airline, had not transferred to BEA – bought Doves for his race meeting charters, as did Captain Morton, Olley's former chief pilot, who had broken away to form his own charter airline, also based at Croydon, also concentrating on upscale charter work. But the independents tended to buy larger aircraft: Vikings, Dakotas, Halifaxes, Lancastrians. Airwork and Hunting, both with substantial passenger charter programmes, bought Vikings. Airwork's customers included the Sudan government, Iraq Petroleum, Anglo-Iranian Oil, Kuwait Oil, Britain's Overseas Food Corporation (in connection with its Ground Nut Scheme in East Africa), and a major operation in Ecuador which saw around ten aircraft flying in support of Shell's oil exploration. Contract flying was only a part, albeit a significant part, of Airwork's business which also comprised engineering, aircraft sales and worldwide ferrying services, flying clubs and training schools, airport catering, and sundry government support contracts. The depth and breadth of Airwork's commercial operations allowed the company to remain sanguine about the ups and downs of its airline operations, at the mercy of volatile government policies; it also had acute political antennae and excellent connections which allowed it to lead, if not dominate, the charter airline industry in the first ten years after the war. Hunting was not dissimilar in scope, with a well known sister engineering company, Field Aircraft Services, and another, Percival, which built training, touring and light transport aircraft; the Hunting group had strong connections with East and Central Africa, and it also had shipping interests. Skyways, a long-haul specialist with an impressive line-up of Skymasters, Yorks, Lancastrians and Doves, flew for blue-chip clients like BOAC and Anglo-Iranian Oil. The other long-haul specialist, Silver City, had by this time completely 'down-sized' its aspirations; the corporate charters to South Africa, Burma and Australia were abandoned, and instead the airline began flying private cars, accompanied by their drivers and passengers, across the Channel from Lympne in Kent to Le Touquet in France, a mere 42 miles. Ferry services from the Channel ports by the newly nationalised shipping lines were cumbersome for those wishing to take their cars to the Continent, as vehicles had to be craned on and off the ship. Silver City had a Bristol Freighter on lease and was looking for new business opportunities; a simple ramp could be used to drive a car up through the clamshell doors into the aircraft. With the help of the motoring organisations, the AA and RAC, and of a blind eye at the ministry, the airline inaugurated the first service on 13 July 1948, flying an Armstrong Siddeley Lancaster saloon belonging to managing director Air Commodore Powell across the Channel. It speaks for the Air Commodore's standing that at a time when it was almost impossible to obtain a new car in England – priority was still given to exports – he was able to buy such a prestigious model.

A number of airlines flew Dakotas alongside BEA and the RAF. Air Contractors used theirs to fly livestock, a new market development; Bristol Freighters were used to carry race horses. Air Transport (Charter) (Channel Islands), a gutsy little airline with a big name, had flown their Dakotas on the Indian airlift, as had Westminster Airways. The operator with the largest fleet of Dakotas, Scottish Aviation, used them to fly for its associated airlines, Hellenic Airlines and Luxembourg Airlines, in both of which Scottish had an interest. Scottish also took over BOAC's Liberator service to Montreal, a throwback to the wartime Return Ferry Service which had continued as a support operation for BOAC's expensive maintenance base at Montreal's Dorval airport.

Kearsley Airways, a newcomer, flew freight charters in its fleet of three Dakotas. Ciro's, owned by a nightclub of that name, used two opulently outfitted Dakotas for passenger work: 'accommodation for 17 passengers has been provided in two compartments. The cabin is fitted with a writing desk, book racks, and a cocktail bar' but no dance floor apparently. Silver City had an even more luxuriously equipped Dakota, named *City of Hollywood*, equipped with just eight armchairs and two settees; it was often used by Winston Churchill. Ciro's was one of the first airlines to be prosecuted under the new Act by the Ministry of Civil Aviation. The men from the ministry had been somewhat dismissive of the airline and were therefore more than a little put out when the magistrate fined the airline only a nominal amount, £10. He had then gone on to criticise the 1946 Civil Aviation Act: 'These are terrific powers given to the Minister. No private individual shall compete with a nationalized undertaking. If they do so, they shall be required to give full particulars of the offence. They shall convict themselves at the arbitrary order of the Minister.'[1] After further, similarly sarcastic comments from other magistrates, which effectively defanged the fierce wording of the Act, which threatened fines of up to 'five hundred pounds, or to imprisonment for a term not exceeding three months, or to both', the ministry stopped prosecuting the airlines for a while.

Other independents flew smaller types, Rapides, Consuls, the boxy Miles Aerovan, some Ansons, but the growing interest in air freight led to the use by some airlines of the Halifax, a four-engine bomber conversion able to carry 6½ tons, which could be fitted with an additional pannier under its belly. In July 1948 BOAC sold eleven of their unwanted Halifaxes, also known as Haltons, to a young entrepreneur, Freddie Laker. *Air Transport* magazine noted in its June 1948 issue that 'Eagle Aviation … started off with a first flight on May 9 with a Halton carrying cherries from Verona to England' and introduced its readers to its founder, Harold Bamberg. Lancashire Aircraft Corporation, dissatisfied with just flying regional services from the north of England, bought a fleet of Halifaxes in 1947 which it based in the south at Bovingdon, and picked up ad hoc charters, flying fruit and textiles into Britain, dispatching ship's spares like propeller shafts worldwide, even on three occasions carrying American ships' crews across the Atlantic to New York. But 1948 was a more difficult year for charter operators; freight rates paid for Halifax charters from northern Italy dropped to between £400 and £500, down from the previous year's level of £800. The most ambitious Halifax operator was LAMS, London Aero & Motor Services, which had grand plans to market worldwide freight tramping services, taking over a former American airbase in Essex, Stansted, and acquiring sixteen Halifaxes. The business did not prosper – its founder, Dr Humby, contracted tuberculosis, a venture into the Australian market failed – and the company ceased operations in July 1948.

Which was a pity, really, for just a few days later, on 27 July, two Lancastrians of Flight Refuelling left their base at Tarrant Rushton to join the Berlin Airlift, heralding the start of a major contribution by the British independents to this enormous undertaking; to keep the western sectors of Berlin and its two million inhabitants supplied by air with all the necessities for living, coal, milk, potatoes, gasoline, medicines, raw materials for Berlin's manufacturers, foodstuffs of all descriptions. Berlin was under the control of the four major powers, American, Russian, British and French, each allocated its own sector. Likewise, Germany after the war had been divided into four zones, each one controlled by one of the four powers. Berlin lay in the middle of the Russian zone, so to get there entailed travelling across the Soviet controlled zone: by train; along the autobahn; or by river and canal. There was agreement on right of access between the four powers, though no formal guarantees on surface links. The only formal agreement covered air transit rights from Berlin to the western zones, along three air 'corridors', defined by height and width; two of them ended in the northern (British) zone, near Hamburg and Hannover respectively, the other in the American zone by Frankfurt. As relations between the western powers and the Soviet Union deteriorated – the start of the Cold War – so the Russians began to make difficulties for road and rail traffic, closing stretches of the autobahn for 'repairs', laboriously inspecting all goods into Berlin, and checking passenger identities on trains. In the meantime the British and Americans were hurrying along the process of industrial and social regeneration in their respective zones, underwritten by the Marshall Plan; for the Russians the limit was reached with the adoption in the western zones of the Deutsche Mark to replace the Reichsmark, implying a more permanent sundering of the two de facto German states, the so-called Bizone of the western powers, and the Soviet zone in the east. On 24 June 1948 the Russians turned off the power, and closed all road and rail connections to the western sectors of Berlin. The city had some limited supplies available, but it was estimated that the population would need at least 5,000 tons of supplies a day to survive, around 3,500 tons of coal and gasoline, 1,500 tons of foodstuffs. The only way to do that seemed to be by air: a daunting prospect. The British had already started flying in supplies to their Berlin garrison, using Dakotas, but it was going to take a lot of planes to keep the whole city supplied: a Dakota carried three tons. However Anthony Eden, Britain's wartime Foreign Secretary, seemed to have few misgivings. Here he is in the House of Commons on 30 June, barely days after the blockade had started:

> I have read many times, and I have heard it said, that it would be impossible to supply by air our sectors in Berlin, with their large civilian population. Well, that may be so, but I should not personally be completely dogmatic about it: remarkable achievements stand to the record of the R.A.F. and the American Air Forces in the war. There is the brilliant record of the American Air Forces in flying supplies to China over the hump, and which certainly made history in efforts of that kind. There was the 14th Army in Burma which advanced on the wings of the Royal Air Force, and was supplied entirely by the Royal Air Force. Since the war there has been the Allied effort in air trooping, which resulted in so many tens of thousands of men being brought home by air for demobilisation.
>
> I only say that it would be rash to assume that air effort cannot meet, to a very considerable extent, the need for supplies in Berlin. Anyhow, if this could be done, whatever effort the Royal Air Force and the joint air forces make, they will be making that effort not in war but in the cause of peace; they will be working to supply a civilian population exposed to cruel suffering; and this time they will be dropping on Berlin not bombs but food.[2]

The allies scrambled to provide the aircraft and crews. The RAF introduced Yorks, which carried nine tons, but had to ask BOAC to take over their trooping flights to the Middle and Far East. The Commonwealth was asked for help, and Australia, South Africa and New Zealand provided aircrews. The Americans brought in around 200 Skymasters from bases around the world, and under the expert leadership of General Tunner, a veteran of 'The Hump', established an orderly flow of machines, travelling northbound along the one-way corridor from Frankfurt, landing at either Gatow or Tempelhof in Berlin to unload, and then proceeding westward along the Hannover corridor, which was also one way. The British organised a not so orderly flow down the northern corridor, flying a mixture of Yorks and Dakotas, even Sunderland flying boats. Split second timing was crucial, with a leeway of 30 seconds over the beacon entering the corridors; an aircraft landed or took off at Berlin's Gatow airfield every two minutes, day and night.

> As soon as a machine stopped, the wide freight doors were opened, and two lorries came up. One was immediately backed up to the hatch, and a chute placed in position from the aircraft to the lorry. Two German loaders in the fuselage then slid the coal sacks down the chute into the lorry, where two more loaders stacked them. As soon as the first lorry had finished, it drove some 300 yards to the light railway, and the second lorry then filled up with the remainder. The aircraft unloading took about fifteen minutes. At the railhead the lorries backed up to the tip trucks and the sacks were emptied into them. As each sack was emptied it was thrown down beside the truck, where more workers rolled them up in bundles of nine, and stowed them in a tenth sack, all ready for the return flight. When the tip trucks were full they were taken to the Havel See, about a mile distant, and there the coal was tipped into waiting barges for transport to the various parts of Berlin.[3]

The British contribution was about to become even more disorderly. The RAF was stretched to its limit providing so many aircraft and crews, between thirty and forty Yorks and as many Dakotas, almost the entire strength of Transport Command, and even with the help of the Commonwealth crews, aircraft still had to be stood down and crews returned to enable Transport Command to resume its now urgently required training programme. Then another problem arose; a shortage of liquid fuel was developing in Berlin, and neither the British nor the American forces had tanker aircraft adapted to carry fuel. The only available aircraft were the converted Lancastrian tankers of Flight Refuelling which had been used experimentally on various transatlantic flights. The British government gagged at the thought of having to use private enterprise to enable it to fulfil its international obligations, but agreed to send the Flight Refuelling Lancastrians to Berlin. The government then had to hold its collective socialist nose even longer when it realised that it needed to use charter airlines to bulk out the British contribution and carry dry goods as well. The Foreign Office agreed to pay, and the operation was given an air of respectability by having it 'administered' by BEA, which had its work cut out trying to organise the motley collection of crews and aircraft that were chartered: Dakotas, Vikings, Halifaxes, Bristol Wayfarers and Freighters, Yorks, Lancasters, Lancastrians and Tudors, the occasional Scottish Aviation Liberator, Aquila's Sunderlands. The first of the additional freighters arrived on 4 August; by the middle of September there were thirty on call; and on 11 November the civil airlift celebrated 100 days of operations, having performed 3,944 sorties and carried 18,585 tons. The independents' contribution continued through the winter; at any one time the number of civil aircraft in use varied between thirty-one and forty-seven; and on 31 May Flight Refuelling carried in the 100,000th ton, flown in by Captain Hanbury, who had delivered the very first civil cargo in July the year before. Twenty-three independent airlines contributed ninety aircraft to the airlift. There was a small contribution by BOAC at the beginning; and a heroic contribution throughout by BSAA, operating two Tudor Is and five Tudor Vs, in essence Tudor IIs with slightly more powerful engines and round windows, bought at an advantageous price from the Ministry of Supply. The Tudor Vs were the biggest aircraft on the airlift, and with their over-size volumetric capacity were champion fuel haulers over the relatively short distances along the Corridor. Avro designed, made, fitted, tested the installation of the internal tanks and cleared ARB approval in just six days. The ARB was helpful all round, temporarily increasing the all up weights, and so allowing bigger payloads; the Dakotas could now carry 3.3 tons, as much as those of the RAF. BSAA's former chief executive, Bennett, was back in business with a new airline, Airflight, and two big Tudors, which he deployed to Berlin early in September. By the end of the airlift the seven 'fat' Tudors had performed 3,167 sorties and carried almost 30 per cent of the liquid fuel required into Berlin; the remaining fuel was flown in by an assortment of forty other aircraft, mainly Halifaxes and Lancastrians. The 'wet' uplift was Britain's unique contribution to the airlift, accounting for two thirds of the civil effort. Even Bevin, Britain's Foreign Secretary, had to acknowledge its worth: 'The civil airlift is admittedly a comparatively small part of the whole, but it is important not only because it is a significant part of our contribution but also because it provides the whole of the wet lift for liquid fuel into Berlin.'[4] He then went on to express his concern that these commercial venturers were in it merely for the money, and worried that they would make 'excessive profits at the expense of the Crown.' *The Aeroplane* estimated that the cost of flying civil aircraft ranged from £85 a flying hour for a Halifax to £120 per hour for the big Tudor, and the Foreign Office confirmed it was spending to £200,000 a week on the Airlift.

The Halifaxes were the most numerous of the British civilian contingent; forty-one were used at one time or another, and they performed over 8,000 sorties, carrying nearly 54,000 tons. Freddie Laker leased his Halifaxes to Bond Air Services and to the parliamentarians of Westminster Airways, and he helped keep them in the air through his engineering and maintenance company, Aviation Traders. Bond also bought surplus Halifaxes from the RAF, at £200 apiece, and used four of them on the airlift. 'The part aircraft from the Lancashire Aircraft Corporation played in the airlift became almost legendary,' enthused Arthur Pearcy in his book *Berlin Airlift*[5] 'and by the end of the humanitarian operation the company had undertaken more sorties than any other charter company, with the exception of Flight Refuelling.' Lancashire developed new tanks for their fleet of twelve Halifaxes, 1,000 lbs lighter than the old ones and increasing the capacity from 1,400 to 1,800 gallons of diesel oil. Fuel was transferred by pipeline from the aircraft to barges on the Havel See, an important means of distribution throughout Berlin. Of course, every charter airline had its own ideas as to how to convert aircraft to carry fuel, so the ground staff at Gatow had to maintain a large assortment of adaptors and hoses of different shapes and sizes to accommodate them all. Eagle flew a distinctive Halifax, registration G-ALEF and painted all-over red, which stood out from the drab olive or aluminium finishes of the other aircraft. Bamberg's airline flew over 1,000 sorties, a creditable achievement for a new airline with just three Halifaxes.

After the Halifaxes came the Dakotas, nineteen of which participated in the civil airlift. But in mid-November the decision was taken to withdraw twin-engine civil aircraft from the airlift, following the lead of the Americans, who had found that it took as long to load a Dakota as the much bigger Skymaster, for a third of the tonnage. Also, the British were finding it more difficult to support the Dakotas with spares, and they were needed in the charter market. That charter airline icon, Air Transport (Charter) (CI), flew 205 sorties on G-AIVZ before it was sent back, Kearsley Airways managed 246 with its two Dakotas, and disreputable Ciro's achieved 328 sorties. Air Contractors was the biggest Dakota contributor, flying 386 missions. The RAF continued flying its Dakotas until the very end, although Transport Command was able to reinvigorate its contribution when the first fourteen of the larger, four-engine Handley Page Hastings joined the team. Other charter airlines made significant contributions. Aquila helped by carrying around 1,000 tons of salt, as well as other bulky items, cigarettes, light bulbs, in its Sunderlands. Despite the difficulties of marine operation, the RAF was able to turn round the flying boats in under 20 minutes. Both Airwork and Silver City contributed Bristol Freighters, highly prized as they were able to carry outsize cargo and load it easily through the clamshell doors in the nose. BEA valiantly continued its Viking passenger services; the operation was completely self-sufficient, the aircraft tankered in enough fuel not only for the return sector, but also to keep its ground vehicles in Berlin supplied. Skyways and Flight Refuelling operated a large fleet of Lancastrians in support of the wet lift, and Skyways was the only independent to use Yorks, which flew over 1,000 sorties with more than 10,000 tons of dry goods.

Alone of the major charter airlines, Skyways was a significant hauler on the Berlin Airlift; with Bond Air Services, BSAA, Flight Refuelling and Lancashire Aircraft Corporation, these five airlines contributed over 70 per cent of the civil lift. Hunting Air Travel, with a handsome contract to support the Ground Nut Scheme in East Africa, stayed away altogether. Airwork was also preoccupied with its other government contracts but contributed two Freighters, as did Silver City during the winter lull in its car ferry services. Scottish Aviation was a disappointing participant; its Liberators were withdrawn at an early stage because of reliability issues, later they were given a second chance as tankers, able to carry 2,500 gallons just in their wing tanks.

By the end the Airlift was bringing in between 6,000 and 8,000 tons a day. Airfields in Berlin were continually strengthened to allow for even larger transport aircraft, like the Boeing C-97 Stratofreighter, a cargo version of the Stratocruiser, able to carry 26 tons. After talks at the United Nations, the Russians lifted the blockade at one minute past midnight on 12 May 1949, but the civil airlift continued flying through to August, as the western allies wanted to build up stocks, and problems with the overland routes persisted. It was not until September that the RAF was finally stood down. Well over three quarters of the total goods into Berlin were flown in by the United States Air Force, helped by the other American services and civil carriers. The Americans also provided the star of the show, Gail Halvorsen, an Air Force pilot who began dropping sweets and other goodies out of his cockpit window to the children he saw playing among the rubble on the approach to Berlin's Tempelhof airport; he would waggle his wings to let them know which aircraft he was flying. Nicknamed the Candy Bomber, his kind-hearted actions led to a full-blown operation, supported by generous contributions from his homeland and a gang of *Rosinenbomber* colleagues, which dropped 23 tons of sweets, chewing gum and other candy, attached to small parachutes, to the children waiting below.

The RAF flew in just under 400,000 tons to Berlin, 17 per cent of the total 2,325,809 tons. The RAF also contributed extensively on the ground; six of the dispatching airfields were in the British zone, and Gatow, in the British sector, was the most heavily used airport in Berlin. The French built an extra airfield in Berlin, Tegel, which was used by the British and had the advantage that it did not interfere with air traffic at the other two airfields. The Germans contributed manpower: building, extending and repairing airfields; unloading the railway wagons that brought the coal, dehydrated potato, flour and other foodstuffs to the dispatching airfields; and loading them onto the waiting aircraft. In Berlin, German labourers, many of them living in the Russian sector, unloaded the aircraft, turning them round in 20 minutes or less. They did not seem to enjoy it much:

> Manual loading is exhausting, and another thing is the language difficulty. On the Lift, the German loaders have no enthusiasm, as they are pretty well exhausted by the loads they have to handle, e.g. flour sacks 220 lb., drums of dried egg 250 lb., coals sacks 110 lb., and so on. This is further complicated by reason of the fact that the composition of the loading teams change almost daily.[6]

Nor did the British government show much enthusiasm, after the Airlift was over, for the civil airlines that had participated. BEA was happy to take the credit for the airlift, claiming that in the four days over Easter 'the B.E.A. fleet of just over 40 aircraft lifted 2,000 tons of liquid fuel and 500 tons of food', which was explained away as 'the British European Airways fleet of civil aircraft owned by charter companies.'[7] There was little more than passing interest in Parliament; Bevin was eventually goaded into saying thank you through a planted question:

> I am grateful for this opportunity of paying tribute to the contribution which the British civil air charter companies have made to the success of this great operation. No less than 26 of these companies have participated in the air lift at one time or another during the past 10 months. Official figures provided by the Air Ministry show that almost a quarter of the total supply tonnage borne to Berlin by British aircraft operating in the air lift was carried by these charter companies. Another fact which is perhaps not sufficiently known is that the entire quantity of liquid fuels, including petrol, diesel oil and kerosene which the Western sectors of Berlin have received by means of the air lift, was carried in British civil aircraft. In the month of April, for example, supplies of this kind amounting to over 400 tons per day were carried in a fleet of civil air tankers specially adapted for the purpose.[8]

It was hard for the airlines after the Airlift finally concluded. Skyways found it difficult to adjust, the more so as the loss of flying contracts coincided with the winding down of its extensive Skymaster operations on behalf of BOAC, and its African operations were also being curtailed. Halifax operators learned that the ARB was not prepared to extend the maximum weight dispensation in effect during the Airlift, so the aircraft shed a ton of payload. Bond Air Services laid up its fleet of Halifaxes, and returned briefly to passenger flying; its founder, David Bond, re-emerged in the 1960s as a helicopter operator. Freight business in Europe was in decline, as was the British economy, which had just had to underwrite the cost of the Airlift, over £10 million, and was about to devalue the pound sterling. Britain had lurched from one economic crisis to another since the war, and had struggled with its huge dollar-denominated wartime debt, to such an extent that Marshall Aid, which should have gone towards replacing plant and repairing infrastructure, was instead used to improve the nation's balance of payments.

The airline that found it most difficult during and after the Airlift was BSAA; the corporation had been eager to participate and as we have seen, played a most valuable role. Pleased with BSAA's success on the Airlift, the government decided to commission ten more Tudor Vs which the corporation would have used to boost Britain's contribution during the coming winter, when the allies planned to fly in enough to give every household 5 cwt of coal. But then the blockade ended, cutting off a serious source of funding and opportunity for BSAA, and giving the various government departments ample opportunity to squabble among themselves as to which should now pay for the additional Tudors. At the same time BSAA had continued its pioneering work in the Caribbean, in 1948 launching service to Miami and Cuba from Nassau in the Bahamas. Then fate struck once more: almost a year after the disappearance of *Star Tiger*, another Tudor IV, *Star Ariel*, was lost on 17 January 1949 on a flight from Bermuda to Kingston, Jamaica, again in circumstances which have not been satisfactorily explained. *Star Tiger* had been creeping across the Atlantic at 2,000 feet against strong headwinds, but *Star Ariel* was at 18,000 feet, in clear weather; in both cases no one picked up any distress calls. The Tudor IVs were grounded, leaving the airline short of modern equipment. It was all most unfortunate. The corporation lacked leadership at this crucial point; Bennett's replacement, Air Commodore Brackley, a veteran of Imperial Airways, had drowned in a bathing accident at Rio towards the end of the previous year, and there was no one to defend BSAA's corner, particularly against the predations of BOAC and its new boss, Sir Miles Thomas. At the time, members of Parliament questioned why modern aircraft were not made available to BSAA to tide it over: the Canadairs were coming on line early, and the government had just bought four more Stratocruisers. But the government performed another u-turn, ignoring all those convincing arguments it had put forward in 1947 as to the desirability of having three corporations, and instead decided to amalgamate BSAA with BOAC. Lindgren claimed that had been the plan all along: 'I make it plain to the House that the disaster of the withdrawal of the Tudors was the decisive factor, although amalgamation had been under consideration for some time.'[9] Now the new Fashion – 'a premature, permanent alteration to correct a passing phase' as Lord Balfour put it – was for BOAC to function operationally as two divisions, respectively eastern and western; the latter would serve North America, the Caribbean, Central America and the northern republics of South America: 'It provides flexibility in the disposition of aircraft capacity to meet varying incidence in seasonal traffic demands in this area,' explained Pakenham on 20 July 1949,[10] as if Caribbean traffic in any way corresponded in volume to the major flows between London and New York. He was at a loss to account for the traffic to Brazil, Argentina and Chile: 'Admittedly, as some noble Lords will wish to point out, the route to Brazil, Argentine, Uruguay and Chile is a separate operational task—I am not disputing that—but it represents roughly only a half of B.S.A.A.'s present activities.' Balfour pressed Pakenham:

> I ask the noble Lord what has altered, beyond a temporary shortage of aircraft at the present time caused by the withdrawal of the Tudors, to cause this Bill to be introduced. Why should we not take a long-term view of civil aviation, in the same way as [we have been] asked to take a long-tem view as regards other nationalised corporations?

Lord Strabolgi made his criticism tellingly, at least to anybody who has ever been reprimanded for a lack of horticultural skills: 'I would like to say how sorry I am that civil aviation is once more being pulled up by the roots to see how it is growing. I am sorry for the changes; I am sorry they are necessary.'

By this stage the quality of the debates in the two Houses had diverged widely. Lord Swinton still led for the Tories; he spoke from experience and with patriotic regret for the deteriorating state of the corporations' finances. He was met with sharp good humour at first by Lord Pakenham, 20 years his junior. Even the independents seemed to like Pakenham, judging from this exchange during a debate in the House of Lords on 2 February 1949:

> Viscount Swinton: I still remain a little surprised at this enthusiasm on the part of the charter companies. The noble Lord met them and knows what they look like.
> Lord Pakenham: They looked very nice.
> Viscount Swinton: I am sure they did, and apparently the noble Lord looked very nice, too.

But the relationship between the two peers changed after a serious difference of opinion over Pakenham's handling of the investigation into the crash of a KLM Constellation at Prestwick; Pakenham had publicly dissented from one of the conclusions in order to protect his ministry's air traffic controllers. The Tory warhorses were somewhat depleted in numbers by now, but with the minister in the Lords, most of the serious exchanges still took place there, and well-crafted speeches followed on from each other in an orderly pattern. The Tories had no such leadership to look up to in the Commons, and in Lindgren, the socialists had a rather obnoxious parliamentary secretary. Air Commodore Harvey would often open the debates for the Tories, but he was no Perkins, unable to keep to the point and for all his professional expertise, no expert. A previous parliamentary secretary, Ivor Thomas, had joined the Tories, so whenever he entered the debating lists, the atmosphere became especially poisonous.

The government was able to push the Airways Corporation Bill, amalgamating BSAA and BOAC, through both houses quickly, and just as BSAA's big Tudors came off the Airlift, it was signed into law on 30 July 1949; it was later consolidated into the Civil Aviation Act 1949. Whatever the rights and wrongs of the take-over, and history suggests that BSAA would have succumbed sooner or later, it did allow the government to sweep under the carpet any residual claims over the Avro Tudor. BOAC provided five Yorks as a stopgap for the South American services, and the Tudors were laid up. To improve their marketability, the Ministry of Civil Aviation withdrew the ban on carrying passengers from the big Tudors, the Marks II and V, but that only helped Bennett's airline, which promptly began using its two Tudors to carry refugees into and out of Israel. Bennett's airline was now called Fairflight. In order to shield the considerable profits that he had made on the Berlin Airlift, he sold Airflight to an old RAF chum who controlled Chartair, retaining the two Tudors for himself, and allowing Chartair to offset Airflight's profits against its own losses.

Another gainer was BOAC. The government had conceded a further change: the corporations could now place orders for new aircraft directly with the manufacturers, rather than going through the Ministry of Supply – 'It is extraordinary how successfully the Ministry of Supply impedes the economic progress of this country' was how Swinton saw the matter – and BOAC promptly ordered twenty-five Bristol Britannias. BOAC had reason to feel smug. After four years of chaotic change, the corporation was at last coming to grips with its fleet, its manning levels, and its direction. Constellations now flew to Australia; the first Argonaut, as the Canadair C-4 was known in BOAC service, flew to Hong Kong and Tokyo in August 1949; the first Stratocruiser was delivered in October and entered service to New York on 6 December. The early delivery of Argonauts saw them taking over the Skyways contract flying, and other services to the Middle and Far East, replacing flying boats, Lancastrians, Yorks; to rub salt into the wounds, Argonauts and Constellations would appear on the South American routes early in 1950. The take-over of BSAA allowed the corporation to expand its network while obliterating a potential competitor, adding route mileage and maybe improving aircraft utilisation. Thomas began some serious cost-cutting; moving out of the plush Mayfair headquarters to Brentford; initiating the slow transfer of engineering to Heathrow, starting with the Canadair fleet; withdrawing flying boats and closing down the marine bases – by 1950 only East Africa still saw the Solents; and reducing manpower levels, from 21,000 in 1949 to 17,340 in 1950. Other losses remained at much the same level, however. BOAC contributed the lion's share – £7.8 million – of the combined deficit of £11.7 million for the three corporations, up from £11 million in 1947–48.

In this BOAC was ably abetted by BEA, which managed a net loss of £2.7 million: 'No small measure of encouragement lies in the fact that it was £800,000 less than the previous year's figure' was *Flight* magazine's gushing comment. More encouraging were the imminent management changes at the top of BEA. For all his experience, as pilot, pre-war director of British Airways, and organiser of the wartime Air Transport Auxiliary, d'Erlanger was not cut out for the rough and tumble that went with the post of managing director, and later chairman, of the ragbag that was BEA. He had friends in high places, of course, especially in the Tory party, but always seemed overanxious to please his political bosses, whichever government was in power. He embraced centralised planning and control, clumsily alienating and eventually dismissing the many professionals who up till then had made domestic air services viable; it is ironic that one of the ostensible reasons for his departure was his disapproval of Pakenham's direction that BEA should operate a loss-making service within Wales. When he appointed Lord Douglas to look into the workings of the 'associate agreements', Pakenham had not intended that Douglas should delve any deeper into the mysteries of BEA. But Douglas could not help himself, and was appalled by what he found.

I doubt whether an organisation with so many General Mangers, whose functions overlap, can be efficient: it would be considerably improved if all the traffic functions were combined under one head. Moreover, there appears to be a lack of drive in the management of the Corporation. Instead of pursuing an aggressive policy and going out looking for business, they seem content to undertake the minimum services required of them and to find excuses for avoiding new work. It seems wrong that a national organisation with definite responsibilities to the public should have decided that the way to reduce their deficit was to curtail the air services provided. Their first stop should, I consider, have been not to cut their services, but to make a vigorous attempt to reduce their costs and to cut out any dead wood in their organisation. The management of BEA appears to lack drive and there is evidence that, in many respects, the Corporation is inefficient.[11]

There was more to this lack of efficiency. Lord Douglas learned that the pre-war services of Channel Islands Airways had been profitable: now they were not, and he put that down to a lack of local knowledge and an inability to delegate.

Channel Islands Airways, who did all their maintenance on the Islands, carried out the main overhauls of their aircraft in the winter and did most of the normal maintenance in the mid-week period in the summer. By this means, they were able to use all their aircraft at the time when they needed them most, viz., at the week-ends in the summer. BEA, on the other hand, spread their maintenance evenly throughout the year, so that the same number of aircraft are undergoing over-haul at any one time. This arrangement may be the best way of obtaining the maximum use from the maintenance base, but it completely ignores the traffic requirements. It also means that the Corporation's engineering staff in the Channel Islands are not fully employed in the winter.

   The Channel Islands representatives told me that there had been a very considerable increase in staff when BEA took over the services, and that, because of over-specialisation of the duties of the ground crews and lack of personal interest, it appeared to the local people that BEA were getting much less work from their staff than Channel Islands Airways did in similar circumstances. It is probably worth recording that Commander Waters, who was Managing Director of Channel Islands Airways and is now General Manager (British Services) in BEA, was most embarrassed when I pressed him to explain (in front of his Chairman) the differences between the operation of the Channel Islands services by his old company and by BEA.

And there is no more convincing indictment of d'Erlanger's harsh treatment of the Scottish aviation pioneers than this:

The Ministry prepared for me a statement comparing the cost of operating the Scottish services with DH89's by the [railway owned] AAJC in 1944 with the cost of similar services by BEA in 1947/8. This showed that BEA's maintenance costs were three times those of AAJC and that the total operating costs were twice as high. BEA's explanation that the increase was due mainly to the higher cost of staff, because of the higher wages and shorter hours which now apply, is not very convincing. I suspect that the real reason is that their standards of operation are too lavish.

Jo Grimond, Liberal MP for Orkney and Shetland, noticed this too, and put an amusing spin on it:

I wonder whether B.E.A. realise the great field of expansion which awaits them in the north. The pioneers of air services went out for custom. They enticed farmers into their aeroplanes. They flew frequent services in small aeroplanes at suitable times. As a result, a habit of air travel grew up and costs were kept down by having small aircraft, well filled, and by having small staffs on the airfields.

Since B.E.A. took over, however—although I must admit that the services which they run are perfectly satisfactory—there is a feeling in the north that we are treated rather as though we were a similar problem to that presented by air services between great cities in the south. Large aircraft fly not, perhaps, very frequently, the staffs have increased, and the whole organisation, it is felt, has become rather impersonal, and of course costs and prices have become very much more expensive.

In a small way my point is illustrated by the sort of advertisements which are to be seen for B.E.A., which are nearly always of gentlemen who, I believe, are known as "business tycoons," flying with brief cases apparently to make astronomical contracts in an atmosphere, if I may so describe it, of cigars and brandy. I have no doubt that these gentlemen exist in some places, but there are not very many of them north of Aberdeen. What we feel most seriously is that there does not appear to be any great anxiety on the part of B.E.A. to increase or even to restore the local services among the Islands.[12]

Of course governments have to keep their secrets, but Pakenham, as a good socialist, was especially concerned to keep Douglas's findings under wraps, highlighting as they did the decline in operating efficiency, profitability and standards since the government had nationalised the railways' air companies. He never published the report, and only ever alluded in Parliament to its recommendations with regard to the 'associate agreements'. But he did act on it. The first thing Pakenham did was fire d'Erlanger, and replace him as chairman with Lord Douglas. Commentators wondered if Douglas was the right man for the job, but then they did not know how thorough had been his investigation of BEA; also, he had some sort of pedigree, having been one of the first pilots on the London to Paris route with Handley Page Transport; and he was on good terms with Pakenham. Next, he appointed Peter Masefield as director-general of BEA, plucking him from out of the coop at the Ministry, where he had been in charge of long-term planning and projects, a role well suited to his erudition. The two of them would lead BEA into its most prosperous era, the golden age of the Vickers Viscount. Then Pakenham had to look to his own backyard, and start defending his turf, as questions began to be asked about the future of his ministry. 'For my own part I consider that the time will soon come—if it has not already arrived—when this Ministry ought to be merged with the Ministry of Transport,' suggested Lord Swinton on 2 February 1949, having just pointed out that the cost to the British taxpayer was not just the £11 million that the corporations had lost that year:

Then there is the cost of the Ministry itself, which has increased greatly. I think the figure for staff alone (if we take headquarters staff, the staff at out-stations and travelling expenses) exceeds £1,000,000. I wonder whether all that is necessary, and whether some of the work could not be eliminated. I think your Lordships will agree that in assessing the real cost of civil aviation all that has to be taken into account, and I would ask the Minister to give us the real aggregate figure. I think your Lordships will be surprised at it. I have tried to calculate a figure from the Estimates, and, allowing £6,750,000 for appropriations in aid, I calculate that we have to add at least £16,000,000 to the Corporations' deficit of £10,000,000 or £11,000,000. If I am right, that means that the true bill to the taxpayer for the year is not less than £26,000,000, and may well be more.[13]

Pakenham pointed out that much of that expenditure was necessarily at the airports his ministry ran, but Swinton had made his point. The huge deficits were not just confined to aviation. Peter Thorneycroft, a Conservative MP, calculated how much the British Transport Commission, responsible under the Ministry of Transport for the nationalised railways, road haulage, some bus companies, the docks, a few former railway hotels, and the canals, was costing the taxpayer:

In 1948, the Transport Commission lost £4¾ million, and that was on a system of accounting which, to say the least of it, was not the most unfavourable towards the Transport Commission. In 1949, the estimated loss is £20 million. In 1950, the estimated loss is no less than £30 million. The nationalised transport industry at this moment is running at a loss of half a million pounds of public money a week. It is a sobering thought that, as we sit here and discuss these matters, the public funds are running out at a rate which I calculate to be £50 a minute.[14]

Then Pakenham announced that he was extending the 'associate agreements' experiment for two years, but setting up a more formal structure. He made it clear that he would not deny the charter airlines these unwanted routes, but with the caveat, 'until British European Airways Corporation is in a position to provide all the scheduled air services in this country for which there is a justifiable demand.' He continued:

If nationalised air transport is the only conceivable form of air transport in this country—as I believe it is—then it is the worst possible service both to nationalisation and to air transport to pursue a "dog-in-the-manger" policy. By that I mean a policy that says "We cannot and you shall not." I am not asking or encouraging these charter companies to step in. If they come in it is their own affair.[15]

Lord Balfour retorted:

Quite a number of them may because they are pretty desperate. I grant that the Berlin air lift has, economically speaking, helped the charter companies immensely, but if it had not been for that, many of them would be nearly on the borderline; and the fact that you allow them to enter a field where conditions are so much against them seems to me to be bad economics and rather unfair.

The task of deciding each application was handed over to the Air Transport Advisory Committee (ATAC), a hitherto largely ignored consumer watchdog. Its chairman, Lord Terrington, was a barrister with a long history in public service as an arbitrator: he is also one of the unsung heroes of British civil aviation. Single-handedly, as the chief regulator over the next decade, he allowed British independents to develop scheduled and charter services to an extent undreamed of by Pakenham and his successors, and without seriously antagonising the government and the corporations. Pakenham claimed:

Lord Terrington [is] not going to play the rubber stamp either to myself or to Lord Douglas…The number of instances in which the Council have differed from B.E.A. is sufficient to indicate that kind of masculine independence which we associate with my noble friend Lord Terrington, while at the same time they are insufficient to suggest a whole series of irreconcilable conflicts.[16]

Pakenham seemed to set some store by this 'masculine' thing; he had earlier referred to Lord Douglas as a 'virile gentleman who is no "stooge" of mine, although I hope he is my friend.'

For the independents the outcome of all these deliberations and changes was mixed. A number were able to apply for longer associate agreements; Silver City could now legitimately run its vehicle ferry services; Air Kruise, a neighbour at Lympne, started an air coach passenger service to Le Touquet; Aquila found regular use for its flying boats by starting a service to Funchal in Madeira, a mountainous Portuguese island in the Atlantic with no airfield, so the Portuguese, who had no flying boats, allowed Aquila full traffic rights between Lisbon and Madeira; Air Transport (Charter) (CI) flew a programme of charters from Newcastle to Jersey, just one of several inclusive tour services awarded; Patrick Aviation, one of many small businesses set up by ex-servicemen, thought it was on to a winner when it was awarded the Birmingham to Jersey holiday route. But associate agreements were only a tiny part of the business needed to support the independent airline industry, and other opportunities were disappearing fast. The bleak outlook for the independents, coming so soon after the hyperglycaemic rush of the Airlift, was not improved by the government's actions. Skyways was forced to sell off its Skymasters as it retrenched, this proud company rapidly dwindling in stature as its long-haul business evaporated, leaving it with not much more than an oil contract in Kuwait for two Dakotas. Westminster Airways closed down 'in view of the restrictive provisions of the Civil Aviation Act and other restrictions on the activities of independent air charter companies.'[17] Hunting also felt the chill wind when its contract with the Overseas Food Corporation was not renewed in November 1949. Instead the contract was awarded to BOAC even though Hunting's bid, at just under £64 a passenger, had been lower. Lennox-Boyd expounded on what had happened to the House on 13 December 1949:

It is our definite charge that on 27th July, 1949, B.O.A.C. had a meeting with the Overseas Food Corporation; that on that day Sir Miles Thomas and Sir Leslie Plummer agreed to B.O.A.C. taking over the contracts; that B.O.A.C. officials were told by Sir Miles to visit the Corporation and work out the details; that, as my hon. Friend said, not knowing that Hunting had quoted at that moment, they quoted £80; that then a message came from Sir Leslie Plummer saying that if B.O.A.C. quoted a figure within 10 per cent. of Hunting's they were to get it; that two officers of the Overseas Food Corporation were then told to work out a figure at an 85 per cent. load factor, and that they came back and said it was £72 10s.; that the representatives of B.O.A.C. were then told that this was a figure which, if quoted, would secure them the contract—they were told this on the quiet; that the next day, 28th July, B.O.A.C. not unnaturally sent in a quotation of £72 10s. and on the following day, 29th July, Hunting's [was] told they were not to have the contract.

That is the sorry story. My hon. Friend says quite rightly that it is not only the case that the Civil Aviation Act has been broken—for it has been broken in the most monstrous way—since the Parliamentary Secretary said that the Exchequer grant would not be used for the purpose of undercutting private operators and we believe that it has been used to break the Act. However, our charge tonight is much more than that. It is that a squalid deal has been arrived at between two Government Corporations which has driven out of this business a highly reputable firm whose members pay taxes to the State to enable us to carry out these risky experiments. Because it is a monstrous breach of the Act and a reckless misuse of public money, I think my hon. Friend was justified in raising this quite scandalous story.[18]

The government could not do much more than smirk, apparently unprepared for the outburst, and agreed to change the rules for government contracts, so that in future BOAC and BEA would not be privy beforehand to the bids, which would now only be considered by the ministry. It sounds a small enough concession, but it was gall to Pakenham, who truly believed in the socialist ideal and wanted to create a British equivalent of the Russian Aeroflot, which controlled all aspects of civil aviation in the Soviet Union, airlines, airports, air traffic control, and flying clubs. In a later debate Balfour categorised these policies:

The Socialist theory, as applied to civil aviation, really does mean in practice that the public must be deprived of facilities, or should be deprived of facilities, that could be supplied and made available. They must be deprived unless those facilities are made available through the nationalised State instrument.[19]

Pakenham's ministry already controlled most of the airports and the two major airlines; and he believed that if charter airlines must operate, they should only do so with the corporations' blessing. His convoluted arguments about not being a 'dog-in-the-manger' came down to this, that 'associate agreements' were acceptable only because BEA 'controlled' the services even if it did not fly them. Likewise Pakenham thought that major government contracts should automatically go to the corporations; it was up to them to subcontract the business to the independents if they so wished, but the corporations should retain contractual control, and of course rake off some of the profits. So when the Overseas Food Corporation had originally given the contract to Hunting a year earlier, thereby saving £100,000 against BOACs tender, it had been very distressing for Pakenham. He could not understand how a government corporation would not play by the rules: support a state-owned industry and pay BOAC to do the job. When the question of government contracts to fly service personnel to and from overseas bases (trooping flights) came up for consideration later, in 1950, Pakenham was again at a loss to understand how the Air Ministry and the War Office could even consider awarding contracts to the lowest bidder when it was surely their duty to allocate the tasks to the nationalised corporations; how the corporations operated the flights was their business.

The government, abetted by its civil servants, continued its attacks on the charter industry. Paperwork increased as the ministry deluged the independents with more and more questionnaires and forms, mainly to establish the bona fides of the chartering organisations, sometimes enlisting the police to check on charterers' credentials. As the government headed towards the finishing tape of its first term of office, labour issues became more significant. 'Mr Lindgren wished to make it quite clear that the lowering of either standards of operations or the undercutting of wages and conditions of service would not be tolerated.'[20] Words like 'union membership' and 'National Joint Council' began to appear, ominously, in parliamentary speeches. Even BOAC was not spared. There were some vicious exchanges over the fate of BSAA employees after the BOAC take over, despite the minister's assurances that the axe would not fall exclusively on BSAA. Overseas governments, too, began to make life harder for charter airlines, requiring prior permission for charter flights and sometimes stipulating lengthy periods of notice; India now wanted fifteen days notice of any charter flight, Greece six days, Italy five days. These requirements were waived if the flight was operated by one of the corporations; *The Aeroplane* explained how the system worked, illustrating the 'Pakenham ideal' of commercial control by the state:

> Last week this clearance period worked to the advantage of B.E.A. A company of radio manufacturers wanted to get a cargo of sets to Greece urgently. They tried the London Air Freight exchange for a charter aircraft and were told of the six day clearance for Greece. B.E.A. then offered a Halifax, sub-chartered from British-American Air Services, and sent the cargo to Greece as a scheduled cargo flight. This circumvented the clearance formalities as they do not apply to scheduled services. We understand that the B.E.A. price was well above the £800 quoted for a Halifax.[21]

There were other setbacks. When BOAC withdrew its Solent service to South Africa in 1950, Aquila applied for an associate agreement to replace it, but was turned down, to the annoyance of many Tories, who seemed to have a nostalgic reverence for flying boat operations. Patrick Aviation also learned the hard way that associate agreements were not for ever, especially if the routes showed promise. Its application to continue the Birmingham to Jersey service in 1950 was turned down because BEA had decided to take over operation of the route. This provoked an irritated response from the local Labour MP, Captain Blackburn, who was duly smacked down by Lindgren using his all-purpose swatter – a

A de Havilland DH. 18 of Instone Air Line, one of the earliest pioneers in British air transport, is seen at Cologne, Germany, in 1922. The eight passengers had a good view through the windows of the enclosed cabin behind the single Napier Lion engine. The pilot can be seen in the cockpit above the two standing figures. (*CMcC*)

Armstrong Whitworth Atalanta, a powerful monoplane built for Imerial Airways in the 1930s, to use at hot-and-high airfields in Africa and India. An advanced design, its four engines were mounted in the wing, giving the aircraft a clean appearance. On African routes the Atalanta could carry nine passengers and up to a ton of mail. (*MAP*)

The Handley Page HP. 42 entered service with Imperial Airways in 1931, and operated in two versions. The HP. 42W, known by the manufacturer as the HP. 45, flew slowly and safely to points in Europe in a thirty-eight-seat configuration. The HP. 42E was used on the eastern services and carried twenty-four passengers and mail. (*MAP*)

Shorts built many fine flying boats for Imperial Airways and BOAC, including the 'C' Class Empires, which first entered service on the Empire Air Mail Scheme in December 1936, just in time for the Christmas post. In this picture, *Capella* is moored on the Nile outside the Winter Palace Hotel at Luxor in Egypt. Passengers would have spent the night in some luxury before continuing to their destination. (*CMcC*)

Three de Havilland DH. 84 Dragons of Scottish Motor Traction Aviation Department. S.M.T. was one of a number of bus companies in Scotland and England which launched air services, this one managed by John Sword who also ran Midland and Scottish Air Ferries. S.M.T. did not last long in the aviation business, starting in July 1932 but ceasing operations early in 1934. (*CMcC*)

De Havilland DH. 86B Express Air Liner was larger than the DH. 84, seating ten passengers and powered by four de Havilland Gipsy Six engines. West Coast Air Services, jointly owned by Olley and the railway companies, flew services to Dublin from Liverpool, Bristol and Croydon, and this aircraft, G-ADYH, continued flying throughout the war for the Associated Airways Joint Committee. (*MAP*)

Jersey Airways flew their DH. 86s in formation to land at Jersey's St Helier beach when tides permitted. It was sometimes unnerving for sunbathers to see the aircraft coming in to land over their heads. The buses served as booking office and shelter. (*CMcC*)

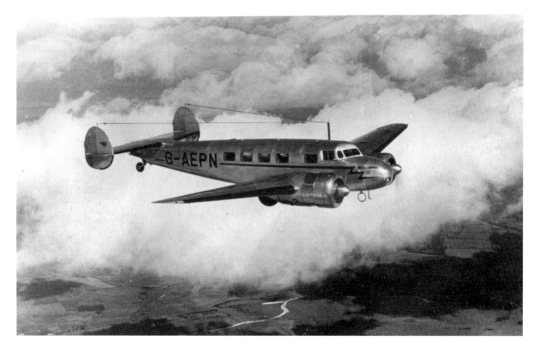

British Airways caused a stir when it introduced fast American-built Lockheeds into service before the war. Up until then British airlines, especially Imperials, flew British-built aircraft. Lockheeds maintained many of BOAC's services in Africa during the war. (*CMcC*)

Railway Air Services used de Havilland DH. 89 Dragon Rapides, a twin-engine development of the DH. 86, for its trunk services. G-ACPR *City of Birmingham* makes a fine sight as it taxies in. It was later sold to the Great Western and Southern Airlines. (*MAP*)

During the war, BOAC used three of these Boeing 314 flying boats on its services to West Africa and across the Atlantic. They could carry up to seventy-four passengers and had a range of 3,500 miles. G-AGBZ was named *Bristol*; passengers entered via the stub wings under the main wing. (*Flight* photography)

The de Havilland DH. 91 was put into service by Imperials in 1938. Originally intended for long haul routes, instead the aircraft were mainly used on services to Paris. BOAC took over the aircraft, but G-AEVW *Franklin* was impressed by the Royal Air Force into No. 271 Squadron as AX903 BJ: W and crashed at Reykjavik in Iceland in 1941. (*MAP*)

After the war, BOAC had to use converted bombers to fly some of the longer routes. This is a converted Handley Page Halifax, known in BOAC service as the Halton. It could carry ten passengers in its slender fuselage, but there was a pannier for extra freight. G-ADHU was the first Halton, converted by Short Brothers and Harland in Belfast.. (*MAP*)

BOAC and the RAF used a large number of Dakotas during the War, and this aircraft, G-ALLI Sir Samuel Instone was transferred to BEA from the RAF in 1949. It was later converted to Pionair standard and is seen here at Manchester Ringway in July 1955. (*CMcC*)

Silver City became famous for introducing vehicle ferry flights across the Channel, first from its base at Lympne in Kent to Le Touquet in France, then later from Ferryfield at Lydd. A Rover P4 is driven on board a Bristol Freighter at Ferryfield, purpose built by Silver City for the service. (*CMcC*)

Skyways Avro Lancastrian G-AHBZ Sky Ambassador was a freight conversion of the famous wartime Lancaster bomber, with gun turrets removed. Other airlines, BOAC and BSAA, also used Lancastrians for passenger duties. (*MAP*)

Skyways was the only independant air line to buy new Avro Yorks. G-AHLV, seen here in 1947, later flew on the Berlin Airlift. Its austere unpainted livery is typical of aircraft of that era. (*MAP*)

Avro built the Tudor as an interim design using parts from the Avro Lincoln bomber, itself a development of the Lancaster. The Tudor had an unhappy history, and was rejected by BOAC, its primary customer. However BSAA used Tudors for its South American services, and the bigger Tudor 5, the so-called 'fat' Tudor, excelled at carrying fuel in the Berlin Airlift. (*MAP*)

Another fuel and cargo hauler that distinguished itself during the Berlin Airlift was the Handley Page Halifax, which was successfully converted to carry liquid fuel. This Halifax, G-AHDV, was operated by Westminster Airways, an airline owned by several Members of Parliament. (*MAP*)

Charter airlines used some smaller wartime conversions, which could be bought inexpensively after the war. Olley Air Service used the Airspeed Consul, seen here at Croydon. Captain Olley was a famous figure before the war as a pioneering pilot for Imperials, before going on to form his own airline; he also participated with the railway companies in some of the leading pre-war domestic airlines. (*CMcC*)

Dakotas were the mainstay of Britain's independent airlines after the war, reliable, economic, adaptable. After the independents were allowed to resume scheduled services, they were put to use on regional services. Here Manx Airlines Dakota G-AMZB comes into land, it was later transferred to Silver City when the latter took over Manx in 1958. (*CMcC*)

When BEA took over all internal air services after the War, it also took over the aircraft of the railways' airline Associated Airways Joint Committe, mainly de Havilland DH. 89 Dragon Rapides. This unidentified Rapide is pictured at Guernsey Airport in the early 1950s. BEA continued flying Rapides until 1964. (*CMcC*)

The Vickers Viking, a development of the wartime Wellington bomber, was ordered to replace the Dakota in BEA service, ironically, the Dakota outlasted the Viking in BEA service. Many were sold on to charter airlines, although this Tradair Viking, G-APOO, had a more distinguished pedigree: it was bought for use by the Royal Family, joining the King's Flight of the Royal Air Force in 1947. (*CMcC*)

AVRO built over 7,000 Ansons before and during the war, and they were used for coastal patrol and flying, navigation and air gunnery training, later they were also used for communications purposes. Transair converted a number into freighters, and used them to carry newspapers and mail to Europe. (*MAP*)

Britain, an island nation, had a long history of flying boat operations, and continued developing them after the war. Saunders-Roe built one prototype of the huge Princess in the Isle of Wight, designed to carry 200 passengers over 3,000 miles, but the type never entered service and it languished at Cowes for many years before being broken up in the late 1960s. (*CMcC*)

Aquila Airways maintained the flying boat tradition after BOAC stopped flying them in 1950. Short Solent G-ANAJ *City of Funchal* is seen in its namesake's harbour on the Portuguese island of Madeira. The Solent's ancestry ran all the way through to Empire Class boats and the wartime Sunderlands. (*CMcC*)

BOAC was quick to buy American aircraft after the war. British manufacturers found it difficult to resume civil airliner production after their heroic wartime achievements, building the bombers and fighters which the nation so urgently needed. The luxurious Boeing Stratocruiser followed the Constellation on BOAC's North Atlantic serives. Note the plain silver finish on G-ALSB *Champion*. (*MAP*)

BOAC also bought Canadian-built aircraft for its Far Eastern and African services, the Canadair C-4, which was a development of the Douglas DC-6, with a shortened fuselage and Rolls-Royce Merlin engines. They gave good service until 1960, and many were then sold to British independents, such as Overseas Aviation, whose G-ALHG is seen landing at Manchester in June 1961. (*CMcC*)

Airwork, a succesful charter airline in the first decade after the war, flew Vikings and the Handley Page Hermes on its trooping contracts and Colonial Coach Class routes. However, it leased Douglas DC-4 Skymaster N4726V from the American airline TALOA to inaugurate its short-lived all-freight serivce across the Atlantic in 1955, seen here at London Airport. (*MAP*)

Freddie Laker was a cheerleader for British-built aircraft, and even found a good use for the ill-fated Avro Tudor, rebuilding them as freighters. Avro Super Trader G-AHNI loads freight for a government charter. (*CMcC*)

The beautiful Airspeed Ambassador entered service with BEA in March 1952, a year later than planned. The type had a short life with the corporation, by whom they were known as the Elizabethan class, in honour of the recently ascended Queen. They had successful second careers, and BKS Air Transport used theirs on scheduled services from Newcastle, later converting them to freighters. (*CMcC*)

Not obviously a passenger aircraft, the Bristol Wayfarer was a conversion of the better known Freighter, but many saw service on the relatively short routes across the Channel, carrying holidaymakers who would then proceed by coach to their destinations. Trans-European's Wayfarer G-AGPV had originally been the first prototype Mk. 1 Freighter, before being converted in 1947 to passenger use. Note the passenger door forward on the starboard side. (*MAP*)

BEA's former Vikings were popular with British charter airlines, faster than the Dakota, and able to carry up to thirty-six passengers. Continental's G-AHPE in this postcard image shows the minimal changes made to its original BEA colour scheme; the cheat-lines over-painted dark blue, but the roof and tail were sprayed an attractive pale blue. (*CMcC*)

The smaller charter airlines bought smaller aircraft! This is a Miles Aerovan, registered G-AJKM of Southend-based East Anglian Flying Services, better known by its later name of Channel Airways. The type could carry ten passengers or a ton of freight, which might have been a very small car, passengers sat very close to the ground. (*CMcC*)

Pristine de Havilland DH. 89 Dragon Rapide G-AKNX beonging to Patrick Aviation, whose vicissitudes were the subject of some parliamentary debate. The luckless airline flew 'associate agreement' scheduled services to the Channel Islands from Birmingham, only to be deprived of them by BEA when they became profitable. Patrick Aviation ceased operation shortly after. (*MAP*)

Intended as a successor to the Dragon Rapide, the de Havilland Dove was an eight-seat feederliner developed under the Brabazon Committee's plans for future post-war aircraft production. Morton Air Services named after Captain Sammy Morton, formerly chief pilot with Olley Air Service. The two airlines competed against each other from their Croyden base until Morton took his former employer over in 1953. (*MAP*)

Miles built a seventeen-seat feederliner in response to the Brabazon Committee's proposals, larger than the Dove and with two more engines. When Miles failed, Handley Page took over production of the aircraft. BEA refused to buy them, but BOAC bought a small number for its overseas associates. West African Airways Corporation was based in Nigeria during the post-war colonial era, and eventually became Nigeria Airways. (*MAP*)

Handley Page built the Dart Herald, powered by Rolls Royce Dart turboprops, as a potential Dakota replacement. Able to carry fifty-six passengers, the aircraft had limited commercial success but those airlines that flew them kept them flying. Jersey Airways and its successors flew Heralds for over twenty years. Herald G-APWC was lent to BEA for evaluation on the Scottish Highland and Islands routes, but the corporation preferred to stay with the Vickers Viscount. (*MAP*)

An earlier product of the Handley Page factory, the Hermes, was developed alongside the RAF's Hasting transport. Ordered by BOAC, the corporation was quick to dispose of them after they entered service, preferring the older Canadair C-4. The Hermes were passed on to the independents and used extensively on trooping contracts throughout the 1950s. Some then had a third career like G-ALDE, seen at Newcastle, flying holiday charters to the Mediterranean. Air Safaris had complicated antecedents and eventually failed in 1961, a difficult year for charter airlines. (*MAP*)

Douglas built a fine range of airliners after the war, none better than the DC-6. Eagle was quick to spot the potential of this excellet aircraft, which could carry almost 100 passengers in pressurised comfort over long distances. This evocative picture, taken for *Flight* magazine inside the terminal at Blackbushe near London, shows G-APON in the snow just before leaving for the sunnier climes of Bermuda. (*Flight* photograph)

When the Bristol Freighters used on the cross-Channel car ferries began to wear out, Freddie Laker's engineering company, Aviation Traders, converted a number of Douglas DC-4 Skymasters into Carvairs, with a high-mounted, opening door at the nose to allow carriage of up to five cars. It was a handy freighter, too. G-ARSD is still in its original Channel Air Bridge colours, but the British United Airways logo has been applied to the tail after BUA took over Laker's Air Charter. (*MAP*)

The Lockheed Constellation first flew during the war. It was used by BOAC for transatlantic services, and later on the route to Australia. Lockheed 749 G-ALAL was first built for the Irish airline Aerlinte, but quickly sold on to BOAC, before passing to Skyways for use on BOAC contract freight services to Singapore. Euravia took over the aircraft when it bought out Skyways. (*MAP*)

A longer range version of the Douglas DC-7, itself a stretched development of the DC-6, the DC-7C was chosen by BOAC to fill the gap when the entry into service of the Bristol Britannia was delayed. Caledonian bought DC-7Cs from the Belgian airline Sabena as well as from BOAC, and G-ARYE, seen here at Paya Lebar airport in Singapore, came from Sabena. (*MAP*)

Not the start of something horrid, just the complicated business of getting the Britannia's undercarriage up as BOAC's Britannia 310 G-AOVC takes off from Manchester. The main undercarriage did a somersault to tuck itself up under the rear of the engine nacelle. The airliner bears BOAC's familiar blue and white colours. (*CMcC*)

Although to Vickers goes the credit of persevering with the development of the Viscount and to BEA the kudos of being the first operator of the type, this image shows Viscount G-ANRR, a 700 series operated by Hunting-Clan and delivered in 1955. It was intended for the company's Northern Network but instead spent two years with Middle East Airlines, before returning for use on the company's enhanced Safari Class services to Africa. (*MAP*)

A lively scene at London Airport, with BKS Air Transport Avro 748 G-ASPL in the foreground, and an executive Airspeed Ambassador of Shell at the rear. In between is a Lockheed Electra of the Dutch airline KLM. (*MAP*)

Another lively scene, this time at Manchester, showing British Eagle's Britannia G-ARKA, Euravia Constellation G-ALAK, a Boeing 707 of BOAC and a Caledonian Douglas DC-7C parked at the end. (*CMcC*)

Cunard Eagle's Boeing 707, registered in Bermuda as VR-BBW, and was the first jet aircraft to fly for an independent airline. Its sojourn in British Eagle's splendid livery was short-lived, however, as it passed to BOAC as part of the BOAC-Cunard joint venture in 1962, assuming British registration G-ARWD. (*MAP*)

An enlarged four-engine version of the DH Dove, the DH Heron feederliner could carry up to seventeen passengers. It resembled a modern version of the pre-war DH.86 Expressliner, illustrated earlier on the beach at Jersey. Jersey Airlines flew Herons within the Channel Islands and to the mainland through out the 1950s. (*MAP*)

British United was the launch customer for the BAC One-Eleven jet, powered by two Rolls-Royce Speys. The aircraft could carry up to eighty-nine passengers, although BUA chose a more spacious configuration for its scheduled services from Gatwick. (*MAP*)

De Havilland Comet 1 G-ALYS was the first jet airliner to receive a Certificate of Airworthiness and was handed over to BOAC on 4 February 1952. It continued in service until all the Comets were grounded in 1954 and withdrawn from service. (*MAP*)

diversionary allusion to the trade-union-supported National Joint Council – in a spirited exchange on 9 December 1949:

> Lindgren: I must make this point—and I would not have done so but for the fact that my hon. Friend rather overstated his case in regard to the effect on ex-Service men and the duties of the country towards ex-Service men. This firm has itself not accepted all the responsibilities it ought to have accepted. As my hon. Friend said, quite rightly, he is a member of the Labour Party and the Labour movement. This firm has not observed even the Act of Parliament in regard to rates of pay and conditions of employment.
> Blackburn: That is a new allegation.
> Lindgren: It is not a new allegation.
> Blackburn: I do not think that is altogether fair. I have been to some trouble over this matter. This is an entirely new allegation made against the firm. I have no desire to defend the firm, but at the same time it goes contrary to everything that I have been told, and I do not think the allegation ought to have been made without my having had notice of it.
> Lindgren: I am sorry about that. But apart from one or two of the larger charter operators, every charter operator in this country is operating below the standards of the airline corporations.[22]

It is always a bad sign when MPs start rebelling against their party bosses. Attlee called an election on 23 February 1950, which the Labour party won with an overall majority of five seats, even though it polled more votes than in 1945. Pakenham remained in situ, but Lindgren was replaced by Frank Beswick as parliamentary secretary. Robert Perkins was back. Almost the first thing he did was to demand an inquiry into civil aviation:

> These Corporations today work in secrecy behind closed doors and very little information is available for any Member of Parliament…The general public believe that there has been gross mismanagement in these Corporations. I believe the general public today would welcome some kind of inquiry into the whole business in order to clear the air.

Commenting on the reduction of BOAC's workforce, he continued:

> But I want to ask the Minister—and I should like to put it before some committee of inquiry: why were these 9,000 people ever taken on? During the time that they were employed by B.O.A.C. what were they doing? Were they playing cards? I suggest that here is something which might usefully be put to some impartial committee charged with the duty of investigating the whole operation of B.O.A.C.[23]

It was too much for Beswick, who confessed that Perkins' 'contribution irritated me in several respects, [he] was, I think, talking utter nonsense when he said the activities were shrouded in mystery.' Perkins did not get his inquiry.

If some doors remained closed, others opened for the charter airlines. Transair started flying newspapers from October 1948 between London and Paris, using specially converted Ansons. Eagle bought three Yorks from BOAC, and began using them on passenger and freight charters, positioning itself in the long-haul market and taking over where Skyways had left off. Air Transport (Charter) (CI) launched a novel kind of service in June 1950 when it carried holidaymakers from Gatwick to Calvi in Corsica for a new tour operator, Horizon Holidays. What made this holiday arrangement different was that everything was included in the cost of the cheap two week vacation, sleeping accommodation, three meals a day, to which was added the glamour of an exotic location in the sunny Mediterranean and the excitement of a trip by air. Horizon structured the programme efficiently so that the sectors were always loaded, the Dakota that took out one group of passengers to Corsica then returned to Gatwick with those who had travelled out two weeks before. Airwork began carrying forces' families to and from the Canal Zone under charter to the War Office, as a shortage of shipping had led to unacceptable delays. It was not the first time that the War Office had chartered passenger flights, but it was the first time it had done so on a regular basis, and the service ministry quickly learned that it was just as cheap, if not cheaper, to effect trooping movements by air rather than by sea, and moreover it meant that service personnel were back 'at work on the jobs they are paid for instead of lying about on the deck of a troopship' as one service chief put it. BOAC took over that contract for the winter, using Stratocruisers, to the intense annoyance of the Tories. But Airwork followed the Canal Zone flights with a six-month War Office trooping contract to West Africa in late 1949, giving it four to six flights a month. The Air Ministry was extremely interested in these trooping flights. The RAF had had to cut back the size of Transport Command, and the Air Ministry had been impressed by the contribution that the charter airlines had made during the Berlin Airlift, so was anxious to establish an air transport reserve, an aviation equivalent to Britain's merchant marine. It called on all the ministries with an interest, the service departments and the Ministry of Civil Aviation, to examine the prospects of trooping by air rather than by sea, establishing a committee under the chairmanship of one of its civil servants, Ronald Melville. For over a year this committee slugged it out, the Air Ministry espousing the cause of the independents, the Ministry of Civil Aviation protecting its state-owned corporations.

The Ministry of Civil Aviation had other matters on its mind. Charter airlines were now finding increasing support in Parliament: 'There is no doubt whatever in my mind that the charter companies are getting a very raw deal indeed,' complained George Ward in the House of Commons on 19 March 1951, 'and it is remarkable that so many of them have been able to survive…if the Minister persists in his present policy of what amounts almost to the persecution of independent operators, he will be doing his best to destroy an invaluable strategic asset.'[24] They were also happily getting business from an unintended source, so-called 'closed groups'. The Act said that only the corporations could operate scheduled journeys 'in such a manner that the benefits thereof are available to members of the public'. Presumably the opposite applied to non-scheduled services, a definition masterfully analysed in later years thus: 'It is a peculiar feature of modern Britain that the provision of a service is most offensive when its benefits are available to the public.'[25] If not to the public at large, then the answer lay in marketing flights to defined segments of the public. Charter airlines increasingly contracted flights with different types of organisation, tour operators, trade associations, church groups, student unions, clubs, which then resold the seats to members at a substantial discount to the equivalent BEA or BOAC fare. 'Anybody can form a club,' said Lord Gifford 'and can by that means pick members of the club and form a party. On the other hand, if a travel agent wishes to get a party together for an inclusive tour, he cannot utilise a charter aircraft without paying the full national air transport fare.'[26] Holiday companies could now find themselves at a disadvantage as they were still obliged to sell their tours at a price that was no less than the equivalent air fare; this requirement, widely known as Provision 1, was to remain an irritant for charter airlines and tour operators for many years to come. Hunting created the East African Club to offer low fare flights back to England for expatriates, and to the chagrin of the Ministry, was awarded a licence by the East African colonial administration, despite objections from BOAC. Even the civil service allowed its staff associations to form Whitehall Travel so that government employees could benefit from cheap holidays abroad. This type of business had not been foreseen. Lord Winster in 1946 had realised that he could not legislate for all eventualities, nor had he wanted to, but now that put the government in a quandary. With no majority worth speaking of, it was out of the question that the Act should be changed, and the government was reluctant to challenge the independents in the courts, following its earlier unsuccessful prosecutions, however far it was goaded by the opposition:

> Surely it would be far better to test the legality or non-legality of the matter in the courts. I do not think it is the right way to deal with the matter for the Government to run these people out of business by the whole weight of the Government machine. That does not seem to be the fair way to do it.[27]

In further exchanges between Balfour and Pakenham, Airwork's Sudan government leave contract and the loss to Hunting of the Overseas Food Corporation business were alluded to:

> Lord Balfour: May I ask him whether he would consider that the Sudan Government leave services come within the ambit of a scheduled service which the Corporations should run, even though that Sudan Government leave service is not available to the public, but only to Sudan Government employees? Which way does that go?
> Lord Pakenham: Does the noble Lord wish me to answer?
> Lord Balfour: Yes.
> Lord Pakenham: I certainly am not going to answer that question to-day. The noble Lord can wag his head, but I am not going to interpret the law this afternoon in relation to particular companies in any conceivable case of this sort. In my place the noble Lord would not dream of doing so.
> Lord Balfour: The noble Lord says he is not going to interpret the law. I wish that he and his Department would not interpret the law. If they feel that these charter companies are encroaching on the field of scheduled services, let them take the charter companies to court, and let the court decide. They should not use the whole resources of the Corporations in an endeavour to substantiate the Government's and the Corporations' position. As things are going at the present time, if the policy of the Corporations in quoting for every repetitive service is to be executed, it will drive these charter companies right out of that particular market. The Corporations can always underquote a charter company, and justify themselves in so doing.[28]

Swinton was also concerned about the ongoing negotiations over the trooping flights: 'In regard to this airlift of troops and stores, which will increase, are the charter companies to be invited to tender, or is it true that the Minister of Civil Aviation wants to seize all this for his own Corporations?' Pakenham replied: 'It is not a question of the Minister of Civil Aviation trying to "do in" the charter companies while the Defence Ministers are trying to prop them up. That would be quite a distorted impression if it got abroad.' But in an increasingly acrimonious debate – 'I was not altogether free from a certain amount of hustling myself, and for a time I had the greatest difficulty in securing the attention of the noble Viscount during my prolonged remarks,' complained Pakenham of Swinton, who retorted: 'I apologise to the noble Lord. At that very moment, I was being asked by my noble Leader to try to explain what the noble Lord had just said! It is very difficult to play this sort of three-handed Canasta' – there was an effective intervention from Lord Montagu of Beaulieu, who presciently pointed the way for the future development of charter services:

> The planning of a route and the development of it is a matter of great importance to air charter firms. I do not think anything has been said today by the noble Lord which is calculated to alleviate the fears of the charter firms that they are to be used as stooges, to pioneer routes, to develop them and spend money advertising them, and then, after they have made a success of them, see those routes taken away.

I put it to your Lordships that one function of air charter firms is to provide tourist or second-class travel for people in this country, at second-class fares. This sort of service exists in America, in France and in many other countries, and it forms an important part of air travel facilities. In France, for instance, second-class facilities are set out in the official time-table alongside the details and fares of the first-class facilities. And it is a recognised fact that the intending passenger is at liberty to choose for himself which form of travel he prefers, having regard to what he can afford.

A further point which I should like to put is that the public which B.E.A. and B.O.A.C. cater for is a public of a completely different type to that which normally travels by charter planes. It seems strange, in view of the great levelling out and socialisation process which has taken place in this country, that the Government have created air services which cater entirely for the rich people, and that private enterprise firms, which are trying to run cheaper services for the ordinary people, should not be put in a position to operate as efficiently. I am not contending that these second-class services should run on scheduled routes. On the other hand, there is no reason why charter 'planes should not fly to the same countries as the scheduled services, though perhaps not to the same airports. Take the case of flights to Italy. It might be that the charter companies should fly not to Rome, but to some other place in Italy. Their object should be to take passengers on different routes at a lower fare, thus providing for the tourist just what he wants. It must be remembered that these people will never fly by B.E.A. They will travel, perhaps, by a charter 'plane run by a company that arranges for its clients to have holidays abroad at an inclusive fee.[29]

Lord Montagu was right on the mark: his ideas read like a manifesto for the independents. Only a few months previously, *The Aeroplane* had pointed out:

The paradoxical effect of the Civil Aviation Act of a Labour Government has been to reserve air transport for a privileged few at high fares, and to deny less affluent members of the community the chance to use air transport at the much lower charges which, again paradoxically, private enterprise operators are able to make available.[30]

The future of charter airlines did indeed lie in offering low fare services, especially to countries within Britain's colonial Empire; in marketing flights to people who would not normally consider travelling – 'ordinary people' as opposed to the affluent – by offering cheaper fares; in flying to airports which would not otherwise see much traffic from the British Isles; and in catering to the increasing demand for inclusive tour holidays.

But for the moment, charter airlines had to wait for these better times. More Berlin Airlift veterans, Kearsley Airways, British Nederland Airservices, and British-American Air Services, stopped flying operations in 1950, Ciro's and Sivewright early in 1951. Worried by these developments, the Air Ministry tried to keep the other charter airlines in the running, and helped as much as it could by doling out short term contracts for the Royal Auxiliary Air Force summer camps, but Pakenham was still fighting a fierce rearguard action against his ministerial colleagues in order to preserve the corporations' right of first refusal on trooping contracts. The Air Ministry postponed any decision on trooping contracts until summer 1951; its civil servants continued to needle their colleagues from the Ministry of Civil Aviation as the work of the committee rumbled on. The award of the 1951 'associate agreements' provoked mixed reactions. BEA took control of the more lucrative services from Manchester to the Channel Islands and the Isle of Man, but some independents received five year agreements; Silver City had carried over 3,950 cars during the summer of 1950, and announced it would reduce its fares the following year, from £27 to £19 for a small car; Lancashire was awarded a number of five year agreements to the Isle of Man from the north, as it developed its coach-air holidays; Scottish Airlines was even awarded a seven year agreement between Prestwick and Liverpool, suggesting that the period of a licence was in inverse ratio to its desirability.

As 1950 wore on, charter airlines were again able to demonstrate their value as a strategic reserve. On 25 June 1950 North Korean forces invaded South Korea, and had captured Seoul by 28 June. The government of South Korea turned to the United Nations for help, and under the leadership of the United States, military units from fifteen other nations, including a Commonwealth division, took part in the ensuing war. At first the pressure was on the Americans to build up their forces in the area, but as British and Commonwealth involvement increased, RAF Transport Command's Yorks and Hastings found themselves committed to many more long distance flights; Britain contributed 60,000 military personnel, the Commonwealth – Australia, Canada, New Zealand and South Africa – a further 50,000. Unlike 1948 there was not much in the way of a strategic long-haul reserve; Eagle had three Yorks and one remaining Halifax, and Fairflight had one Tudor, having lost the other with great loss of life at Llandow in Wales earlier in March. Lancashire had three Halifaxes, but they were freighters. By September they were all flying down to Singapore or Iwakuni in Japan, carrying servicemen and military cargo. The War Office had to resort to using Silver City's Bristol Freighters, which gamely undertook the journey to Singapore in five days. Freddie Laker saw an opportunity arising, and pondered how he could re-enter the market. He had disposed of the Halifaxes and although he had his engineering company, Aviation Traders, he did not have an operating licence, so in 1951 he began buying up charter airlines – Surrey Flying Services, a venerable relic going back to the 1920s, and Air Charter, a post-war new entrant – and then bought two Yorks to get them aloft. Later he would buy Fairflight as well. Lancashire Aircraft Corporation also had its eye on this gap in the supply chain, at the same time eying BOAC's fleet of surplus Yorks, and satisfied both scores by relieving the corporation of twenty of them. It was to be the start of an excellent business relationship between the corporation and Lancashire: 'It has been pointed out that as these aircraft are public property they should have been put forward for public tendering,' observed *The Aeroplane*. 'One cannot blame Lancashire for getting in whilst there was a chance to negotiate privately, but there is a certain feeling among other companies who were not given a chance to quote.'[31] As the Korean War continued, American owners began buying Dakotas as well as all available modern four-engine American transports, taking them off the British market. The reduction in inventory coincided with the decision by BEA to upgrade its existing fleet of Dakotas, so the corporation needed to charter additional aircraft while its own were modified by Scottish Aviation at Prestwick; then BEA had to continue chartering in to cover delays in the delivery of its first Airspeed Ambassadors. Those charter operators that had stayed the course, like Air Transport (Charter) (CI), found their services in demand; it moved its operations up to Blackbushe from Jersey, and added a fourth Dakota to its fleet. Other Dakota operators remaining were Scottish Airlines and Skyways, now joined by two new airlines, Liverpool-based Starways and Crewsair at Southend; the latter was backed by three names, Barnby, Keegan and Stevens, who would remain partners in a later venture, BKS Aerocharter, and soon split off from Crewsair. Airwork and Hunting already used Vickers Vikings, but as Dakotas disappeared from the market, smaller operators began to buy Vikings, including Crewsair. The shortage of aircraft capacity made things difficult for freight forwarders and brokers, on whom the independents usually relied to secure *ad hoc* charters; moreover the government was about to become the largest single charterer in the market and it did not pay any commission at all. This meant trouble for brokers representing British airlines on the Baltic Exchange, but firms like Davies & Newman, which represented the South African airline Tropic Airways, were less affected.

Trouble was breaking out for the British all over the world in 1951. As well as the Korean War, there were problems in Hong Kong with the new communist Chinese government on the mainland, an ongoing 'emergency' in Malaya, another never-ending dispute with Iceland over fishing rights, continuing unpleasantness with the Argentines over the Falklands and British dependencies in the Antarctic, renewed Russian provocations in Berlin, unrest in Egypt after the Egyptian government abrogated the 1936 Anglo-Egyptian Treaty (which guaranteed Britain's bases in the Canal Zone), and now, the nationalisation by a new revolutionary government in Iran of Britain's strategically vital Anglo-Iranian Oil Company. Britain responded in due course by withdrawing all personnel and shutting down the refineries. Eagle was already busy helping out the Korean war effort, Airwork and Hunting were unable to commit more aircraft in view of the impending trooping contracts, Scottish and Air Transport (Charter) (CI) were flying for BEA, yet the British Foreign Office needed all available aircraft for the evacuation of approximately 4,500 staff and their families from Abadan, site of Anglo-Iranian's oil refineries. BOAC and Lancashire used Yorks to supplement the RAF, and by the end it was all hands to the sheets, even Aquila's Sunderlands did their bit. After that, Yorks and Vikings were diverted to help carry reinforcements for British troops in the Suez Canal Zone, a two month airlift, during which RAF Transport Command's Hastings acquitted themselves magnificently, flying in over 10,000 troops and 350 vehicles. Meanwhile the British government dispatched Fairflight's remaining Tudor to Berlin to help with the export of manufactured goods which increasingly were delayed by the Russians at the zonal crossing points.

In the middle of this hyper-activity, in August 1951, Hunting was awarded the first of the new two-year trooping contracts, or Tasks, for forty to fifty flights a month to Malta and Gibraltar, using thirty-seat Vikings. It was a coup for Hunting, providing guaranteed year-round flying. Additional contracts were awarded to Airwork for the Medair Task, shuttling personnel around the many British bases within the Mediterranean and Middle East; and to Lancashire to operate daily flights to Fayid in the Canal Zone. Lancashire also won the Caribbean contract, two flights a month to Jamaica, a laborious operation for the unsuitable, and payload restricted, Yorks which had to fly the long way round via Iceland and Newfoundland. Neither BOAC nor BEA tried very hard to get the contracts; the Air Ministry's Director of Contracts was dismissive of their tenders which were not only considerably more expensive than the independents' but also so hedged with reservations that they were virtually 'cost plus'. Poor Lord Pakenham was not around to see the final denouement of the 18-month interdepartmental drama, as he had been moved to the Admiralty in June, and was spared the final ruthless machinations of the Air Ministry as it successfully completed its Tasks: to ensure flexibility for Transport Command, and allow it to cope with unexpected demands on its resources; to establish a strategic civil reserve of air transport aircraft which could undertake the more mundane tasks like regular trooping flights less expensively than the RAF; and to award civilian contracts without interference. The final irony is that the Ministry of Transport, a bit-player in the show, promptly ordered two new troopships for delivery later in the decade.

Whatever the reasons for it, the Air Ministry's actions helped the independents turn the corner. *The Aeroplane* noted the change:

During the coming Winter opportunities for private operators seem to be considerably better than ever before. In previous years the Winter months meant a general lay-off of aircrew and a semi-retirement of the aircraft fleet. Thanks, however, to a more general demand for air transport and a long awaited measure of support from the Government most charter companies should be able to keep black figures on their ledgers through the months ahead. The road leading to this better deal for the private companies has been a long and bitter one and the mortality rate high. It does seem, however, that the industry has at last stabilized.[32]

Ironically, a Labour government that had tried so hard to squish the independents at first afforded them the means to survive the following decade. Perhaps the fact that the two corporations had also turned the corner helped; now they did not need so much protection. In 1951 BEA carried more than a million passengers for the first time, and brought its deficit down to less than a million pounds, also for the first time. The corporation was looking forward to the delivery of the Ambassadors, and had finally ordered twenty turbine-engine Vickers Viscounts; it was experimenting with helicopter operations, an area that fascinated Lord Douglas, and had begun flying internal services within Germany, a privilege it was to enjoy for the next 40 years. BOAC still produced vast deficits, £4.5 million in 1951, but that was down £3 million from the previous year, and the corporation had a more or less decent fleet, with some exciting new aircraft on order, de Havilland Comet jets and Bristol 175 Britannia turbo-props. Actually, there was an embarrassment of new aircraft, as BOAC had belatedly taken delivery in 1950 of its fleet of Handley Page Hermes, which it did not really need as it had bought the Canadairs, and did not really want, as the Hermes were troublesome to bring into service – 'it flew wearily with its tail down, which induced an appalling amount of drag, and we had a whole sheaf of troubles to eliminate before it was route-worthy,' complained Thomas in his autobiography *Out on a Wing*. Still, they were slightly less expensive to operate than the Solent flying boats on the African routes, and did allow BOAC to withdraw from flying boat operations altogether, but BOAC still wanted to dispose of the Hermes as quickly as possible. Pakenham had tried to force the Air Ministry to let BOAC fly these surplus aircraft on trooping flights to the Canal Zone, on the grounds that this route required four-engine aircraft, but again the Air Ministry demurred; it had plans for the Hermes, and they were not the same as those that Pakenham had in mind. At least BOAC was no longer bothered about the big SR.45 Princess flying boats. They would now be operated by the RAF: 'Each boat will have the equivalent lift of one Hastings squadron, and they will, therefore, be a most valuable addition to our transport resources in time of war.'[33]

The King was planning to go on a long Commonwealth tour in 1952, but was concerned at being away from the country when the government held such a small majority. The signs were propitious for Attlee, and so he called an election for 25 October 1951, hoping to increase his party's small majority.

CHAPTER 6

1951 to 1959
Basking in the Pale Sunshine of Conservative Government

Attlee lost the election, even though the Labour Party polled more votes than it ever had before or has since, at just under 14 million, about 230,000 more than the Conservatives. The Tories, with the help of the National Liberal Party, won with a majority of seventeen seats. The Liberal Party was reduced to just three seats.

Churchill returned as Prime Minister, and was immediately confronted by an economic crisis, leading to an emergency budget within 10 days of Parliament reconvening, which, among other imposts, restricted the amount of sterling tourists could take out of the country. The costly conflict continued in Korea, and now the country needed to rearm for the Cold War. His Foreign Secretary, Anthony Eden, inherited a dangerous situation in Egypt, although the effective and speedy reinforcement of the garrison in the Canal Zone eventually controlled the violence. In Iran, after the evacuation of the British technicians, the Abadan refineries closed down, and countries to the east, especially India and Pakistan, suffered fuel shortages which disrupted flights to the Far East. Churchill appointed a National Liberal, the Hon. John Maclay, as both Minister of Transport and Minister of Civil Aviation, although the two departments were run separately until October 1953. Maclay came under a newly created transport and energy supremo, Lord Leathers, a former businessman and Minister of War Transport, who now became Minister for Coordination of Transport, Fuel and Power. When in opposition the Tories had heckled the Labour government over the treatment of the independents, and their spokesman, Alan Lennox-Boyd, had even appeared to question their commitment to state ownership of the corporations: 'Can the hon. Gentleman explain the statement by the right hon. Member for Mid-Bedfordshire [Lennox-Boyd] who did say that the Conservative Party intended to restore a measure of private enterprise in this field?'[1] asked Frank Beswick of Maclay in Parliament on 5 December 1951. But Maclay denied there was any intention to change the status of the corporations. The Conservatives froze all major developments, asking the ATAC to limit new 'associate agreements' to no longer than one year while they pondered, now that they were in power, what to do about the relationship between the corporations that they now had in their charge, and the free enterprise they espoused.

While the new government was coming to grips with its mandate – among other promises was one to build 300,000 new homes a year – there were still some final tweaks needed in the air trooping negotiations. Pakenham had wanted the Air Ministry to use BOAC's Hermes on the longer flights, especially to the Canal Zone, but misunderstood BOAC's stance; at the time the corporation wanted rid of the aircraft, not additional business to keep them in the air. Later BOAC remixed its version of history and claimed that it had wanted to keep the aircraft all along. Sir Miles Thomas skilfully portrayed his corporation as unfairly discriminated against in the matter of trooping contracts, eliciting much sympathy in Parliament. But BOAC would not have been able to tender competitively with the Hermes anyway, a fact somehow overlooked in the ensuing arguments, and possibly not understood by parliamentarians. The Hermes was a new and therefore relatively expensive aircraft, further burdened with at least part of BOAC's substantial overhead; early corporation tenders were two or three times more expensive than those of the independents. After Pakenham left the Ministry of Civil Aviation, and following further negotiations between the latter and the Air Ministry, BOAC agreed to sell four of the Hermes to Airwork on hire purchase, and Airwork was then awarded the major Canzair Task to the Canal Zone. It would be some time before the Hermes were ready to enter trooping service, however, so Lancashire continued sending its Yorks on the 13 hour journey down to Fayid in the Canal Zone; it carried around 30,000 service personnel and their families in the first year, and flew fifty round trips a month.

The War Office had to rely on Yorks for most of the long range tasks, for they were all the independents could afford. BOAC was offering its Hermes for sale at £198,000 each, way beyond anything the charter airlines could pay, and Treasury rules required the War Office to accept the much lower bids made possible by written down aircraft like the Yorks. They were sometimes used on quite unsuitable routes. There was an outcry after a Skyways York was lost over the Atlantic en route to Jamaica, but Sir Wavell Wakefield MP, a director of Skyways, defended the use of obsolescent types and pointed out presciently that they could be more reliable than newer aircraft which had still to settle down in service:

> These Yorks have been operating for over 10 years and are known to be safe. All the "bugs" have been taken out of them, but we know that the Comet is still in a state of development. Yet the Comet I is now obsolete, and there is now a Comet II and Comet III. There are the Rapides which are known to be very safe, and the Dakota is recognised as one of the safest aircraft in the world. They are obsolete, but they do a useful job of work satisfactorily and successfully.
>
> The hon. Member (Ian Mikardo) tried to convey the impression that the disaster over the Atlantic occurred because an obsolescent and unsafe aircraft was being used. He referred to French troops being carried in Stratocruisers. No doubt he will recollect, when I remind him of it, that the type of aircraft to which he referred was lost in the Atlantic about the same time as the York. It disappeared just as the York did, and nothing was known about it. I am sure the House will regret deeply that the hon. Member should have tried to convey the impression that our troops are being uncomfortably carried in aircraft which are not safe.[2]

As a footnote, Skyways suspended their Caribbean flights, and BOAC then took over this task; when there was no competition from independents, BOAC could gain contracts! Until the War Office began to demand minimum flight service standards, troops and their families continued to put up with the results of lowest cost tenders. Douglas Whybrow, in his book *Air Ferry*, is candid about the realities of the early trooping flights:

> The Yorks were converted freighters with a speed of about 160 mph, some with little soundproofing to take the edge off the lusty roar of the four Rolls-Royce Merlin engines, and all too often with dirt and damage to the interior lining from previous freight flights. The flights were long – anything from ten to thirty hours – and the discomfort astonishing; aircraft seats did not recline, some did not even have headrests and the rules specified that children under two should not be provided with a seat. Even the simple matter of providing seats with headrests could not be settled. There was also the argument about rearward facing seats. These had proved to save lives if there was a crash – something that then was not all that uncommon…The Treasury would not permit them to be specified for charter flights as the heavier seats meant at least two less passengers carried on each flight and consequent increased cost.[3]

The RAF was scarcely better; it may have used rearward facing seats 'but the spartan qualities of the Hastings's interior do not make for luxury travel. In particular, the seats, without head or arm rests, and with their rigidly vertical backs, not to mention the lack of leg space, seem to have been ingeniously devised to prevent the unfortunate occupants from enjoying a moment's rest.'[4]

And for this the War Office was charged the full scheduled air fare. Some charter airlines, like Eagle and Laker's Air Charter, improved their in-flight and operational standards on their own initiative, and the gradual introduction of the Hermes onto the trooping rosters brought higher levels of comfort, but it was always the case that trooping flights were performed by the previous generation of aircraft; the turboprop Britannia was the mainstay of trooping in the 1960s, flying alongside the Boeing 707 and Douglas DC-8 jets of the world's scheduled airlines. In other respects, the savings were real enough. Charter contract prices came down over the years; in 1961 the Ministry paid a rate for a single passage on the Cyprus task which was just 70 per cent of the rate it had been charged in 1955. Sea passages cost four times as much to Malta, twice as much to Singapore, as comparable passages by air.

The last Labour Minister of Civil Aviation, Lord Ogmore, who had succeeded Pakenham for all of four months, pressed the new government for a statement on aviation policy. Maybe Ogmore thought that the Tories were seriously considering amending or even removing the corporations' monopoly on air services, something that went to the very heart of socialist doctrine, which itself went back to the ideals of internationalism. Pakenham sounded quite upset when the matter came to be debated in the House of Lords on 5 December 1951: 'I do not want to adopt a tone of violence, let alone of threats, but I must inform the noble Lord that if he…took steps which, in our view, damaged the Corporations, we should fight him by every constitutional means, here, elsewhere and everywhere.'[5] He need not have worried. Lord Leathers had no intention of changing the status of the corporations, nor did the Prime Minister want any serious contention with the Opposition:

> It is the intention of the Government to help forward the sound development of civil aviation, to reduce the cost of air transport to the taxpayer and to give greater opportunities to private enterprise to take part in air transport development, without in any way impairing the competitive strength of our international air services. We have no intention of undermining the existing international networks of the Air Corporations, B.O.A.C. and B.E.A. However, there are also other ways of expanding our air transport effort, and we shall explore directions in which it is possible to provide opportunities for the private companies to play a valuable part in this expansion.[6]

That seemed to suggest that domestic services were not sacrosanct. And maybe BOAC's charter activities, noticeably on the increase during the past 12 months, were not necessary for the corporation's competitive strength. There was much concern on both sides about the merger of the two transport ministries and the way forward – 'I am a little apprehensive about the whole situation, because civil aviation is such a restless subject; it is never the same for a year,' was how Brabazon put it – but the man with the clearest vision, surprisingly, was Lord Balfour.

Balfour had had a lacklustre career in government, overseeing BOAC's wartime activities without conspicuous success, and had then been forced to play second fiddle to Lord Swinton in debates after the war. But he must have learned something along the way because his contribution on 5 December 1951, complementing the ideas of Lord Beaulieu which were referred to in the previous chapter, became a blueprint for his party's policy on the future development of Britain's airlines over the decade. He outlined his ideas in four steps: 'First, open up those routes not being run by the Corporation but on which, at the present time, the exercise of the Corporation's monopoly rights prevents anyone else from operating,' he suggested. 'One envisages a licensing board, people applying to that licensing board, and so on.' Then: 'The next proposal I make to the noble Lord is that there should be a more liberal interpretation as to what are scheduled services available for the public. There has been a great deal of doubt as to whether an inclusive tour was a scheduled service available for the public.' Thirdly: 'It is unfair that the Corporation's picture should include the social services and I should like to see these lifted right outside. Let the Government, if you like, charter these services from the operators, taking to their own credit any income derived therefrom.' Balfour concluded his wish-list: 'The last suggestion I make is that the charter companies should be allowed to take over more of the Army and R.A.F. trooping work. I should like to see R.A.F. Transport Command confined almost to the operational aspect of Transport Command work—such as carrying parachutists, towing gliders, and moving troops about in the operational theatres. I cannot see any logical reason why the R.A.F. should do, as it were, carriage work.'[7]

When the government came to launch its 'New Deal' on 27 May 1952, it followed Balfour's guidelines, only coming unstuck on the subsidy issue. The idea that social services should be paid for by the government, rather than through cross-subsidisation, was at odds with the Treasury 'view', even though economists recognise that it is unfair for one section of the community to subsidise another randomly selected part of the community, however well deserving: that is the job of government. I was sorry to read that later in life Balfour recanted. When challenged 20 years later over whether BEA ought to be allowed to continue their charter operations in order to make sufficient profit to subsidise the Highlands and Islands services and other unprofitable services, Balfour responded: 'Certainly, my Lords, and in order to help keep going less profitable services of the scheduled variety. That would be eminently suitable and right.... Let them have every advantage and go to it, and good luck to them!'[8] The new minister, Alan Lennox-Boyd – Maclay had had to resign for health reasons – announced that the independents would not be allowed to challenge the corporations on any of BEA's or BOAC's existing routes, but they would be allowed to apply for any new routes:

> We have decided that the development of new overseas scheduled services shall be open to the Corporations and independent companies alike. Applications will be made to the Air Transport Advisory Council, which will administer a procedure on licensing lines...
>
> We have hopes of independent companies developing the all-freight market, which is a growing field with great possibilities. There are also opportunities for special types of service such as seasonal inclusive tours and services at cheap fares not directly competitive with the Corporations to places within the Colonial Empire.
>
> Charter operations are in the main the domain of the independent operator. The Corporations will keep the right to engage in charter work in those cases where they have special facilities. They will not, however, maintain aircraft specifically for charter work.
>
> United Kingdom internal services present a special problem. Their cost to the taxpayer is considerable. We are still examining the best way of dealing with this.[9]

Somebody got cold feet, or maybe took a reality check, because the original wording of the last sentence was: 'We are still examining the best way of relieving the tax-payer of this burden as soon as possible.'[10] The Cabinet Conclusions of 27 May 1952 note: 'Applications to operate private internal services had not been forthcoming from suitable sources to the extent expected by Ministers.'

'Profound disappointment' was the initial reaction of the charter airlines to the Minister's New Deal. There was some bitterness that so little was on offer in the way of more opportunities. What new routes were available? BOAC and BEA had spread their tentacles far and wide by now, and the corporations could always argue that there would be material diversion if new routes ran parallel to their own existing ones. Charter airlines already flew freight services, which seemed better suited to ad hoc arrangements rather than regular line services. The independents would find it difficult to raise new capital, so buying new aircraft would depend on tapping into other resources. Aircraft like the Viscount and Britannia were expensive, and banks would look askance at the short term nature of their business; trooping contracts were for one, maybe two years at most, not long enough to justify investing in new aircraft. By contrast, government contracts for the remaining three chartered troopships were for 15 years; it was little consolation for the airlines that the Ministry of Transport had to pay substantial cancellation fees when the troopship contracts were prematurely terminated. Air fares were coming down on the major transatlantic routes, after Tourist Class travel had been introduced on 1 May 1952, but the independents were denied that business, even though their lower costs made them well suited for this type of traffic; instead they were only allowed to introduce new 'C', or Colonial Class, fares on routes to Africa, under severe restrictions, limited frequencies and with uncompetitive aircraft types. As for inclusive tour services, the independents could but hope that Lord Terrington would continue to be sympathetic towards them. Disillusioned, Bamberg decided to pull out of the business, selling his Yorks and the long-haul contracts to Skyways, leasing his Vikings to Airwork, but he kept the Dakotas. Both Crewsair and Air Transport (Charter) (CI) closed down their air operations at the end of October; BKS Aerocharter took over the pioneering Corsica route for Horizon Holidays, flying it twice a week, and added Palma, Majorca, in 1954.

'Sober assessment' was how Charles Orr-Ewing MP described the statement in the Commons debate on 16 July 1952. Nevertheless Airwork and Hunting were quick to apply for C Class licences, and in June 1952 started a joint weekly low-cost 'Safari' service to Nairobi. The leisurely flights resembled BOAC's and Imperial's flying boat services in pace, taking three days, with two hotel night-stops, in each direction; BOAC responded by offering Tourist Class fares to East and Central Africa. More important, the independents were awarded substantial trooping contracts, their mainstay for the next 15 years. After the government asked BOAC to dispose of its dedicated charter fleet, the corporation was no longer able to tender for the main government contracts, giving Labour MPs the opportunity to indulge in endless griping. Government contracts did not just mean trooping; related institutions like the NAAFI and other welfare services also used charter aircraft to support their missions at Britain's military bases overseas. The Foreign Office had kept Fairflight's Tudor on the Berlin run, so when Freddie Laker took the business over, he found himself with an important role to play as the so-called Little Airlift intensified. As well as shifting freight out of Berlin, it also became necessary to cope with the increasing numbers of refugees from the Russian sector who were streaming into the western sectors of Berlin; they then had to be evacuated by air to West Germany. Laker coordinated the effort to clear the backlog and keep Berlin's industries active, bringing in his own Yorks, Bristol Freighters from Silver City, and Dakotas from many of the charter airlines; among the latter was a newcomer, Dan-Air Services, formed in May 1953 by ship-brokers Davies & Newman, who held a lien on Dakota G-AMSU of Meredith Air Transport, and decided to put it to good use on their own account. Colonial C Class, trooping, freight services: they all helped, despite the independents' gloomy prognostication, but led increasingly to a two-tier charter industry wherein the favoured airlines received government contracts and scheduled licences; the rest had to make do with BEA associate agreements, and flying 'off the record' for closed groups. What the government did not do was ease up on the monopoly that the corporations held on scheduled services, leaving some very anorexic third level routes to be operated by the next tier of airlines, which struggled with seasonal summer-only holiday routes as best they could. Captain Olley sold out to his rival – and former employee – Captain Morton, who continued to run both third level airlines, flying Doves and Rapides, under their separate names. Airlines like East Anglian Flying Services, better known by its later name of Channel Airways, and Cambrian Air Services persisted, and eventually won through. Lancashire bet both ways on its future plans, retaining its North Country coach-air services to the Isle of Man, but investing heavily in four-engine aircraft for ministry work. Its chairman, Eric Rylands, bought the goodwill of Skyways early in 1952, and used the name 'Skyways of London' for trooping and other long-haul flights. Laker simplified his trading names, amalgamating Surrey Flying Services and Fairflight under the Air Charter banner.

Now that the Labour Party was in opposition, it suddenly became the friend of the independents, not just the champion of the corporations. Lord Ogmore, the last Labour Minister of Civil Aviation, sounded almost enthusiastic:

> First of all, we have helped them in the matter of the trooping contracts. Practically every soldier, sailor or airman who goes abroad by air—and a very large number do nowadays—is carried in a charter plane, so far as I am aware…I hope that the charter companies will play a very considerable rôle in civil aviation in this country in the future. I say that, in the first place, because I believe in a certain amount of competition and, secondly, because it gives a wider range of opportunities of employment to pilots and others. Thirdly, it ensures the maintenance of a great reservoir of machines and men—air crews and the like—which can be drawn on in case of war.[11]

The government found it difficult to reconcile its free enterprise credentials with the responsibility of airways ownership: support for the corporations had to be balanced with opportunities for the charter airlines. It did try. Protection of the scheduled service monopoly was offset by trooping contracts worth millions of pounds. Aircraft were made available directly through the Air Ministry – sixty Dakotas and ten Yorks were disposed of to private operators, Laker acquired the government's entire stock of Tudor aircraft – or via its proxy, BOAC, which sold off its fleet of Hermes aircraft to the independents, giving them access for the first time to modern, four-engine, pressurised aircraft. Maybe the latter were a mixed blessing: Airwork lost two of its Hermes within weeks of their entering service in 1952, as a result of fatigue fracture in the crankshaft of the almost new Hercules engines. Lord Leathers also beefed up the charter airlines' financial backing, by having a word or two in the ears of his shipping colleagues and inducing them to take a stake in some of the airlines; there was some synergy, especially on the freight side, between shipping companies and airlines, and Airwork, Hunting, Britavia and Skyways all acquired new shareholders from among the shipping lines.

Britavia, or British Aviation Services, was the parent company of Silver City, and had bought out Aquila early in 1953. Silver City had made over 10,000 vehicle ferry flights by 1 July 1952, and added two more routes, Southampton to Cherbourg, and Southend to Ostend. It was also a major freight hauler, especially during the slacker winter months; the Berlin Little Airlift kept the Freighters busy and the airline had recently ordered six stretched Bristol Mk. 32 Freighters, able to carry three cars and twelve passengers, and at £575,000, the most expensive purchase made by an independent up to that point. Aquila had acquired the Short Solent for its Madeira service, and was even picking up trooping contracts, to Singapore and West Africa. The Air Transport Advisory Council was approving of their efforts:

> Nearly half the total traffic carried on associate services during 1951 was on international services. The two outstanding services were the Lympne–Le Touquet service…and Aquila Airways Ltd.'s service from

Southampton to Madeira via Lisbon. Between them these two Companies carried over 80 per cent. of the total traffic on international associate services.[12]

Lord Terrington also considered the arguments about material diversion overdone:

> The Council's general conclusion…is that, while under the present arrangements their scope is limited, these services have been of considerable benefit to the public in that they have carried 91,000 passengers, the greater number of whom would not have been catered for by the Airways Corporations.

The government gave the ATAC revised terms of reference in view of its enhanced role, which included a long list of all the corporations' existing routes on which the independents were not to be allowed to compete; Lord Terrington was confirmed as its chairman, though the effect was a little spoiled by the government naming Gerard d'Erlanger to the Council.

'A triumph of compromise' was how the New Deal was being described one year later, in July 1953. Indeed, Bamberg's disillusionment had been short-lived; now he decided to concentrate on short haul flying, buying BEA's stock of Vikings. Both he and Airwork took the government at its word and applied for new routes, and then rather wished they had not. Eagle tried Belgrade, Aalborg and Gothenburg, Airwork wanted to start transatlantic freight services. Hunting's, now renamed Hunting-Clan after the Clan Line bought an interest in the airline, took a different approach and applied for a small domestic and northern European network out of Newcastle, hoping to charge lower fares; it ordered Viscounts, the first independent to do so, and launched its Northern Network in May 1953. A number of independents sought new Colonial Coach Class services, but found the ATAC was rather stingy in doling them out: services to Africa were approved sparingly, with strict limitations on frequency and aircraft type, but routes to the Far East were turned down; Cyprus was allowed a very low frequency operation, but services to Malta and Gibraltar were refused.

Balfour's suggestion regarding social services was not taken up in the end, but it was considered seriously, and debated in Parliament. Labour's spokesman in the House of Commons, Beswick, thought it a good idea too: 'In Scotland, for example, I believe that the value of the services should be estimated by the Scottish Office and paid for by them. Otherwise, it is quite unfair, and, indeed, damaging, to stick to a profit or loss figure as an accurate indication of the efficiency of B.E.A.'[13] One of his colleagues, Wing Commander Shackleton, nailed the culprit:

> They are social air services, and I can see no reason why that matter should not be clearly indicated and why there should not be a specific subsidy borne on the Scottish Vote. I realise that the Treasury have many good reasons administratively for not following a particular course, but I urge that this should be borne in mind.[14]

In the end a lack of suitable candidates – only Scottish Aviation really qualified – and Lord Douglas's rearguard action in defence of his airline prevented Scotland's air services being devolved to an independent.

Douglas had other pressing concerns to deal with. For a start, BEA had slipped back into major deficit mode, gloomily describing 1951 to be the corporation's 'most difficult year' as it announced a loss of £1,423,611, an increase of 45 per cent over the previous year. There had been inflation, strikes, additional taxes, restrictions on taking sterling out of the country, all of which had affected traffic; BEA claimed that the deficits would have been eliminated if the corporation had bought American equipment instead of relying on its fleet of Vikings and Dakotas, and now the new British aircraft were being delivered late. The Airspeed Ambassador, ordered in 1948, should have entered service early in 1951; instead the first regular flight, to Paris, took place on 13 March 1952. There was also worrying talk of merging the two corporations, for by contrast, BOAC had turned the corner in 1951, recording a profit for the first time, small at £275,000, but a profit nevertheless, followed by its best year in 1953, with profits over £1 million. Chairman Thomas had begun sorting the corporation out – there were now only two maintenance bases, at Heathrow and Filton, and even Filton's days were numbered; 50,000 more passengers had been carried following a major sales effort; productivity by any measure was up; and he presided as BOAC inaugurated the world's first regular jet passenger service on 2 May 1952, when de Havilland Comet 1 G-ALYP left London for Johannesburg with thirty-six passengers on board. By the end of the year Comets were flying to Colombo and Singapore. Equally encouraging, the first Bristol 175 Britannia had flown in August. The government had established a super-priority list for resources which now included civil aircraft, the Comet, Britannia and Viscount.

But on 2 May 1953, one year after its introduction into service, BOAC lost the first of its Comets when G-ALYV broke up after taking off from Calcutta during a severe storm. The remaining aircraft continued flying, and contributed to BOAC's gradually improving results, so much so that grant deficiency payments stopped after 1952. The corporation withdrew its almost new Hermes in 1953, replacing them on African services with Canadair C-4s of somewhat older vintage. Just under a year later, BOAC lost another Comet, G-ALYP, which disintegrated in the air off Elba, on 10 January 1954. The Comets were withdrawn temporarily, but were back in service by the end of March. A Constellation crashed at Singapore, on 13 March. Then a third Comet, G-ALYY, flying for South African Airways, crashed into the sea south of Naples on 8 April. The remaining aircraft were grounded and the type's airworthiness certificate revoked. Unlike the BSAA Tudors which were never found, the remains of Comet G-ALYP were located, and with the help of the Royal Navy, salvaged and brought back to the Royal Aircraft Establishment at Farnborough, where it was painstakingly reconstructed; other Comets were put through severe ground fatigue and water tank pressure testing, and eventually the failure was pinpointed to the rear ADF window. BOAC drafted in the redundant Hermes for a few months to fill the immediate gaps in its schedules, but in the longer term preferred to buy second-hand Constellations and Stratocruisers to bolster its fleet. The corporation's bad luck continued through to Christmas Day 1954, when a Stratocruiser crashed at Prestwick. 'A swine of a year' was how Sir Miles Thomas came to stigmatise 1954.

BEA, meanwhile, introduced its first Viscount into service on 18 April 1953, flying from London to Rome, Athens and Nicosia, at the same time as it was busily introducing the new Ambassadors, which it called the Elizabethan in honour of the newly ascended Queen, on domestic and short haul European routes. Jersey Airlines, a sprightly post-war new entrant, upheld the honour of the independents by introducing the de Havilland Heron on its Channel Islands routes, a robust seventeen-seat airliner that resembled a stretched de Havilland Dove with four engines; and Silver City put into service its larger Bristol Mk. 32 Freighters. By now a sizeable operation, Silver City had carried over 24,000 cars across the Channel in 1953; when conditions at the Ministry's grass airfield at Lympne became intolerable, Silver City built a new airfield nearby, at Lydd, which opened in July 1954, custom built for vehicle ferry operations. Silver City had not persisted with its Southend route, and came to regret it when Laker opened his first car ferry service late in 1954 between Southend and Calais, at first using the smaller Bristol Freighter, which he upgraded a few months later to use long-nosed Mk. 32 Freighters; he named the service Channel Air Bridge. Laker was by now stretching himself; he still participated in the Little Air Lift, but had insinuated his Yorks into cargo flying from Germany and trooping, breaking into the circle of favoured charter airlines: Airwork, Eagle, Hunting, Silver City, Skyways. Anxious to upgrade his fleet but reluctant to pay the going rate of £185,000 for a Skymaster and unable to secure Canadair C-4s from BOAC – interestingly, he did not think the Hermes was up to the job – he bought the Ministry's entire stock of Avro Tudors, many of them unused, and started rebuilding ten of them, some as passenger aircraft. These rebuilt Tudors, 'thin' Marks I and IV, were given new certificates of airworthiness, and Laker applied for a Colonial Coach Class licence to Nigeria; he also hoped to use them on trooping contracts.

It was time for the other charter airlines to look to their long-haul aircraft fleets, too. BOAC had been unable to sell any of the Hermes on the open market, and began offering the aircraft to the independents at around £100,000 each, with the added proviso that they could only be used on trooping flights. Britavia set the ball rolling, offering to buy four of them, but immediately ran into union resistance from BOAC's maintenance staff, whose cooperation was needed to prepare the aircraft for service. BOAC then came up with a much better idea, to its way of thinking, one moreover that would simultaneously allow it to re-enter the trooping and charter market through a surrogate, and also deny the Hermes to other operators. Why not sell the aircraft to Skyways at an advantageous price, in exchange for a small shareholding in the company? Relations with Skyways were already excellent, and Sir Miles Thomas and Sir Wavell Wakefield quickly agreed terms: the Hermes would be bought for £90,000 each, without restrictions, and BOAC would acquire a 25 per cent shareholding in Skyways. The minister, Lennox-Boyd, saw nothing to object to but said he needed a few days to think about it. When Britavia complained about the terms of the Skyways deal, managing director Powell was told that the deal with Britavia was now off; BOAC even returned the deposit cheque. Powell, a man renowned for his temper, was furious and immediately passed on the bad news to his colleagues in the industry; within a short time a number of very irate airline operators, some of them supported by their new and influential shipping backers, gave the minister what is commonly known as an ear-bending. He was not amused, and told Thomas to call off the deal with Skyways:

> I informed the B.O.A.C. on 19th March that I was prepared to approve the agreement. I confirmed this to the Chairman on 22nd March. Later that day I asked him to defer signature of the agreement. On 26th March, when it had become clear to me that the proposed agreement would discriminate against other independent operators, I told the Chairman that I could not agree to it.[15]

BOAC redid its sums, and a few days later agreed to sell four Hermes, later increased to six, to Britavia, three more to Airwork, and the remaining ten to Skyways; its maintenance staff found they had to return the aircraft to service anyway because they were needed in the short term to shore up BOAC's African services following the grounding of the Comets on 8 April 1954. The Hermes played their role as troopers over the next five years, being used mainly on the Far Eastern and some African contracts. Airwork and Skyways shared the Singapore and Hong Kong tasks, Britavia used its Hermes to Cyprus and East Africa. There is a chronology of the trooping contracts in Appendix 1. Ministry contracts also covered major freighting tasks, to the Middle and Far East, and support for the Commonwealth rocket facility at Woomera in Australia; Yorks were still in play, operated by Air Charter, Dan-Air and Scottish. Air Charter suffered a setback in its plans when the War Office absolutely refused to allow any members of the services to travel on the rebuilt Tudors, and the ATAC turned down the request for a service to Nigeria. So Laker bought Skymasters, and successfully bid for trooping flights to Cyprus; the Tudor IVs were instead converted into freighters, which he used for service flying and on the Woomera contract, until they were finally withdrawn from use in 1959. For the record Air Charter did perform thirteen trooping flights in 1953 using G-AGRY, the former Fairflight 'fat' Tudor II. Eagle, with a large fleet of Vikings, took over the West African service and many of the Mediterranean tasks, which included a leave service for servicemen from the Canal Zone to Cyprus. Hunting-Clan concentrated on its Northern Network, and the Colonial Coach Class routes which it shared with Airwork; Hunting-Clan was finally awarded a C Class licence to Gibraltar, initially for one flight every four weeks! At least Skyways was able to fly its Crusader C Class service to Cyprus once every two weeks. Trooping numbers ran to between 150,000 and 200,000 a year, declining after Britain finally withdrew from the Canal Zone in 1955; C Class carryings never amounted to more than 17,000 passengers a year.

New air cargo routes, which the incoming government had indicated would be offered to the independents first, were a disappointment. Airwork eventually launched its transatlantic freight service in 1955, using a Skymaster chartered from the American airline Taloa, and introduced feeder flights from Europe, but the venture did not succeed and was withdrawn after only nine months. Both Britavia, now owned by P & O Steam Navigation, and its subsidiary Aquila wanted to fly cargo to Australia, but were frustrated by Qantas, which resented any incursion on its turf. Hunting-Clan had more success with its Africargo service to East and Central Africa, and eventually on to Johannesburg, which used Yorks, later upgraded to Douglas DC-6s. Skyways built on its relationship with BOAC, in 1954 contracting to fly the corporation's all-cargo services to Singapore with Hermes; when BOAC withdrew its Constellations in 1959, Skyways bought the last four. Silver City continued to fly freight across the Channel, export cars, livestock, French cheeses, but the Little Air Lift from Berlin was wound down in 1954; Laker built up his Channel Air Bridge from Southend to Calais and Ostend, later introducing day-trips for which passengers did not have to have a passport.

If there was nothing much to say about aviation in Parliament, apart from once yearly reviews of the corporations' annual reports, it was because the industry flew into the doldrums during the second half of the decade: the New Deal became the Status Quo. 'I think that the industry is settling down to a pattern of orderly development' was the government's take on it. In the same debate, Ernest Davies, a Labour MP with an impressive background in transport economics and policy, showed what little progress the argument over the corporations had made in the last ten years:

> Are these public corporations to be operated as business concerns and to be judged entirely by commercial standards or are they to be operated as public services, which means that other considerations have to be taken into account? Up to the present we have endeavoured to combine public and commercial services; we have endeavoured to operate them commercially and yet to provide a public service. We expect them, on the one hand, to operate commercially and, on the other, to serve the British aircraft industry, and to establish British civil aviation services throughout the world.[16]

BOAC successfully overcame its capacity shortages following the withdrawal of the Comet, but that left it without the kudos of flying jet aircraft; the corporation flew the same aircraft as other long-haul carriers. Any competitive advantage to be derived from the introduction of the turboprop Britannia was fast ebbing away, as the aircraft, a technically complex project, endured a protracted development. Thomas recognised the signs and insisted the corporation be allowed to order long-range Douglas DC-7Cs to protect itself against further delays; but he also remained steadfastly loyal to the Comet, ordering the re-engineered and lengthened Comet 4. BEA finally turned the corner in 1954/5, making a small profit of £63,039. A year later, the tenth anniversary of the corporation, profits were higher, at £603,614, and for the first time, BEA carried more than two million passengers in a year. The fleet had stabilised, with twenty-eight Viscounts and nineteen Ambassadors as its first rank aircraft; the Vikings had all gone by this time, but the corporation still fielded no less than forty-six Dakotas.

So did the independents; Dakotas were the most numerous type in the independents' inventory. There were also thirty-seven Vikings and twenty-eight Bristol Freighters, and fifty-four larger four-engine aircraft, plus Aquila's five Solents; nineteen Hermes and twenty-seven Yorks made up the bulk of the long-haul fleet. Vikings were used mainly on trooping flights, usually with thirty-six backward facing seats. There was an unwritten understanding that ministry contracts entailed use of British-built aircraft; it says much for Laker's excellent reputation that he was nevertheless able to use Skymasters. Vikings had to be used on Colonial Class services; there was no getting around that. So it was up to the Dakotas to have fun, flying holiday makers to the Mediterranean and affinity groups to Europe. It was often very much easier to organise a holiday programme through a closed group; no problems with licences and tiresome objections from BEA – 'The main concern of the Corporation was that Inclusive Tour Services should only be approved for one season at a time and then only for operation at week-ends during the peak Summer months,' noted the ATAC[17] without comment – and fares did not have to be set at BEA's fare levels, the Provision 1 clause. After a while BEA and the ATAC got wise to this development: 'Air services chartered to "closed groups" are not subject to regulation by the ATAC,' BEA complained. 'Almost as many passengers travelled to Europe on services of this kind in summer 1958 as on inclusive tours'.[18] Inclusive tours followed one of two patterns. Passengers could travel all the way by air, in the manner pioneered by Horizon Holidays, especially to the island resorts of the Mediterranean, or they could fly across the Channel, and then continue to their destination by coach or train. Ostend was a popular jumping off point for the continent, as was Basle in Switzerland. Silver City's sister company Air Kruise used its Dakotas to fly for Blue Cars from Lydd to Le Touquet, Calais, Ostend and Basle. BKS and Transair flew to the Mediterranean, newcomer Starways specialised in pilgrimage traffic from Liverpool for the Cathedral Touring Agency. Inclusive Tour passengers doubled between 1955 and 1956, a sign of things to come. The versatile Dakota was also used for short haul freight work – now more specialised, newspapers to France and Germany, for example – and on a very few scheduled services.

For the most part internal associate agreement services were flown by Rapides; there were thirty-four in regular use, and BEA still had six which it used to the Scillies. A few airlines upgraded to Herons and Doves, but many holiday makers flew in the 'gentleman's carriage of the air' to the Isle of Man and the Channel Islands, the main destinations approved by the ATAC. Not everybody was charmed:

> I was beguiled by advertisements of the facilities provided by going by this airline from Shoreham to Paris instead of making the journey from my home in Brighton to London and taking one of the main services. When I tried Channel Airways I found that all the company had was a de Havilland Rapide, which takes four or five passengers with a pilot who sits and reads his one-inch map with one in the cabin.

Donald Chapman, a Labour MP, in the House of Commons observed. 'When I complained, I was told that, of course, there was not sufficient traffic to justify a larger plane and that the company was not big enough to be able to run a bigger plane.' His fellow MP, Stephen McAdden, defended the airline, summarising the plight of the small independents in a kindly way:

> Channel Airways, together with many other independent operators, have started from small beginnings. This firm, which was subjected to attack by the hon. Gentleman, was started by a chap with a distinguished career in the war. He had very little money but managed to build up a service very much appreciated by the people who saw fit to use it. It is true that he had not at that time the resources to buy a more modern

plane, but, as a result of his hard work and energy, his business is improving. He is improving his planes every year, and I should have thought that that was something worthy of praise.[19]

It was hard for the independents to create viable schedule services. Hunting-Clan struggled with its Northern Network, eventually handing them over to its newly acquired subsidiary Dragon Airways, which deployed Herons for a time before it in turn was sold on to Britavia. Britavia was in acquisitive mood, also buying Manx Airlines and the remnants of Blackpool based Lancashire Aircraft Corporation, both of which were consolidated with Dragon into one unit and operated under the Silver City name as its Northern Division. Lancashire's founder, Eric Rylands, decided to exploit his coach-air services elsewhere, buying the Ministry's now unwanted airfield at Lympne, lately abandoned by Silver City, to start a cheap coach-air service in September 1955 between London and Paris. Passengers travelled by East Kent coach to Lympne, closer to London than Lydd, and served by better roads, followed by a one hour flight in a Skyways Dakota to Beauvais, 56 miles north of Paris, then a one hour coach ride to a terminal in north Paris conveniently near the Métro. The journey took six hours, not much faster than the train and ferry journey, but an easier journey, and considerably cheaper than flying on the London–Paris services of BEA and Air France. Five years later the service was carrying 100,000 passengers a year. Silver City responded with its own rail-air service a year later, taking passengers by coach from Victoria to Lydd, flying them to Le Touquet which had its own railway station, and then transferring by *Autorail* to the Gare du Nord; the service was marketed as 'Silver Arrow', a tribute to the Southern Railways' legendary 'Golden Arrow'. In time Laker's Channel Air Bridge inaugurated similar coach-air services from Southend.

Other independents worked out different solutions. No one knew for sure that inclusive tour holidays would prove to be the format best suited to the skills and low costs of the independent airlines. At this time, the mid-1950s, holiday flying provided some benefit, but only during the summer months and usually only at weekends; such low utilisation required written-down aircraft and temporary staff. Government contracts allowed year-round utilisation, but were keenly contested and priced, and lasted at most two to three years. Scheduled service licences, some of which could be granted for seven or ten years, offered a measure of security, long term profitability, and possible opportunities for investment, if only the airline were granted decent routes. But all the best had already been assigned to the corporations, and were securely and aggressively ring-fenced, so independents had to come up with new ideas, like the vehicle ferry services, a brilliant innovation but restricted in the long run. Hunting-Clan had tried its Northern Network; Eagle went for new international destinations, and launched services from Manchester; BKS established itself at Leeds/Bradford. Airwork lost money on its transatlantic freight service. Cambrian and Jersey Airlines specialised in their geographical niches, not unsuccessfully, but found it better to collaborate with BEA, which benefited from their lower costs. It was not for want of trying, but with the Treasury setting the tone, and resolutely opposed to any kind of competition in the market, the independents had precious little opportunity.

Unless they looked abroad, or diversified. Bamberg successfully applied for rights to fly between Bermuda and New York, establishing a local company, Eagle Airways (Bermuda), and started Viscount services in May 1958. Both Airwork and Hunting-Clan already had overseas and other interests. Airwork's ancestry went back to before the war, when it had been involved in India and the Middle East, working there for oil companies and participating in the new Egyptian airline Misr-Airwork. After the war the airline launched freight service between New Zealand's North and South Islands, using Bristol Freighters. Later the airline would manage the Viscount operations of Sudan Airways. Crop spraying and helicopter operations were also part of its portfolio. Hunting's was part of a group that manufactured aircraft and owned a major servicing facility, Field's; it also had extensive air filming and surveying expertise. Both companies had invested in colonial Africa, at times owning subsidiary air companies. Hunting's had long pockets, ordering Viscounts, and later Britannias. When opportunities failed to develop in the United Kingdom – the Colonial Coach services, the Northern Network – the airline proposed buying out Central African Airways (CAA), an airline corporation owned by the governments of the Federation of Rhodesia and Nyasaland; the Britannias could then be used on the London route. BOAC, horrified at the prospect, flew to the rescue of CAA, taking over its loss-making long-haul flights in exchange for royalty payments. Thwarted, Hunting-Clan now had a number of modern aircraft in service or on order, and no work for them. The Viscounts could not be used on Colonial Coach Class services, so Vikings were competing against BOAC's new Britannias: 'It is extraordinary,' said Maurice Curtis, Hunting-Clan's managing director, 'to suggest that you must never replace your aircraft with more up-to-date ones.' He sold some of the Viscounts, leased out others, and pondered what to do with the Britannias: maybe inclusive tours to East Africa?

The independents were not the only ones frustrated. There was a changing of the guard at the top levels of the corporations and the ministry, the three not unconnected. Peter Masefield was sent off by the government in November 1955 to try and instil some sense of urgency at Bristol's and help bring the delayed Britannias into service. A new minister was appointed early in 1956, Harold Watkinson, the tenth incumbent in the ministry's short life. He stumbled more or less immediately on entry into service, claiming in a newspaper interview that BOAC should expect to be a proving ground for British aircraft whether or not there were any successful British aircraft available. He had to backtrack quickly, adding, 'It is equally my responsibility to see that B.O.A.C. makes a profit and maintains its position as a leading world airline.'[20] But by that stage he had lost Sir Miles Thomas, who resigned suddenly in March, complaining of 'irksome political interference' and 'uninformed criticism from back-benchers'.[21] Watkinson then had to find a replacement, and showing a singular lack of imagination, tapped Gerard d'Erlanger for the job, he of the inglorious years at the helm of BEA in its early days. To give d'Erlanger credit, he really did not want the job, and only accepted it on a part-time basis, insisting that a deputy chairman be appointed to control the day-to-day running of the corporation. Watkinson's next mistake was to appoint a senior civil servant, Sir George Cribbett, as the deputy chairman. BOAC's board scented danger: if Watkinson really thought that BOAC was there to showcase Britain's aviation products then appointing a government insider as deputy chairman implied renewed assertion of the minister's powers of control. In scenes reminiscent of BOAC's upheavals during the war – when readers will recall d'Erlanger was the only director not to resign in 1943 – resignations and threats of resignations flew back and forth, and after a palace coup orchestrated by the corporation's financial comptroller, Basil Smallpeice, Watkinson backed down. Smallpeice was appointed managing director, and Cribbett was shunted off to the 'branch lines', as the overseas subsidiaries were referred to in the BOAC annual report. Smallpeice, whose dislike of Cribbett had precipitated the crisis, was told by d'Erlanger not to interfere in the associated companies. Cribbett was responsible for international relations, and overseeing some thirteen subsidiaries and associates, which included Bahamas Airways and British West Indian Airways (BWIA), Middle East Airlines (MEA), Gulf Aviation and Aden Airways; under his stewardship these associates, with the honourable exceptions of Gulf and Aden, racked up accumulated deficits of around £12 million over the next six years.

Watkinson had to do more backing down only a few months later. 'It is and always has been Government policy for the Corporations to fly British,' he had asserted in May, but five months later he unobtrusively admitted, in a written answer, that he had given BOAC permission to order fifteen Boeing 707s:

The purchase of American aircraft in this instance has proved necessary in order that the Corporation may hold their competitive position on the North Atlantic route from 1959–60 when the Boeings will be in service with foreign airlines. At that time no suitable new British aircraft can be available for that purpose and this purchase is therefore regarded, both by the Government and by B.O.A.C., as an exceptional measure to bridge the gap until a new British type is produced.[22]

Funny how BOAC's front-line American aircraft, Constellations, Stratocruisers, DC-7Cs, Boeings, were always explained away in generally similar terms as 'a stop-gap operation to preserve [BOAC's] position on the North Atlantic route.'[23] To sugar the pill, Watkinson then claimed BOAC was waiting to agree final specifications for a developed Comet, the de Havilland DH.118, before buying the type. BOAC was ordering up a very impressive inventory of aircraft, and nobody seemed to be paying attention. In 1956 the corporation had twenty-one Canadair C-4s, sixteen Constellations and sixteen Stratocruisers, and was awaiting delivery of the first of ten Douglas DC-7Cs at the end of the year. Now BOAC had ordered fifteen Boeings and nineteen Comet 4s, and was down for fifteen medium range Britannias and a further eighteen of the longer range 300 series. Including the DC-7Cs, that was seventy-seven new aircraft, bigger, faster, and more productive. But did the government really mean for BOAC to increase capacity threefold over the next five years? The DC-7Cs should have been disposed of after the Britannias came into service, but that did not happen; the corporation was moreover in complete denial in its amortisation calculations, blandly depreciating the aircraft over seven years, when clearly some of the propeller aircraft would be in service for far less. And there was Watkinson saying they needed to buy a British built competitor for the Boeings as well. D'Erlanger took it all on the chin, meekly signing up for thirty-five Vickers VC10s the following year, 1957, the rear-engine jet ousting the DH.118 as favourite.

Watkinson's influence showed how far the government had managed to gain control of the management of the corporations, BOAC especially. The 1959 House of Commons Select Committee Report[24] commented on the 'the extent to which the Corporations tacitly allow powers to the Minister which the statutes do not.' It went on to enumerate a 'formidable collection':

Although the Minister has no express statutory control over the Corporations' capital expenditure, they always seek his approval (and that of the Treasury) for orders of aircraft. They have agreed not to open new routes without [his] consent. They fly on various routes, domestic and international, because he asks them to, and they lose money in the process. They seek his approval for all fares and rates on non-international routes. They refrain, at his wish, from keeping aircraft specifically available for charter work. They come to him for permission before creating or investing in a subsidiary company.[25]

In the same spirit, the government, by condoning BEA's losses, extended subsidies to Scotland's air services without attempting to gain parliamentary approval; the process was underhand, informal, sloppy, muddled. Maybe the government as owner, sole shareholder and holder of the purse-strings was entitled to these privileges, but it was far removed from Lord Reith's advice in 1945: 'The chief characteristics of the public corporation system is that it is established and owned by the State, but not—repeat not—managed by the State.'

BOAC's Douglas DC-7C entered service across the Atlantic in January 1957, followed a month later by the first Britannia passenger flights, to Africa, the Far East and Australia. BEA put into service its first Viscount 802, larger than the 700 series and able to carry ten more passengers, and began disposing of the Ambassadors, some of which went to BKS and Dan-Air. Up until now BEA's fleet development had been in better shape; its main supplier, Vickers, had come up trumps with the

Viscount, which had enjoyed some export success, and both BEA and Trans-Canada Air Lines had ordered the Vanguard, a much larger follow-up turboprop design. A solid body of opinion in Britain favoured the turboprop over the jet. 'I wonder whether the future is not with the turbo-prop,' said Lord Winster. 'There is an economic argument involved in this question, because, especially if our aim is to get the populace into the air, to arrive at what I would call mass travel, the propeller is still the most economic way of transmitting thrust.'[26] But however enticing the economics of a large turboprop might be, its appeal receded against the glamour of the new jets. BEA realised this: it would be competing not only with the new long-haul jets, Boeing 707s and Douglas DC-8s, but the French were building a short-haul jet, the Caravelle, which in turn pulled the procurement strategies of European airlines inside out. Apart from KLM and Germany's relaunched Lufthansa, and of course BEA, every European airline bought Caravelles. During his time with BEA, Masefield had encouraged the development of the Vanguard; now, as managing director of Bristol's, he must have regretted his earlier enthusiasm, for BEA paid little attention to Bristol's products. So Britain designed two large, obsolescent, turboprop airliners, neither of which sold well; and for all its faults, the Britannia was a flexible aircraft, as much at ease carrying passengers between London and Glasgow as it was hauling freight to the Far East. To ease competitive pressures, BEA ordered Comets adapted somewhat for shorter hauls, and relentlessly pursued pooling agreements with every single European airline, sharing revenue, agreeing capacity limitations, coordinating flight departures; it took the existing fare cartels to a new dimension. Pools divided capacity 50/50 between the national carriers of each country, but there were consequences. First, each country could claim half the traffic as its legitimate share, regardless of the origin of the passengers; there is an obvious imbalance between the populations of Britain and Malta, for example, but the Maltese could still claim half the traffic as 'their' passengers. Secondly, with only BEA operating European routes, the 50 per cent share became its entitlement; a second British airline would have to carve its share of frequencies out of BEA's allocation, a loss of capacity and thus market share to the corporation. But in the meantime the policy seemed to work for BEA. By 1959, the corporation was carrying 3 million passengers a year in its fleet of sixty-two Viscounts, turning in bigger and better profits: 'The vista ahead of BEA in the next five years is exciting', a refreshing note in its 1960 Report.

Behind the scenes, Watkinson was trying to cobble together a benefits package that would bring him some relief from the independents' griping, without attracting too much ire from Lord Douglas and his friends in Parliament. Attacking the government over trooping was a useful public relations exercise for BOAC, diverting attention away from its own unequivocal monopoly and other shortcomings, but the ministries never wavered from the policy of reserving trooping for the independents. They were vindicated when the independents played a major supporting role in the Suez Crisis of 1956, Britain's last hurrah as an imperial power. Charter airlines evacuated British civilian personnel from Egypt, and helped position armed forces in Malta, Libya and Cyprus before the joint Anglo-French invasion, an attempt to regain control of the Suez Canal after it had been peremptorily nationalised by the new Egyptian leader, Colonel Nasser. When the mission failed, the charter airlines were used to bring the servicemen back. A few months later, following the Hungarian uprising, the independents were called on to help with an airlift to Austria, flying relief supplies out, and bringing back 5,000 refugees. There were nevertheless upsets. Scottish Airlines lost two Yorks in accidents during 1956, finally provoking the War Office to ban their use on passenger flights. The Hermes troopers, too, were barely adequate, their performance stretched on the long hauls to the Far East. The aircraft carried up to sixty-eight passengers on these flights, but the ventilation system had been designed to BOAC requirements, predicated on fifty-four passengers and much lower load factors; temperatures inside the cabin could reach 87° F (30 C). The government realised that independents would find it hard to buy more modern equipment, so the Ministry of Supply ordered three Britannias for future civilian trooping, without however giving much thought as to how the aircraft would be made available to the independents. The Ministry of Transport and Civil Aviation wanted the War Office to issue contracts for five to seven years to encourage investment by the charter airlines, but the War Office would not oblige, pointing out that garrison requirements overseas were always changing, especially now that Britain was beginning to divest itself of its colonies in Africa and the Far East; the War Office did relent a tiny bit, and agreed to three-year contracts for the major tasks. The independents were nervously aware that the RAF was beginning to accumulate a larger transport fleet, having taken over BOAC's original order of Comet 2s, and with Britannias and Comet 4s on order. The Treasury had a light bulb moment, and began manoeuvres to steer trooping contracts in-house and utilise the increased RAF airlift that was now becoming available.

Aside from trooping contracts, Watkinson decided he had little else to offer the independents. He made one further concession, changing the terms and conditions of the Colonial Coach Class services, a name which by now was no longer appropriate as African colonies began to seek independence. Instead, a new 'Safari' service would be introduced; furthermore, following a recommendation from the ATAC, there would no longer be restrictions limiting independent airlines to the use of sub-standard aircraft. But in future BOAC would receive a share of the traffic; actually, BOAC would be allowed to have most of the traffic, as the government stipulated that its share would be 70 per cent, however that was to be arrived at, and the independents would get the remaining 30 per cent. At least Hunting-Clan and Airwork could now start deploying Viscounts on their African services, and were quick to do so. Viscounts were also about to appear on trooping rosters for the first time. Transair, recently bought by Airwork, won the West Med contract to Malta, Gibraltar and Libya in October 1957, and must have felt vindicated in the calculated risk it had taken in ordering its two Viscounts; the contract was worth 3,700 hours of year-round flying, whereas Transair could only count on 1,000 hours in inclusive tour flying during the peak summer months. Transair opened a base at London's new Gatwick airport, bought a third Viscount, and also started flying for Air France.

'Cinderella airlines' is how *Flight's* Transport Editor Mike Ramsden described the independents at this stage.[27] He pointed out that their share of UK output appeared to be decreasing. It had been running at around one third, now it was approaching one quarter; one half was accounted for by trooping, another third by charters (mainly inclusive tours), and the rest by scheduled services. He estimated total revenue for the independents in 1956 at £17 million, and from that deduced their operating costs to be between 25 old pence and 30 old pence per mile. These he compared with BOAC and BEA: 38 old pence and 41 old pence, respectively. Noting that the independents, with their much lower costs, could probably operate more of BEA's loss-making domestic services profitably, he urged them 'to come to terms with the Government. The words "come to terms" mean more than a readiness to associate with the Corporations operationally. The independents cannot progress by hammering away at the political resistance which is the biggest bar to progress.'

Somewhat supine advice, but probably what the minister wanted to hear. What he did not need was the independents telling him that 'the limits of current Government policy have been reached'.[28] A year later they were loudly calling for proper licensing arrangements and the abolition of 'predetermined criteria', that is, the corporations' monopoly powers. Watkinson had exhausted his agenda, and now his civil servants were also grumbling about closed groups and the legal status of associate agreements. At first he hoped that licensing arrangements under a new ATAC could be reconstituted within his existing powers, but then realised that any further changes would have to involve new legislation, for the existing arrangements were stretching the ATAC to the limits of legality. The British can live with muddle, but not their administrators. There might have to be a new Fashion, something along the lines promised by his predecessor in 1952, 'to throw the lines open to private competition under proper regulation, and to have some system analogous to the Civil Aeronautics Board in the United States.' But he shied away from further confrontation with Beswick, a nationalisation diehard, and his socialist team; instead he dropped a few hints about possible future arrangements, and then did nothing. The government's only advice to the independents was to start amalgamating with each other: 'The Government would welcome some reduction in the number of companies if this is likely to result in the formation of larger and more firmly based companies.'[29]

Silver City celebrated the tenth anniversary of its car ferry in 1958, when its large fleet of Bristol Freighters carried over 47,000 cars and 340,000 passengers. Interestingly, half of those passengers were on inclusive tours; eight of the original short-nosed Freighters and two of the bigger Type 32 had by now been converted to all passenger layout. Silver City continued to stimulate demand by cutting its fares and increasing efficiency; the airline carried more cars in 1958 than in 1955, but with eight fewer aircraft. Routes to the Channel Islands and Northern Ireland were tried, and dropped; none proved as effective as the core routes from Lydd to Le Touquet, Calais and Ostend, on which a rate of seven cars per aircraft/hour could be achieved. Sister company Aquila just made it to its tenth anniversary. The Solents were getting older and more beat-up: 'Their noise is incredible,' complained Donald Chapman MP.

They are very old machines developed during or shortly after the war. The journey is interminably long because they fly so slowly. On the occasion when I travelled we flew overnight. The heating system in the wretched thing did not work at all and everybody was so perishingly cold that it was beyond description.[30]

He made no allowances for the unique operating difficulties Aquila faced: 'Conditions are such at Madeira that these flying-boats cannot take off in the slightest swell, and there are Heath Robinson devices for running people up and down the island and taking them off from small coves when there happens to be a break in the weather.' Difficult sea conditions that year around Madeira had made operations especially trying. There was no replacement in sight for the Solents, and the government declined the company's offer to take over the Princess flying boats, still looking for a home, so the decision was taken to close the airline down at the end of the season, on 30 September 1958, ending a fine tradition of British seaplane service. By contrast, Eagle soared past its tenth anniversary, flying ever higher. The airline re-entered the long-haul market, buying Douglas DC-6s, surely the most efficient piston engine airliner ever built, to complement the Viscounts and Vikings which continued to fly European routes. One of the DC-6s, G-APOM, flew over 3,800 hours in its first year of operations, a record for a British registered aircraft. Although the early services to Sweden and Yugoslavia proved unsuccessful, Eagle persisted with international scheduled services, adding Luxembourg, Innsbruck, Pisa and Rimini to its destinations, as well as continuing with a considerable programme of inclusive tour and trooping flights. One of the Viscounts was based in Bermuda, and Eagle applied for Colonial Coach Class services between London and Bermuda, and on to the Bahamas and Jamaica. Predictably the ATAC refused the application, so Eagle resubmitted the application through its Bermuda subsidiary. Bamberg then stirred up more trouble by applying to the ATAC for a number of low frequency routes to colonial points – Aden, Hong Kong, Singapore, the Caribbean, Nigeria, Nairobi, Nicosia, Malta and Gibraltar – using DC-6s and offering Very Low Fares, around half the existing Tourist fares. Air Charter was in the news too. Laker sold a controlling interest in Air Charter and Aviation Traders, his

Southend-based engineering firm, to Airwork, which was beginning to accumulate airlines; later in the year Airwork took over Morton and Olley, the specialist operators flying Doves, which migrated to Gatwick from Croydon. Laker opportunistically bought two Bristol Britannias from a cancelled order and started flying them on government flights to Christmas Island in the Pacific, where Britain was testing its nuclear bombs. The War Office was enthusiastic about the upgrading of the independents' long-haul stock; as Britannias and DC-6s entered service the days of the Hermes were numbered. Nevertheless the Ministry of Supply still could not make up its mind what to do with its Britannias, nor for that matter could Hunting-Clan. Hunting-Clan was now part of an ambitious shipping consortium, British & Commonwealth Shipping, formed when Clan Line merged with Union Castle, but the new owners did not know what to do with the Britannias either. When Peter Masefield delivered them to Sir Nicholas Cayzer, chairman of British & Commonwealth, at the end of 1958, the aircraft were left unpainted.

By 1958 BEA was hitting its stride. Not so BOAC; it was beginning to produce gloomy results again, accompanied by much whining from its board. The corporation posted a loss of £2.8 million. Just about everybody got it in the neck: the manufacturers, especially Bristol, for late delivery of the new Britannias, which proved troublesome in service and had had to be expensively rectified; the government, for insisting on a return on its capital, and by inference, for granting independence to its former colonies, thus depriving BOAC of monopoly cabotage rights; the independents for introducing Viscounts on Colonial Coach Class routes, despite their reduced frequency of operation. Unfortunately, just as the corporation was boosting its output, traffic began to tail off. On the Atlantic routes in 1958 BOAC increased capacity by almost 50 per cent, but traffic growth was below 30 per cent; load factor and utilisation suffered. For reasons that are not entirely clear, d'Erlanger prioritised load factor over utilisation; daily aircraft utilisation had declined since Thomas's day, although increasingly expensive aircraft really needed to be flown more intensively. Concerns over depreciation of the new aircraft coming on line were put to one side. Maintenance standards remained lavish:

> In their engineering workshops, B.O.A.C. were employing 3,000 more staff than they needed. They employed more than twice as many staff per aircraft or per flying-hour as did the others; they employed between four and six times as many inspectors and supervisors as did the other airlines investigated.[31]

On any given day one in four of BOAC's aircraft would be in a hangar on the ground rather than earning its keep in the air. BOAC flew its last Constellation service on 6 October 1958, just two days after its first Comet 4 flight to New York; it had to stop at Gander to refuel. And after a four year hiatus, services to Venezuela were resumed, using Britannias; Comets reopened the main South American routes, abandoned after the Comet crashes, in January 1960.

If the outlook was unpromising for BOAC, it seemed terminal for Airwork. The airline had an extended portfolio of airlines, Air Charter, Morton, Olley, Transair, a freight airline in New Zealand, an operating agreement with Sudan Airways, but its own operations were to be put on the block. The Hermes contract to the Far East was about to end in May 1959. The Vikings were no longer needed as Viscounts could now fly Colonial Coach Class, and the entire fleet was put up for sale; two Viscounts were transferred to Transair which took over the operation of the African services. It was a turn-up for the airline that had dominated the independents since the war, and it was not quite the end of the story. Britavia also had to face a rather stark future as its trooping contracts came to an end in 1959; the Hermes were repainted in Silver City colours and deployed to Manston in Kent, where they operated the coach-air services and even gained the first of the War Office's trooping contracts to Germany, the last of the major tasks, replacing the ferry and train link via Hook of Holland. Hunting-Clan finally landed the major Far East trooping contract for its two Britannias. It was a significant upgrading for the War Office; flights would now take 24 hours, rather than 3½ days in a Hermes. Outfitted with 114 rear-facing seats, the aircraft also acquired a coat of paint, not however Hunting-Clan's handsome colours with the dayglo orange tail, but instead lettered for 'British and Commonwealth', the airline's shipping backer. A few months later the company gained further contracts, to Kenya, Cyprus and Aden. The Ministry of Supply gave a little sigh, and sold its three 'civilian' Britannias to the RAF.

As the end of 1959 approached, and with it the prospect of new elections, Watkinson realised that his ministry was losing control. Bumbling along within the existing legal framework, hoping that he could safely delegate everything to the ARB or the ATAC, was a policy that came unstuck when safety became an issue. On 2 September 1958 a Viking of Independent Air Transport crashed into a house in Southall, killing the three crew members and four people on the ground. It subsequently transpired that the aircraft had been overloaded, was significantly off-course, and that the captain had been flying in excess of recommended duty hours, and 'the operating and maintenance standards of the airline involved left much to be desired.'[32] There was an outcry, and calls for the airline to be shut down. But Watkinson did not have the powers to do that. His ministry had previously prosecuted Independent over flight time limitations. He revoked the airline's licences, but then realised the airline did not need them: by flying for closed groups, it could go on trading without recourse to the ATAC. After the accident, Independent changed its name to Blue-Air and went on flying for another year.

There had been a sudden and explosive growth in inclusive tour charters and the airlines to service them, and the ministry had little control over either. When the ministry prosecuted Milbanke Tours for re-categorising an ITC flight as a closed group charter, after the ATAC had denied a licence to the operating airline, Hunting-Clan, the magistrates threw the case out, pointing out that the airline, not Milbanke Tours, was carrying the passengers, and the airline was entitled to carry closed groups. The ATAC had to cope with over 700 applications in 1958–9, and that was just for the inclusive tours that needed a licence; possibly as many holiday flights were flown unlicensed. It is a measure of the ministry's dysfunction that it had no statistics for these unlicensed flights; indeed, the only sources of information were provided by the corporations, the ATAC and the members of the British Independent Air Transport Association, itself an unrepresentative body. Beyond the pale, and not members of the association, was a batch of new airlines – Air Safaris, Continental, Independent, Orion, Overseas, Pegasus and Tradair – all of which had plans for expansion; two of them, Independent and Overseas, acquired four-engine aircraft. The ministry was overstretched: Watkinson was just as likely to be taken to task over the state of the Kingston bypass as the control of competition on Colonial Coach Class, and even his friends thought it was time for change. 'The policy of this and any subsequent Government,' explained Frederick Farey-Jones, an industry expert, to the House of Commons on 28 February 1958,

> should be directed to giving a wider sphere of influence to the people whom we now call the independents, and to developing the Ministry of Civil Aviation itself, because I should like to see the Ministry of Supply pooled with the Ministry of Civil Aviation and made one Ministry.[33]

Watkinson conceded change was due, but it would fall to take place in the next parliament, after the election in October 1959. In his valedictory, he looked to the future:

Any Government who wish to expand in the air would be absolutely wrong not to try to exploit the pioneering work of people who are prepared to put in their own money and risk their own capital in this job. That does not mean, as I often see in trade union journals, that one is deliberately trying to take business away from the Corporations. We are trying to increase the totality of that business so that the cake that we all cut should be bigger. I challenge anybody to deny that that is the right and sensible policy for civil aviation as a whole. I make no apology, therefore, for continuing this policy, and it remains the Government's view that independent operators have a valuable contribution to make to our prosperity and development in the air.

For the future, I think that in the new central licensing authority there will be a new plan for the air which will allow greater freedom, a quicker rate of expansion and a fair deal for both the Corporations and the independent airlines….In the Department we have put much painstaking work into this concept of a new central licensing body that will license both operations and the organisations themselves. That will have two advantages. One is that it will get the Minister a bit more out of this business of trying to sort out routes and services, which I think is right, and, secondly, it will give the Ministry…the power, which it now has on the roads, of withdrawing the licence of an unsatisfactory operator; in other words, a clear mandate to control the situation more satisfactorily than we can under the present Acts.[34]

CHAPTER 7

1959 to 1963
A New Charter for British Civil Aviation?

The Tories won the election with an overall majority of 100 seats. It was a come-back for a party that only three years previously had been humiliated by the Suez Crisis, and a tribute to its leader, Harold Macmillan, who had taken over in 1957 following the anguished resignation of Sir Anthony Eden. The Prime Minister immediately began making changes to his departments. He was anxious to promote the development of civil aviation, especially the building of aircraft, and to achieve that, he created a new Ministry of Aviation, which took over the former Ministry of Supply, responsible for procurement on behalf of the RAF, to which were added the civil aviation bits of the Ministry of Transport and Civil Aviation, which included responsibility for the state-owned corporations. The Ministry of Transport would revert to sorting out the Kingston bypass, Britain's merchant marine, London Underground and British Railways, about to undergo its own reshaping in the capable hands of Dr Beeching. Macmillan thought the independent airlines were of some value – 'They really are,' he wrote in 1957 'like the merchant navy in the old days, our second line of defence so far as air transport is concerned' – but for him the immediate priority was the creation of jobs; he wanted to restore Britain's industrial prowess. The new Minister of Aviation, Duncan Sandys, was given the remit of sorting out both the aircraft industry and the airlines.

He started off with the aircraft industry. Within two months he had corralled them into five major groupings: two aircraft and missile manufacturers, Hawker Siddeley and the British Aircraft Corporation; two aero-engine firms, Rolls-Royce and Bristol Siddeley; and one helicopter builder, Westland. They were all privately owned but susceptible to government pressure, dependent on ministry orders. Hawker Siddeley (HS) took over Blackburn and de Havilland, adding them to its cluster of previously acquired companies: Armstrong Whitworth, Folland, Gloster, Hawker and Avro. Hawker Siddeley also had a half stake in engine manufacturer Bristol Siddeley, which it shared with Bristol Aeroplane. Bristol's, meanwhile, joined forces with Vickers and English Electric, later adding Hunting Aircraft, to form the British Aircraft Corporation (BAC). Bristol's then sold its helicopter interests to Westland, which emerged as the dominant helicopter manufacturer, having in turn taken over Fairey and Saunders-Roe's helicopters. Fairey had designed and built the Rotodyne, a sophisticated if noisy compound gyrocopter – and source of endless fascination in the House of Commons – subsequently cancelled by Westland. Saunders-Roe had turned to helicopters after building the hulls for the Princess flying boats, still languishing on the beach at Cowes.

In return for their compliance, the government undertook to help new civil projects by giving them launch aid – the Trident, VC10 and the new Argosy freighter – but was ambivalent as to its responsibilities if it were to oblige the corporations to buy British built airliners: 'The Government may be prepared to contribute towards the cost of proving a new type of civil aircraft and of introducing it into regular air line service'.[1] The government's pixie dust would no longer fall on Handley Page, however, which naughtily refused to join either of the airframe combinations; fortunately the government had previously undertaken to buy three of the new Herald turbo-props, which were lent to BEA for its Scottish services. The Herald had a rival, the Avro 748, of similar size, seating up to forty-eight passengers, also powered by two Rolls-Royce Dart engines. Both aircraft were billed as DC-3 successors, and Skyways ordered three Avros for its Coach-Air service out of Lympne. Left in limbo were Scottish Aviation at Prestwick, which built specialised short take-off and landing transports which did not sell, and Short Brothers & Harland in Belfast, owned by the government, now building Britannias for the RAF and which had just launched a large freighter, the Britannic, later renamed the Belfast, which used the wing design of the Britannia.

Then it was the turn of the airlines. Sandys' predecessor Watkinson had set the ball rolling, but it was left to Sandys to introduce the new legislation in March, the 1960 Civil Aviation (Licensing) Bill. Even the opposition – without its spokesman, Beswick, who had lost his seat at the election – was impressed at the speed with which Sandys tackled the task. The Bill set out to do two things. First, the government wanted to tackle the lack of proper regulatory oversight of its airlines. The Airworthiness Registration Board supervised the safety of airliners, but the government needed to get a grip on the airlines which operated the airliners, to ensure they were properly financed, organised, competent, fit for purpose. It proposed introducing the Air Operator's Certificate (AOC), which an airline would be obliged to hold before it could even begin thinking about starting up. Sandys explained the issue which had come to prominence after Independent's Viking crash at Southall:

> At present, no new scheduled service is approved by the Minister unless the Director of Aviation Safety at the Ministry of Aviation certifies that the operator's equipment and organisation are safe and satisfactory for the service proposed. On the other hand, and this is our difficulty, we have no power to insist that the same standards of safety are observed by operators of charter services, who do not have to go through the procedure of obtaining the Minister's approval.[2]

That part of the Bill was uncontroversial.

The other main element of the Bill, the abolition of the corporations' monopoly powers and the institution of an independent Air Transport Licensing Board to award new route licences, should have been controversial, but was not. Reaction was muted, even disparaging. 'The proposed Board will not be the powerful autonomous instrument that had been hoped for,'[3] commented *Flight*. 'Neither the Corporations nor the independents are likely to be very pleased with the contents of the Bill,' agreed *The Aeroplane*, pointing out the independents 'will be able to recognise little practical change other than a tightening of the licensing arrangements.'[4] Discussion in Parliament was described as 'not very searching', 'affable'; perhaps it was the absence of Beswick, with his diehard commitment to nationalisation, or maybe it was because Sandys bent over backwards to assure MPs that the corporations' interests would be safeguarded at all costs:

> I can tell the House what the Bill will not do, and is not intended to do. It is not intended to undermine the position of B.O.A.C. or B.E.A. Those two corporations are our main flag carriers on the air routes of the world. Large sums of public money have been invested in them and they have to face fierce competition from foreign rivals.[5]

Parliamentarians learned to always mention 'fierce competition' when debating the corporations, even though Sandys went on to deconstruct the ferocity of the competition:

Another thing that the Bill will not do is to break up the partnership agreements the corporations have concluded with Commonwealth and foreign airlines. These pooling arrangements have proved valuable in eliminating wasteful duplication and promoting productive co-operation and harmonious international relations in the sphere of aviation. I shall certainly take care to see that nothing is done to upset these arrangements.

These pooling arrangements had a dark side; they were opaque, anti-competitive, restrictive, exclusive. One example: the attempts by Britavia to fly to Australia had caused much anguish, and as a result:

> The B.O.A.C.-Air India International-Qantas Tripartite Partnership Agreement… contains a stipulation by Air India International and by Qantas to the effect that they will regard the Agreement between them as valid only so long as B.O.A.C. remains the only United Kingdom airline authorised by the United Kingdom Government to operate in or out of the United Kingdom on the main routes covered by the Agreement.[6]

BOAC had further pooling arrangements in Africa and Canada, the latter a regulatory Neanderthal. BEA used its many pooling agreements within Europe, equally opaque, to deny access to the independents. Both corporations deployed extensive international relations departments whose job was to keep the pool partners happy, on the one hand, and cosy up to the government on the other. The government seemed oblivious to the devolution of its authority to the corporations. *Flight* commented sharply:

> In recent years the bilateral-agreement negotiators in the Ministry of Aviation have left largely to BEA and BOAC the job of striking better bargains for British air transport. The corporations have done this by negotiating pooling agreements—agreements which the Ministry does not even see. The Ministry must accept responsibility for the powers it claims…There would be cause for disquiet even if the Ministry does sit up, switch off the corporations' pooling autopilots, and take over the controls. The Ministry has a vested interest in BOAC and BEA, so it need not try hard to win for the independents the traffic rights that are needed…The Ministry's powers over traffic rights can make a mockery of the whole licensing system.[7]

The only routes on which there were no pooling arrangements, and coincidentally the only routes on which more than one British airline would have been allowed to compete, were those to the United States, at this time limited to New York, Boston, Chicago, Detroit and San Francisco.

Sandys was nervous about the corporations, especially BOAC – 'I am a little hesitant about prophesying for B.O.A.C. sunshine round the corner' – and was under pressure from his civil servants and the Treasury not to take anything away from them. The Treasury did not want to imperil BOAC's worsening finances, and the only way it knew how was to eliminate possible competition. The men from the ministry did not want change either, for their own reasons, and set about subverting Sandys's well-meaning proposals. They certainly did not want to encourage the independents, and furthermore, the rules needed to be ratcheted up: no more so-called 'associate agreements', when the airlines were in reality competing with the corporations; and definitely no more flying off the record, no more closed groups. In future all flights for which each passenger paid a 'separate fare' would need a licence. When Sandys realised how little he was giving the independents, he tried to push back against the combined forces of the Treasury and his civil servants, and suggested that maybe not all the corporations' licences need be transferred under the new legislation. He was ruthlessly steamrollered, and had to explain to the House in the debate that all current licences and agreements would, after all, be transferred to transitional licences; 'A transitional licence…will be issued by the Board without application from the operators, and without examination and discussion, merely to legalise the continuance of the existing position.' So that was that. Sandys put a brave face on it:

> As I have explained, the Bill withdraws from the corporations their statutory monopoly. This gives to the independents something for which they have long been asking—freedom to apply for licences in their own right on the same footing as the corporations. Whether or not any particular application is successful will, of course, depend upon a number of factors, including the ability of the applicant to convince the Board that his company possesses the resources needed to provide an effective and a reliable service.

But he was also careful to explain that the Board would not make the final decision, which, in the event of an appeal, would rest with the minister.

Some MPs sounded enthusiastic about the proposals: 'I believe that the independent operators, who have engaged in a magnificent struggle in the last ten years against almost impossible odds, have earned what we now seek to give them—that is, a place in the sun in British civil aviation.'[8] But William Shepherd had also recognised the dangers of a sickly BOAC.

> The truth is that the board as at present constituted does not give the Corporation the leadership, the direction and the drive that it ought to have.…We have tolerated this situation in silence for quite a long time. The time is now overdue for my right hon. Friend to deal with this situation. B.O.A.C. is a vast national asset. Its performance, in all parts of the world, is a matter of supreme importance to us. It is not at the moment as virile and as efficient an organisation as it could be or ought to be.[9]

That masculine thing again. Just as well that his colleague Frederick Burden in the House was able to offer some reassurance: 'There is no question of denationalising the corporations, or of emasculating them in any way, or reducing their activities.'

Sandys also wanted amalgamations in the independent airline sector, and looked to Airwork to provide a lead. Airwork had already scooped up a number of operators; Bristow Helicopters was the latest to succumb, in January 1960, and on 1 March, Myles Wyatt, Airwork's chairman and managing director, duly complied, announcing the impending merger of his airline group with Hunting-Clan. The combined group – Air Charter, Airwork, Airwork Helicopters, Bristow Helicopters, Channel Air Bridge, Hunting-Clan, Morton and Olley, Transair – would deploy over fifty fixed-wing aircraft, including four Britannias, two DC-6s and ten Viscounts, held significant trooping contracts, and was the main operator of Colonial Coach Class services. Four shipping lines, Blue Star, Furness Withy, Clan Line, and British & Commonwealth, together with Whitehall Securities, were the principal backers. Channel Air Bridge was spared, but the rest all took the name British United Airways on 1 July 1960. The name harked back to Blackpool-based United Airways, formed in 1935 by Whitehall Securities and a forerunner of British Airways; perhaps Lord Balfour, now on the board of BEA, and d'Erlanger, both of them former directors of British Airways, appreciated the historical allusion. D'Erlanger was about to become part of history himself, stepping down from the chairmanship of BOAC in July, shortly after he had been bullied by Sandys into ordering another ten VC10s. He was succeeded by Rear Admiral Sir Matthew Slattery, who had enjoyed stints at Short Brothers & Harland and Bristol's, and arrived just in time to post a tiny improvement in BOAC's results, to the extent that the loss was only £833,795. Sandys was also moved along at this time, after less than a year in post, to oversee the dismantling of the colonial empire; he was succeeded by Peter Thorneycroft. At British United Freddie Laker took over, beating Transair's Freeman to the post of managing director.

Not a merger, but a sea-change of sorts, came about in March 1960 when Cunard Steamship announced it was going to buy Bamberg's Eagle. Cunard was being solicited by the government to build a replacement 'Q3' for the *Queen Mary* on the Atlantic crossing, but had always been keenly aware of the potential rivalry with, and opportunities in, air transport. Eagle was making progress in the western hemisphere; the Bermuda operation had grown and now included the Bahamas as well, with frequent Viscount service between Miami and Nassau, curiously in competition with Skyways, which had taken Bahamas Airways off BOAC's hands. Still outstanding was the licence for the Bermuda to London route, which had been granted by the Bermuda authorities, but two and a half years later was still awaiting reciprocal approval from the British. Even at this stage Cunard sounded dubious about its future partner, Eagle. 'We are talking to BOAC about a mutual arrangement', said Cunard's chairman Sir John Brocklebank, and BOAC admitted it was exploring 'possible ways and means in which Cunard and BOAC might collaborate to further British interests across the Atlantic.'[10] How the new Cunard Eagle would fit into a possibly tripartite arrangement could only be guessed at. For the time being, Cunard saw promise in the Bermuda to London route, and Eagle acquired the first of a large fleet of Britannias.

Britannia production closed down in 1960, with eighty-five built. BOAC's Boeing 707s entered service on 27 May 1960 to New York. BOAC had cleared out its stock of piston-engine aircraft in 1959, retaining its Douglas DC-7Cs, but disposing of fourteen Stratocruisers, twenty Canadair C-4s and sixteen Constellations. BEA had retired its Ambassadors, and taken delivery of the first of its Comets, but otherwise relied on its huge fleet of Viscounts, twenty-three Viscount 701s and eighty-nine of the larger 800 series Viscounts, and a still impressive wing of thirty-four Dakotas. The independents fielded around 200 multi-engine aircraft, of which 114 were twin-engine, short range, vintage piston-liners, Dakotas, Vikings and Bristol Freighters; there were just nineteen turboprops, fourteen Viscounts and five Britannias. The disparity in fleet composition highlighted how far investment in new aircraft by the independents had lagged, but that did not extend to their ambition. Barely days after the new Bill received Royal Assent on 2 June 1960, Cunard Eagle announced it wanted to apply for scheduled routes across the Atlantic.

It was a busy time for everyone. The ATAC was to be dismantled, replaced by a new Air Transport Licensing Board (ATLB); for a time the boards operated in parallel, under the same chairman, Lord Terrington, which provided some continuity. Many airlines found that they had to apply for transport licences for the first time now that closed groups and non-systematic flying were no longer exempt; rules for affinity groups were much tougher now as well. New ARB regulations were also making it harder to operate older aircraft profitably; Vikings, unless rebuilt, would have their payloads reduced, which meant fewer passengers. The government did a deal with the corporations, colonial airlines and the independents over the Very Low Fare issue. After much argument, IATA had agreed to introduce new Economy fares, to replace the old Tourist class. Now Sandys sanctioned a new Skycoach fare on cabotage routes, those to Britain's remaining colonies, which was set at levels 20–30 per cent lower than Economy. Traffic would be split 70/30 between the corporations and independents, and participating carriers were limited in what they could give passengers: no bar service, cold meals only, no reassuring hand-written route maps from the captain; it was a long way from Imperial Airways' standards. Frequencies were laughable, fortnightly to Africa and the Mediterranean, monthly to Bermuda and the Caribbean. BOAC could also offer Skycoach to Hong Kong and Singapore. In return Cunard Eagle finally received approval for the Bermuda to London route, which it would operate in parallel to its Skycoach services. Because the airline already held Bermuda–Nassau–Miami rights, it could market the service from London through to Miami. British United, also awarded Skycoach routes, still flew its twice weekly 'Safari' services to Nairobi, and once a week to Accra, and continued the weekly Tourist Class services to Gibraltar; note how the frequencies had improved over the years! Whether intentionally or not, the government killed off the Very Low Fare concept with the austerity Skycoach; it had fizzled out by 1964.

In other ways 1960 proved an eventful year. Three airlines shut down, Air Condor, Continental and Orion, but over 200,000 inclusive tour passengers were carried, and possibly as many again on closed group and other exempt charters. BEA benefited too, confessing it had increased its inclusive tour traffic by 24 per cent, to over 219,000 passengers. Independents jostled for transitional licences under the new regulations to cover their 1961 programmes. Expansion was in order; Overseas bought fifteen more Canadair C-4s to add to its fleet of six, Falcon arranged to buy four Constellations, Air Safaris had five Hermes on its books, Tradair bought Viscounts. The Air Transport Licensing Board opened its doors on 1 December 1960 and was promptly deluged with applications for new scheduled services. The very first application was from Cunard Eagle for routes to New York, but British United was quick off the mark, applying for a large route network from Gatwick to Europe and Africa. Cunard Eagle also applied for European and domestic routes from its new base at Heathrow, where it had transferred its services after the closure of Blackbushe on 31 May 1960.

The ATLB veered off course almost immediately. Lord Terrington, its first chairman, died on 7 January 1961. A pragmatic regulator, he had steered the airline industry against strong headwinds and would, I feel sure, have adapted to the new regime with the same realism and discipline that he had displayed during his years at the ATAC. He was eventually succeeded by an economics professor, Daniel Jack; there was always an element of academic nonchalance in the Board's decisions. Although it was supposed to be quite independent – 'The Act does not provide any positive guidance on policy…It appears to have been the intention of the legislature to leave the Board unfettered…and free to exercise their judgment' – the new Board could have used some help from the very beginning, noting it was 'without the guidance of a permanent Chairman during the important formative period of our existence.'[11] Appeals against decisions were to be heard by a commissioner, usually a former judge, bringing in a modicum of legal process, except that the appeals commissioner could rehear the whole case, even to the extent of allowing new evidence. It was then up to the Minister to examine the Board's original decision, consider the commissioner's recommendation, and then decide; sometimes the Minister ignored both! Licence applications became a lengthy three-part process: first the Board; then the appeals commissioner; and finally the minister, who had the last word, advised of course by his civil servants.

The Board ran into trouble with Cunard Eagle's New York application, its very first, number A.1000. The airline had ordered two Boeing 707s, at a cost of £6 million; Cunard came in for some flack when it transpired that it was about to receive £18 million from the government towards the cost of the new Q3. But neither this allegation nor BOAC's claims of 'material diversion' deterred the Board, which with a fine show of bravado gave Cunard Eagle what it wanted, a daily service to New York. Even in the euphoria of the moment, however, *Flight's* transport editor, Mike Ramsden, remained sceptical:

> It is by no means a foregone conclusion that Cunard Eagle will get their licence, particularly as the Minister must be as concerned as BOAC about the corporation's really serious surplus of capacity on the North Atlantic. But if he vetoes the Board's first major decision he will confirm what has always been suspected— that the Board is only as independent as the Minister, guardian of the corporations, wants it to be.[12]

BOAC appealed the decision; it also announced increased losses in its 1960–61 results, citing among other causes the decrease in traffic across the Atlantic just when the corporation had increased capacity by a third. Things just got worse after that at BOAC, so much so that by the end of 1961 the minister was softening up Parliament in the expectation of horrible results; deficits over £10 million were hinted at.

BEA was also facing challenges. Like many other carriers, it had an excess of capacity as new aircraft, Comets and Vanguards, joined the fleet, and faced the prospect, after seven profitable years, of losses in 1961–62. On the credit side, it managed to sell its remaining thirty-three Dakotas, nineteen of them to British independents. But then it also had to tussle with the independents before the Board; not that it was over-concerned, despite the thunderous language of Lord Douglas, its chairman, because all its existing European scheduled routes were stitched up under pooling and restrictive air service agreements. No European government was going to concede its national carrier's 'entitlement' to half the traffic, so any new British entrant would have to encroach on BEA's share, something the government had pledged would not happen. Domestic services were a different matter, as were the dwindling number of cabotage routes, because for those the government did not have to take into account international agreements. That meant that only 'new' routes within Europe would qualify for route approvals, something that had always been the case since the Tories had introduced the New Deal in 1952. And there were still some routes that had not been developed: Genoa; Marseilles; Madeira (now that Aquila was no longer around); and Malaga, a new airport on Spain's Costa del Sol. BEA continued to put a lot of effort into raising objections to charter licences, so the process continued as a lottery, with applicants never certain as to what would be permitted; in its first year the ATLB refused 246 of the 673 inclusive tour applications it received. In the past, this problem had often been resolved by reclassifying the flights in another category, closed group charters for instance; now that was no longer possible. Instead tour operators transferred their business to foreign airlines, knowing that the British authorities would not dare to refuse them traffic rights; retaliation on British airlines would have been too severe. In 1962, as a result, around 25 per cent of inclusive tour charter flying was performed by foreign airlines. One of the duties of the Board was to further the development of British civil aviation: forcing charter business on to foreign airlines seemed an odd way to go about it.

But first, everybody had to get through the rest of 1961, an epic summer of chaos and disruption. Although airlines were now required to have an Air Operator's Certificate, there were still lingering concerns over the safety of charter airlines. The fall-out from the Southall crash continued, and then in 1961 there were three fatal accidents involving charter airlines. One of the largest independents, Overseas, was getting a lot of publicity, but was also having trouble operating its aircraft to schedule and paying its bills; the airline suddenly went into liquidation on 15 August, in the middle of the summer holiday season. Another airline in difficulties, Falcon, found itself without the Constellations it needed to operate its services; it was then prosecuted over safety infringements following a transatlantic flight it had undertaken in March. Of the four Constellations it had bought, all of which needed to be brought up to ARB agreed standards, one had been sold to another new British airline, Trans-European, one was put on the Austrian register, one spent long periods out of service, and the fourth was stored and never flown; Falcon had to transfer many of the contracts to Air Safaris. The ministry would not allow the Austrian Constellation to fly for Falcon; it only relented after the failure of Overseas, when every airline seat was needed to rescue over 5,000 stranded British tourists. It was a temporary reprieve, however, for the ministry withdrew Falcon's AOC on 21 September. Derby Airways lost a Dakota in the Pyrenees on 7 October. The Board's more stringent financing requirements bit hard: Pegasus put up its shutters in October; Air Safaris did the same early in November; both Tradair and BKS went into receivership. Could there be any more bad news?

Yes. Late in October, Cunard decided not to proceed with the Q3 project, embarrassing the government, which had gone to some trouble to pass legislation covering future ship-building subsidies. The Transport Minister, Ernest Marples, claimed Cunard 'has withdrawn from its side of the bargain, and, to put it crudely, has said, "All bets are off."'[13] Indeed they were. One month later, on 21 November, Thorneycroft, the Aviation Minister, announced that he was upholding BOAC's appeal against the Cunard Eagle New York licence, overturning the Board's decision and simultaneously undermining its authority before it had really started, delivering a nasty kick to the independents, and punishing Cunard. He based his decision on the recommendation of the appeal commissioner, who felt that BOAC had adequate capacity on the route for the next five or six years, further enhanced by the three additional Boeing 707s that BOAC had opportunely been allowed to order at the time of the hearing. Although MPs have notoriously thick skins, even Thorneycroft must have squirmed a little when he was congratulated by the Labour opposition on his decision. But maybe he put that down to all the irony in the air, his own included:

> In the first place, I would say that the decision or appeal in no way implies the slightest loss of confidence in the Air Transport Licensing Board—far from it…This decision does not freeze the pattern of air traffic as it is at present, and anyone who assumed that it did would be very wide of the mark.[14]

It was left to Southend's MP, Stephen McAdden, to tell it as it was:

> It is most unfortunate that in this, the first major instance to come before the Minister, he should decide to turn down the recommendation of the Board, whose excellence he has praised and whose chairman, he says, is beyond praise. What I am saying, in particular, is that if the Corporations are to be put in a privileged position of being able to say, "We have ordered enough aircraft and the introduction of any competition means that some traffic will be diverted from us", and these are to be paramount considerations in the Minister's mind, it is a waste of time for independent operators to go to the Licensing Board at all.[15]

The corporations went further, threatening a reduction in their orders for British built aircraft if licensing decisions were made in favour of the independents.

This was gall to British United; the airline had just ordered VC10s in June, and had launched a promising short-haul jet in May, the BAC One-Eleven, with an order for ten. It felt that its applications to Africa were vulnerable to the 'adequate capacity' argument of the appeals commissioner, and abruptly withdrew them. The airline could take some encouragement from the next batch of decisions which the Board presented, which granted British United a number of European routes, albeit with limited frequencies: Paris, Amsterdam, Zurich, Basle, Genoa, Milan, Athens and holiday routes to Barcelona, Palma, Madeira and Malaga, the latter in pool with BEA. But the response was muted: 'It will be interesting to see if the Government, in its triple role of judge, jury and father confessor to the corporations, will see fit once again to upset the decisions of the Licensing Board.' Actually, Britain's new Aviation Minister, Julian Amery, upheld the Board's decisions, this time round, with the exception of Zurich. But more to the point, would his department try and negotiate traffic rights? Eagle was given a number of domestic routes, but at absurd frequencies; the airline had asked for fourteen flights a week to Belfast, Edinburgh and Glasgow, enough for twice daily flights. In the interest of 'carefully regulated competition' the Board, studiously academic, cut the frequencies in half, just seven a week on each route, which in the case of Edinburgh was reduced to five flights a week in winter. Using words like 'pathetic' and 'farce', Cunard Eagle pointed out that BEA 'can drive us off the route by putting on even more than the 59 services they currently operate on the [Glasgow] route.'[16]

Other airlines got short shrift. Starways, Silver City, Tradair and Channel Airways all had their applications summarily refused. Somewhere between the opportunism of the new, and now largely defunct, holiday charter airlines and the gravitas of the established independents – British United, Cunard Eagle, Silver City, Skyways – there flew a swarm of ambitious airlines with variegated business plans, all of them making steady progress, all of them destined for greater things. BKS might be in temporary difficulty, but it was building up networks from Newcastle and Leeds/Bradford with a fleet of Viscounts and Ambassadors, and had just ordered the new Hawker Siddeley HS 748, previously known as the Avro. Cambrian, associated with BEA, used its Dakotas to serve South Wales and the West of England. Channel flew holidaymakers from East Anglia and the South Coast to the Channel Islands, Ostend and Rotterdam, squeezing passengers into its fleet of Dakotas, Wayfarers and an eighty-eight-seat Skymaster; it would later take Tradair off the receiver's hands. Dan-Air flew anything, anywhere, having shifted its base from Blackbushe to Gatwick: increasingly it used its Ambassadors for inclusive tour flying, and stood to gain from the premature collapse of so many operators in 1961; its Yorks tramped cargo worldwide, the Freighters took rocket parts down to Woomera, an 11-day journey; and it operated some scheduled services, including an embryonic Link-City, from Cardiff and Bristol through to Liverpool and Newcastle; it also bought the airline remnants of Scottish Aviation – a Dakota and the route from Prestwick to the Isle of Man. Derby Airways operated its eight Dakotas on charter flights and scheduled services from Derby, and specialised in flying to the Channel Islands. Jersey Airlines, which had recently severed its connection with BEA, carried a quarter of a million passengers in 1960 in its fleet of Heralds, Dakotas and Herons, second only to Silver City's half million. Starways was just as happy sending its Skymasters to the Congo to help the United Nations as it was flying them full of pilgrims down to Tarbes in France.

And there were some new names. Autair, a significant helicopter operation for some years, began flying Dakotas out of Luton on holiday flights. Caledonian was at the other end of the spectrum, using a Douglas DC-7C to fly for a travel club, Overseas Visitors' Club, which had previously used Overseas Aviation's Canadairs. Lloyd International was backed by shipping interests, and flew a Skymaster on freight and seamen's charters from Cambridge. Both Lloyd and Caledonian suffered early setbacks, Lloyd losing its DC-4 when it caught fire at Malaga, without loss of life; Caledonian crashed its DC-7C early in 1962 on take off from Douala, killing all 111 on board. Euravia had a happier start. Captain Langton, a tour operating entrepreneur who had earlier launched Blue Cars and now ran Universal Sky Tours, had been badly mauled in his operations over the last three years, contracting flights with a string of airlines that had all met unseemly ends: Independent, Continental, Falcon, Air Safaris. He thought there had to be a better way to ensure quality of service, and joined forces with J. E. D. Williams, an aviation economist, and John Harrington, formerly an operations director at BOAC, to launch Euravia, based at Luton, the first 'vertically integrated' charter airline, dedicated to carrying inclusive tour passengers in a rational and economic manner. Part of the inclusive tour problem lay in the mismatch between summer and winter business, with so much holiday demand squeezed into the peak weekends of June, July and August. Euravia's solution was initially to purchase reliable, low cost aircraft; it bought three Constellations from El Al in Israel which were more than adequate to fly to destinations in the Mediterranean, but did not have the globe-trotting qualities of the Douglas DC-6, capabilities that Langton and Euravia did not need. Being inexpensive, the Constellations could be written off relatively quickly and did not need to be flown intensively. The plan then was to move on to more desirable turboprops, but before they could do that, the airline and tour operator had to work at creating a better economic model for the business, and that meant, among other innovations, offering alternatives to the traditional holiday format, and moving on from weekend departures and the two-week holiday.

British United stayed with the programme, whatever the disappointments. Laker was naturally ebullient, optimistic, and could act quickly, to stave off a problem, to grasp an opportunity. His chairman, Wyatt, was good at putting together deals, and early in 1962, did another (without telling Laker about it), bringing in Silver City, a company that was now floundering just as British United was gaining leeway. The two airline groups were complementary. British United was a long-haul carrier, with a growing commitment to inclusive tours. Silver City had failed in its long-haul operations, but had built up an extensive network of domestic scheduled services; it was also an active participant in the holiday market. Silver City was unable to come to grips with the problem of how to replace the old Bristol Freighters, so they kept chugging along, but were becoming more expensive to keep in the air and were running out of wing spar life. Channel Air Bridge acted decisively, choosing to build its own replacement for the Freighters when it was unable to identify a suitable replacement. Aviation Traders converted relatively inexpensive Skymasters to carry five cars and up to twenty-three passengers by the unorthodox process of grafting a new nose to the fuselage; the resulting 'Carvair' cost less than £200,000, was faster than a Freighter, had greater range, and carried more cars. On some of the longer runs, Southend to Rotterdam or Ostend, Channel Air Bridge estimated that the Carvair was twice as productive as the Freighter; it also allowed the company to introduce 'deep penetration' routes into Europe, to Basle, Geneva, and Strasbourg, rather than being limited to the short cross-Channel routes. Silver City and British United formed a holding company, Air Holdings, which was soon in the news again when it announced that it was going to buy Jersey Airlines as well.

Saturday 5 May 1962 was significant for at least two new ventures. Euravia inaugurated its operations with flights from Luton, Manchester, and Birmingham; and Cunard Eagle started flying its 135-seat Boeing 707, registered in Bermuda as VR-BBW, three times a week from London to Bermuda and on to the Bahamas, Miami and Jamaica. BOAC and Cunard Eagle had both done well in Bermuda, especially on the route to New York. After Eagle's arrival in 1958, BOAC's share of the traffic actually increased, and subsequently never fell below 20 per cent. BOAC carried 28,000 passengers in 1957; by 1961 the combined figures for the two British airlines had more than doubled, to 58,000, of which BOAC still carried the greater part, 32,000. That suggests three things: competition from another British airline was not necessarily damaging to BOAC; the share of the traffic gained for British aviation if two or more British airlines participated was substantially improved; and Cunard Eagle, which had gone from zero to 26,000 passengers in four years, could more than hold its own against BOAC and major US airlines. But read how BOAC interpreted the situation, standing the truth on its head:

> In particular, the emergence of Cunard as an Atlantic air carrier through their wholly-owned subsidiaries in Bermuda and the Bahamas produced a big new factor for us to reckon with. This was not just another competitor—we have always had plenty of foreign competition. This was British competition, splitting the British effort, dividing the British market and—because of the way international air agreements work—inevitably having to siphon off most of its traffic from the British share.[17]

BOAC struggled with its subsidiaries; it had had to buy back Bahamas Airways from Skyways, and with some relief disposed of British West Indian Airways to the government of Trinidad. Now its Britannias were competing with Eagle's Boeings out of Bermuda, and the latter was expanding in the Caribbean, having recently gained rights from Jamaica. More important, Cunard was still a force to be reckoned with in the corridors of Whitehall, despite the North Atlantic licensing setback; there was even talk of re-applying for the London to New York route. But as he smiled for the cameras on the inaugural flight to Bermuda, Bamberg knew that the aircraft steps were about to be pushed away from under him. Sensing danger, BOAC had approached Cunard about a joint venture only a few days earlier, knowing that both the corporation and Cunard were sustaining heavy losses on their transatlantic routes. Cunard, anxious about the £6 million invested in the Boeings, disillusioned by broken promises – 'private enterprise air lines, financed by shipping companies, have not in practice been allowed as much opportunity as, in their opinion, they had been led to expect'[18] – still faced continuing losses on its shipping operations; it was happy to see a way out of this imbroglio.

On 6 June BOAC and Cunard announced the formation of a joint venture airline, BOAC-Cunard, to take over the transatlantic operations of the corporation and Cunard Eagle in the west. BOAC's share was 70 per cent, and it contributed eight Boeings to the deal; Cunard Eagle held the remaining 30 per cent, and put in its two Boeings, thirty pilots, and all its operations in Bermuda, the Bahamas and the eastern seaboard. BOAC had no intention of collaborating with its junior partner; it merely painted BOAC-Cunard on the side of its aircraft, and closed down Cunard Eagle's western hemisphere businesses, successfully eliminating the competition out of Bermuda and the Bahamas. No wonder managing director Smallpeice sounded triumphalist: 'Aircraft will have 'B.O.A.C. –Cunard' on their sides, sales offices may have the new name across the front, and notepaper may carry the new heading, but our staff will still be B.O.A.C.'[19] Bamberg joined the board of the new venture, and still had the remnants of Cunard Eagle to manage, but it was a sorry end for his feisty Bermuda outpost.

And for what? BOAC announced in October a huge increase in its losses for 1961–62. The corporation lost almost £20 million on its operations, much worse than expected; it had increased passenger capacity by 31 per cent, but passenger traffic to the United States, BOAC's biggest market, flattened out – which led to a fall in load factor of 10 points, from 59 per cent to 49 per cent; it had too many aircraft; it suffered from costly strikes; and it was still unable to stanch the flow from its unprofitable subsidiaries. Chairman Slattery looked at a number of options, including a drastic reduction of the route network, retaining just those profitable routes from London to Hong Kong and Sydney, to Johannesburg via East Africa, to Lagos, and to New York and Toronto; that would have meant abandoning Japan, Malaya, Ceylon, Ghana and South America. In the end he thought that was too drastic, and would have led to unacceptable levels of redundancy. He wanted a much closer commercial relationship with BEA, possibly a merger, in order to better 'Sell British' between North America and Europe; BOAC was limited in its pick up rights in Europe, and any attempt to negotiate more points in Europe interfered with BEA's elaborate pooling arrangements. Slattery also tried to come to grips with the capital losses that were now inevitable for the Britannia and Comet fleets, as well as the losses on the subsidiary companies, suggesting that the government should write off around £70 million of the lost capital. Slattery submitted these ideas in a memorandum to the Minister in late 1962, but found him somewhat unresponsive: 'I hate saying this, but I suppose I have to give you the facts,' Slattery told the Select Committee in 1964, 'he just failed to do anything at all …from 16th August, 1962, to the 31st December 1963.'[20] So instead Slattery and the corporation's board decided to accelerate the amortisation of the now largely redundant fleet of Comet 4s, Britannias and Douglas DC-7Cs, adding another £30 million to the pile of accumulated deficits, which was now up to £64.5 million. Slattery complained that too many VC10s had been ordered, and griped about the interest charges the corporation had to pay on its accumulated losses, using unusually robust language for the time. Unwisely, he added: 'A day of reckoning must come.' When Amery came to debate the corporation's losses with his fellow MPs – he had to ask for an increase in borrowing powers for the two corporations – the minister was not a happy man: 'Frankly, this is rather steep,' was his comment on BOAC's deficit, 'and calls for searching inquiry.' He went on to criticise:

> The other major item in the deficit—the loss on operating account. This is, in my view, much the most serious side of the picture, because it arises not so much from decisions taken many years ago as from current policies, and it also casts a long shadow into the future. It is, of course, true that this item includes interest charges on earlier losses, notably the losses incurred in the previous year, and it is these charges—the payment of interest on the accumulated loss—which Sir Matthew Slattery has dismissed with a characteristically salty expletive….to dismiss as "bloody crazy" the idea that one should pay interest charges on borrowed capital was not something which commended itself to me.[21]

Possibly encouraged by the Prime Minister, who had a low opinion of the corporations' bosses – Macmillan thought Slattery an 'ass', Douglas was 'clever but shallow' – Amery decided he needed outside help with the searching inquiry, and asked an accountant, John Corbett, to investigate BOAC, and advise on what needed to be done to put its house in order.

BUA and Air Holdings felt they needed to clean up house too. BUA had absorbed a number of airlines by this stage, many of them still operating as semi-independent fiefdoms. Late in 1962 the vehicle ferry operations were combined into one operation, and the engineering base was moved to Southend; 600 staff were made redundant. The group decided to drop the well known brand names, Silver City and Channel Air Bridge, for the more corporate British United Air Ferries, or BUAF for short; a pity that many users shortened it still further to Boo-Af. Douglas Whybrow, Channel Air Bridge's general manager, points out that whatever may have been gained in increased efficiency was lost through bigger overheads, after BUAF moved into grandiose new office buildings in London which it shared with its parent company; it also came as a shock to the Laker team to discover that, despite the shortcomings of Silver City's management, its operation was extremely efficient, the aircraft immaculate, and the engineering and flying costs considerably below those of Channel Air Bridge and its associate, Aviation Traders. 1962 was to prove the vehicle ferry's finest year, with 134,888 cars carried across the Channel. Wing Commander Kennard, a refugee from Silver City after it had earlier bought his airline Air Kruise, took over where Silver City left off at Manston, starting a new charter airline using Skymasters and Vikings, which he called Air Ferry; the name annoyed British United Air Ferries, so much so that two years later, Air Holdings bought that company too, adding it to its stash of small airlines. Irrepressible, Kennard merely started another charter airline at Manston, this time calling it Invicta, a suitably Kentish name, and annoyed British United again by taking many former Air Ferry clients with him. Silver City's northern network was assimilated from 1 November 1962 with Jersey Airlines' routes under another catchy new banner, British United (Channel Islands) Airways, the whole sprawling operation controlled from Jersey, with three engineering bases, at Jersey, Blackpool and the Isle of Man. That arrangement did not work out, and the Isle of Man operation was consequently given back its autonomy. Morton became the jack-of-all-trades airline, at Gatwick, also with its own dedicated engineering company, using Dakotas on Transair's former newspaper contracts; the Doves and Herons flew Channel Islands services, especially to Alderney, whose short grass runway limited operations by other aircraft types. British United operated its Britannias on trooping flights out of Stansted, but the other Britannias and Viscounts were based at Gatwick. Stansted was a legacy of Skyways' trooping operations; now Skyways was about to become part of history too. The coach-air operation at Lympne had been hived off into a separate company, Skyways Coach-Air, leaving the long-haul operations at Stansted and Heathrow, where the company's Constellations flew BOAC cargo services, and the Yorks were available for emergency AOG flights. When BOAC terminated the contract for its Far East freight services at the end of March 1962, Skyways was left with three Constellations, four Yorks and no visible means of support. Euravia bought out the airline, adding the Constellations to its fleet, and continued to operate the Yorks for another year, still in Skyways' colours. After Trans-European closed down in 1962, Euravia bought their two Constellations, making eight available for the next summer season, 1963.

BEA had to announce losses for 1961–62 as well, £1.5 million, blaming a slump in traffic and an inability to reduce capacity in line with the reduced demand; the corporation glibly pointed out that 'foreign competition on BEA's international routes remains intense' and complained about the ATLB's 'misconceived' awareness of its licensing duties. Fifty-nine Viscounts flew alongside twenty Vanguards and thirteen Comets, and the corporation carried well over four million passengers. BEA had applied, as it transpired, unsuccessfully, to the government for subsidies to operate services in the Highlands and Islands of Scotland; and in other ways sought to reduce its costs. One solution was to transfer unprofitable routes to a low-cost associate, and BEA tried this with Cambrian, passing on the route network out of Liverpool and the Viscounts to operate it. BEA still had to go through the process of a public hearing at the ATLB; British United also applied for the Liverpool routes, and made a better case, but this time the Board decided to go along with BEA. It was a turn-round for Cambrian, an airline which had almost ceased operations only three years earlier; but led by its determined managing director, Wing Commander Elwin, the airline had picked itself up, brought in Dakotas from BEA, which acquired a one-third shareholding, and went back to developing its routes from Cardiff and Bristol. By 1962 Cambrian was carrying 123,000 passengers a year, a figure that had doubled by 1963 with the start of the Liverpool services; in 1965 the airline carried 400,000 passengers. Also changing course was Derby Airways, which took up some of the slack after the collapse of Overseas Aviation in 1961. It acquired three of the Canadairs for inclusive tour flying, changing its name to British Midland Airways late in 1964. Two years later its first turboprop entered service, a Handley Page Herald; this aircraft was swapped with British United for a Viscount early in 1967, the first of what was to become a large fleet, and the backbone of the airline's subsequent successful development.

BEA and BOAC kept the flame of righteous indignation burning brightly over the issue of trooping contracts, applying to the ATLB for rights to carry troops and families on scheduled services at a discounted fare, arguing this was a quid pro quo for the enhanced scheduled services the independents were purported to enjoy. So far, the ministry had gained just two new foreign route rights out of London, to Genoa and Amsterdam, both for British United. The government's lack of success in acquiring traffic rights for British United exasperated Laker, who put the blame squarely on BEA, accusing the corporation of 'actively frustrating' the intentions of Parliament, the minister and the Air Transport Licensing Board, after it had emerged that the corporation's overseas managers told their foreign pool partners that BEA 'would not be happy if independents were given traffic rights. Representations would be strong in some cases.'[22] Aside from some seasonal holiday destinations, and minor regional services, it is a matter of record that only these two routes were successfully negotiated by the British government during the eleven year incumbency of the ATLB. Fortunately traffic rights for charter services were not dependent on the negotiating skills of Britain's Aviation Ministry – charter airlines applied directly to the authorities concerned – and traffic numbers were beginning to increase. Amery allowed that over one million passengers had been carried in 1962 on non-scheduled services by British carriers, up from 750,000 two years previously. He also admitted: 'Foreign operators carried 371,000 passengers to and from the United Kingdom on non-scheduled flights in 1962. In 1960 they carried 100,000 passengers.'[23] Euravia reported that bookings in 1963 were 'fabulous'; it succeeded in persuading a reluctant ATLB to allow ten and eleven-day holidays, part of the airline's strategy to spread the demand for peak departures. Its tour operator parent, meanwhile, was securing the best hotel accommodation by paying for it in advance, to the consternation of smaller tour operators. Caledonian, having re-equipped with three Douglas DC-7Cs, now abandoned the travel clubs and decided to pursue the North American charter market, successfully applying to the United States Civil Aeronautics Board for a charter permit to fly affinity groups. Cunard Eagle had been able to operate over 100 transatlantic charters in 1961, using existing rights it held over Montreal to New York, but the airline's upheavals in 1962 had prevented a repetition of the 1961 programme. In 1963 it tried again, under a new name, British Eagle. To no one's great surprise, Bamberg had been unhappy in his position in the new BOAC-Cunard combine, and early in 1963 he abruptly resigned from the board; a few weeks later he bought the remains of Eagle from Cunard. After that there was no stopping him. He took on seven Britannias from BOAC, changed the airline's name to British Eagle, bought out Starways in Liverpool, and in November launched domestic routes in competition with BEA, from Glasgow to Heathrow, and from Heathrow to Edinburgh and Belfast. BEA increased capacity on those routes, putting on extra flights around Eagle's timings, and dutifully copied all British Eagle's service improvements. Bamberg went back to the ATLB to get his frequencies increased, and was refused; he appealed the decision.

Bamberg was not the only independent launching new services. Autair started flying between Luton and Blackpool, having acquired the licence in a roundabout way. The route was originally awarded to Silver City, now British United, but on appeal was taken away and given instead to newcomer Autair. This seemed to be part of a new pattern, brought about by the increasing disconnect between the government and the ATLB. Having seen its first major decision, Cunard Eagle's New York route, dumped by the government, the Board then realised that its carefully crafted methodology for granting European licences was also leading nowhere, as the government was unable, or unwilling, to deliver on its side of the deal, the negotiation of traffic rights. As for inclusive tour licences, the Board became more pragmatic, and stopped forcing charter business on to foreign airlines:

> We have continued to follow an increasingly liberal policy in the granting of [these] licences…we had over the years come to the conclusion that there was no evidence that Inclusive Tours had been responsible for any diversion of traffic from the scheduled carriers.

For 1966 the ATLB granted 552 licences and only refused five. In other areas, involving more contentious issues –domestic tariffs, the trunk routes, international services – the Board went its own way, deaf to entreaties from the corporations, the independents and especially the government. The various appeals commissioners and the minister would then overturn the decisions of the Board on appeal, helping to create a dysfunctional process in which none of the parties found common ground. The Board noted punctiliously in its annual report:

> The outcome of the forty appeals duly processed were as follows:
> a) Twenty-three of our decisions were upheld, although in one instance with a modification and in three others subject to re-hearing of part of the issue.
> b) Re-hearings were ordered in five cases;
> c) As a result of appeal findings adverse to our decision two new licences, nine variations of licence and one variation of the United Kingdom Domestic Air Tariff were granted.[24]

The teams seemed to be in the same game but on different playing fields. The Board kicked off first, basing their decisions on whatever criteria were favoured that day; the commissioners, usually a different one for each appeal, reheard each case on quasi-legal grounds; the ministry processed the appeals according to whichever way the political winds were blowing: 'I asked my new masters by what criteria the reports of Appeal Commissioners were assessed,' recalled Ray Colegate, a senior civil servant, 'and was told there were no such criteria. If anything, I was told, it was a convenient rule of thumb to decide in favour of a state corporation one week, and an independent airline the next; on that basis the Minister would not be unduly exposed to criticism.'[25] An amusing take on the subject, leading one to speculate how other decisions were arrived at: for example, the two corporations' re-equipment plans.

Not so amusing was BOAC's day of reckoning, which arrived on 19 November 1963. A day of high drama, chairman Slattery and managing director Smallpeice were asked to submit their resignations to the Aviation Minister – code for getting sacked – as a result of the minister's study of the report he had commissioned from Corbett. Amery had received the report in May, but claimed not to have read it until late June, and then put off answering questions about it in July, finally conceding that he would publish a White Paper on BOAC after the summer recess, by which time there was further upheaval following Macmillan's resignation in October. To his colleagues in Cabinet he explained:

How are we to put B.O.A.C. on its feet? Many of the mistakes that have been made stem from decisions taken when Sir Gerard d'Erlanger was Chairman, if not before. Sir Matthew Slattery has undoubtedly done a good deal to improve the position. I have, however, reluctantly come to the conclusion that the Corporation will not make a full recovery and measure up to the problems ahead under the present management.[26]

Finally, with some leaking to the press, he published a dismal fourteen-page White Paper, *The Financial Problems of the British Overseas Airways Corporation*, its contents having been pared down somewhat from the original draft document of sixty-three pages. Even then the final version included much padding to eke out the few elements taken from the bowdlerised Corbett Report. He made a statement to Parliament on 21 November, announcing the forthcoming retirement of Lord Douglas, mentioned the resignations of Slattery and Smallpeice, said he had appointed a new chairman to BOAC, Sir Giles Guthrie, and had given him a year to come up with a plan to get the corporation back on its feet.

Amery blamed BOAC's top management for fudging the rate of amortisation of the DC-7C, Britannia and Comet 4 fleets, and for not taking heed of warnings given by government ministers. Indeed Watkinson had said in Parliament late in 1956: 'I have asked both Chairmen to apply a stricter standard of amortisation for their aircraft.'[27] But six months later, in a letter to them both, he backtracked, agreeing 'with some reluctance' to their proposal that 'as a minimum, new aircraft should be written off over seven years to a value of 25 per cent of cost as from 1956–57.'[28] Even though the House of Commons Select Committee in 1959 devoted some time to the issue – 'With so many aircraft remaining unsold and unused on their hands, it is not surprising that they should now regret that higher depreciation was not allowed' – Corbett noted in his report that subsequently 'no one in any quarter pressed for an increase in the obsolescence charge', which he regarded as 'entirely inadequate.'[29] However all references to Watkinson's change of heart were excised from Amery's statement, in order to leave 'fewer flanks open.'[30] The issue of amortisation, and who was to blame, was comprehensively thrashed out by the House of Commons Select Committee in 1964; it generously attributed the debacle in part to a misunderstanding between the Minister and the corporation. The Treasury almost ate humble pie over the episode: 'We are not very proud of this piece of work.'[31]

As for the overseas subsidiaries, both Corbett and the government agreed that the benefits were illusory, and implementation unsatisfactory. No attempt was ever made to try and estimate the amount and value of feeder traffic. The Treasury was especially supine: 'We were told by the Ministry of Aviation, that the prospects of these companies the next year would be much brighter than they had been in the immediate past. This is very difficult to refute.'[32] The government acknowledged the value to British aircraft exports of the corporations' involvement in its associated companies – MEA, Kuwait Airways and Turkish Airlines as well as British West Indian and Bahamas Airways had all bought British built airliners with the corporations' help, a familiar story with an exotic twist. But the corporation had paid dearly for its overseas investments, its Middle Eastern ventures alone accounting for £5½ million over the four years to 1961–62 before BOAC was finally able to extricate itself. Corbett put BOAC's commitment to its subsidiaries down to a feeling that 'it was acting in the national interest in making these investments'. The government did respond to that suggestion:

> The Government think it necessary to reaffirm that the Corporation must operate as a commercial undertaking. If the national interest should appear, whether to the Corporation or to the Government, to require some departure from commercial practice, this should only be done with the agreement or at the instance of the Minister of Aviation.[33]

Both Corbett and the government agreed that BOAC's traffic forecasts were too optimistic; the engineering function over-manned – too many unproductive 'supervisors' – and much too expensive; the financial controls generally too lax. The Chairman of the 1964 Select Committee, Sir Richard Nugent, asked: 'What have the Treasury watchdogs being doing in the last few years to allow this situation to come about?' Not much, was the answer, which the Sir Richard summed up: 'You refrained from action because you felt it would have been to interfere too seriously with the actual management of the Corporation.'[34] Corbett was extremely critical of the management at BOAC, especially Smallpeice, but had nothing to say about any proposed merger between BOAC and BEA, so Amery decided on his own initiative to kill that idea. Corbett did however have a great deal to say about the Vickers VC10, deploring the muddled thinking that had led BOAC to over-order this aircraft, again because it thought it was acting in the national interest, and for deluding itself that there was any benefit in operating the type, when it was clear that the fleet of aircraft ordered would have higher costs than the rival Boeing 707-320C, to the tune of £11 to £12 million a year. Amery reduced the pages of argument to: 'Much will depend on how far the passenger appeal of the VC10 will lead to increased load factors and revenue and will offset its higher capital charges.' This was to become a familiar mantra, one that Corbett rejected: 'It is suggested that the benefit which may flow from the better load factor should be treated as some offset to the higher operational costs in any assessment of the penalty of operating the VC10 rather than the Boeings. I do not agree.'

Others were puzzled by the lack of reference to the VC10. Labour MP John Cronin chronicled the story accurately:

> I turn now to the VC10. One of the conspicuous omissions in the White Paper is the absence of any reference to this excellent aircraft. I know that Mr. Corbett went into the question of the VC10s, and it seems odd that in these circumstances there should be no reference to them, until one realises the Government's actions in the matter. In 1960 the right hon. Gentleman, who is now the Colonial Secretary (Duncan Sandys), was then in the process of forming the big aircraft mergers. He put great pressure on Sir Gerard D'Erlanger to order 10 VC10s in addition to the thirty-five already ordered. Sir Matthew Slattery was appointed chairman

of the B.O.A.C. in July, 1960. Before he took up his office he specifically requested Sir Gerard D'Erlanger not to commit himself to the purchase of these extra ten aircraft—and it must be remembered that they cost about £2 million each—but Sir Gerard, under pressure from the Colonial Secretary, went ahead and finalised arrangements to buy them. Only last May the B.O.A.C. announced that it could not properly use ten of these aircraft. Once again, as a direct result of Ministerial interference, the Corporation was not able to use its commercial judgment, and it has been saddled with extra aeroplanes which are greatly superfluous to its requirements.[35]

Amery brushed off the criticism: 'No part of the deficit has resulted from the VC10 because it has not yet been introduced into service.' The press soon had other matters to occupy them. The controversy over the BOAC affair and the sacking of its top management was tragically overtaken by world events: the following day President Kennedy was assassinated.

Unlike his colleagues at BOAC, Lord Douglas left BEA in a blaze of glory. The corporation announced the results of its 'most successful' year, 1963–64, with traffic at record levels, over 5½ million passengers carried, more freight carried than ever before, profits of over £3 million. In his 15 years, Douglas had overseen the introduction of turboprop and jet equipment, had pushed out the route network through the Iron Curtain, and beyond to the eastern Mediterranean, and he had done much to promote the use of helicopters, the small experimental unit eventually morphing into BEA Helicopters, which introduced a regular helicopter service between Penzance and the Scilly Isles in 1964; that service continued, under different guises, for just under 50 years.

British United was doing well, too, it announced record profits of over £1 million in 1963, which saw it launch service to Genoa and anticipate the arrival of its first jets. But it was British Eagle that seemed to have the wind beneath its wings. In a rare reversal of fortune, the appeals commissioner overturned the Board's decision and allowed the airline to increase frequencies on its newly launched domestic services, not by much, but enough to permit twice daily services from Heathrow to Glasgow and Edinburgh. British Eagle had added Liverpool to its network when it took over Starways. It began to develop its portfolio of tour operating companies, Sir Henry Lunn, Poly Travel and later Rickards. The airline had picked up the long-running government contract from Dan-Air to support the rocket range in Woomera, Australia in 1962, using DC-6s, later Britannias. In May 1964 it was awarded an even bigger contract, taking over the Far East trooping task from British United. The good news continued; in October Qantas gave the airline the job of carrying British emigrants to Australia under the assisted passage scheme. British Eagle bought more Britannias from BOAC, taking twelve in all, and successfully applied to the Americans for a charter permit, following Caledonian's first season. Bamberg wanted to return to his former stamping grounds in Bermuda and the Caribbean, but in this he was thwarted by the Aviation Minister, who at BOAC's behest imposed a new condition on colonial administrations, that any route from the colonies to London would now be subject to licensing by the ATLB if it was to be flown by aircraft registered in their countries.[36]

Also buying Britannias was Euravia, now ready to move on to the next phase of its development. British Eagle needed its Britannias to perform a wide variety of tasks, from domestic scheduled services to worldwide charter flying, but Euravia just needed them for inclusive tour flights to the Mediterranean, so settled for six of BOAC's original Britannia type 102, with more modest range, able to carry 117 passengers; the first entered service in December 1964. BKS also decided to invest in Britannia 102s, buying them for its Newcastle to London service during the week, and flying them on ITC charters at the weekend, an elegant solution to existing business and holiday demand. BKS had terminated its receivership and now flew two promising trunk routes out of London, to Leeds-

Bradford and Newcastle, arousing BEA's interest; in June 1964 the corporation acquired a 30 per cent shareholding, at a similar level to its existing stake in Cambrian.

The Aviation Minister's agony over BOAC continued. Although the corporation was profitable in 1963, there were further adjustments made to its capital account so that the deficit had risen to almost £90 million in the 1963-64 accounts. The Select Committee of the House of Commons on Nationalised Industries, in July 1964, already cited above, blamed both the government and the corporation for the mess, which by now had moved beyond the issues of aircraft write-downs and associate companies, to focus on BOAC's VC10 orders, which, as Labour spokesman Cronin had pointed out, were 'greatly superfluous to its requirements'. The report covered familiar ground, but its conclusions remind us that Britain's muddled airline/aircraft manufacturing/aviation policy did no one any favours. 'Today, in 1964, the Ministry of Aviation have recognised that the logic of B.O.A.C.'s commercial policy should be to determine first the route mileage and then to adjust the size of the fleet to it.'[37] BOAC had placed speculative orders in advance, greatly in excess of its needs, to ensure the launch of the VC10 and the larger Super VC10; Vickers had built an aircraft to BOAC's specifications which few other operators wanted to buy. The government was vulnerable on both counts; and in the slipstream, the independents were penalised in a bizarre tangle of regulatory process and policy muddle.

Appendix 1
Government Trooping and Other Contracts Chronology

Prior to 1951, the War Office, Admiralty and Air Ministry chartered aircraft on an ad hoc basis; RAF Transport Command undertook most of the trooping and other supply commitments. Commercial contracts could be for single flights, or less commonly, for a series of flights. BOAC operated a regular schedule for the RAF to the Far East during the Berlin Airlift (1948–9) and Airwork performed a number of charters from Cairo to clear a backlog of forces personnel and their families in 1949, an operation which the airline repeated the following year, carrying out thirty such flights between June and November. When the West African troopships were withdrawn, Airwork was given a six month contract from January to June 1950 to operate between four and six flights a month to Kano, and on renewal this contract was awarded to Hunting Air Transport, to operate up to ninety round-trip flights over the next nine months. The references to 'Troops carried' should be understood to include forces families and other civilians entitled to travel on trooping flights. The sources are either BIATA figures from its annual reports or those given in evidence to Sub-Committee E of the Estimates Committee, and printed in its report of 20 December 1961.

1951

The year was to see the award of the first major trooping contracts under the new Government policy, gradually transferring the trooping task from troopships and the RAF to the independents; however, even before the new policy officially came into effect, the Service Ministries were relying increasingly on the independents for air support. The Korean War effort was undertaken by the RAF using its own resources, but Eagle was awarded a number of contracts to carry out medical evacuation and trooping flights. During the Canal Zone crisis BOAC and Airwork operated an emergency airlift to ease some of the pressure on the RAF's Transport Command.

April	Hunting West Africa contract renewed for one year.
May	Cyprus Airways awarded contract for Cyprus Leave Scheme (Cyprair), May–October, with Dakotas.
August	Hunting awarded Task 1, to Malta, and Task 2, to Gibraltar (West Med). 40/50 flights per month, with Vikings.
September	Airwork awarded contract for services between bases in Malta, Cyprus, Libya, Kenya, Aden and Baghdad (Medair), with Vikings. Airwork awarded Task 3, to the Canal Zone (Canzair), with Hermes, starting March 1952. Lancashire/Skyways awarded short-term Canzair contracts in the interim, with Yorks.

Troops carried during 1950/1: 18,500 by air, 423,000 by sea (Estimates Committee)

1952

April	Crewsair awarded West Africa contract, eighty flights/year between April and October.
May	Cyprus Airways re-awarded Cyprair contract.
June	Airwork assumes responsibility for Canzair, although Skyways continue to operate extensively throughout 1952 and 1953.
July	Skyways awarded Task 4, to the Caribbean, 3/4 flights per month, with Yorks.

Short-term contracts also awarded to East Africa (Airwork), to Livingstone, Rhodesia (Eagle, subsequently Skyways) and to the Far East (Eagle, Airwork and Aquila).

Troops carried during July 1951 - June 1952: 53,876 by air (BIATA)

1953

January	Airwork awarded 18 month East Africa contract.
April	Airwork assumes West Africa contract, following financial failure of Crewsair. Air Charter awarded one year contract to operate fortnightly service to Fiji (via Singapore) with Yorks.
May	Skyways awarded Cyprair contract.
August	Hunting renews West Med contract for two years.
September	Airwork renews Medair contract for two years.

During the year, Scottish Aviation was awarded a one year contract to operate to Canada (Montreal). Air Charter, Airwork and Skyways flew to the Far East on short-term contracts.

Troops carried during July 1952 – June 1953: 88,285 by air (BIATA)

1954

May	Air Charter take over West Africa contract from Airwork, with Yorks. Eagle awarded Cyprair contract.
July	Britavia wins East Africa contract. Britavia awarded new UK/Cyprus contract.
August	Air Charter awarded Canzair, taking over from Airwork/Skyways. Daily flights.
September	Airwork awarded new long-term 2½-year contract to Singapore and the Far East, with Hermes.

Troops carried, July 1953 – June 1954: 147,825 by air (BIATA)

1955

March   Air Charter gains contracts to fly to Australia in support of the Woomera test establishment, and to Christmas Island, in connection with atomic bomb testing, with Tudors.

August   Air evacuation of the Canal Zone, and related contracts, end. Skyways awarded UK/ Cyprus contract for one year.

September   Eagle wins West Med and Medair contracts for two years, with Vikings.

During the year, Skyways was awarded long term contracts to fly alongside Airwork to the Far East, using Hermes. Airwork flew between Singapore and Calcutta in connection with Gurkha jungle training exercises over the next two years.

Troops carried during July 1954 – June 1955: 214,594 by air (BIATA)

Troops carried during 1954/5: 172,400 by air, 616,000 by sea (Estimates Committee)

1956

June   Eagle awarded West Africa contract, with Vikings.

July   Scottish Aviation wins freight contracts to Cyprus, the Middle East and Aden, with Yorks and Dakotas. Dan-Air awarded freight contracts to Singapore and the Far East, with Yorks, which the company held until 1959.

August   Air Charter takes over UK/Cyprus contract from Skyways.

Having just completed the evacuation of the Canal Zone in 1955, British charter airlines participated in the build-up to the Suez Crisis of 1956, and its aftermath.

Troops carried during July 1955 – June 1956: 204,700 by air (BIATA)

1957

September   Eagle re-awarded Medair contract, with three Vikings based at Nicosia.

October   Transair gains West Med contract with Viscount equipment, first turboprop aircraft on regular trooping services.

Britavia holds East Africa contract and adds Aden service. Air Charter awarded the Singapore/Calcutta Gurkha contract for the next two trooping seasons. Airwork and Skyways retain the major Far East contract for another two years.

Troops carried during July 1956 – June 1957: 157,035 by air (BIATA)

1958

July   Eagle takes over the East Africa, Aden and Cyprus contracts, to be operated mainly by Douglas DC-6As; the airline adds these contracts to its existing Medair and West Africa Viking services.

Britavia gained a weekly contract to Tripoli, Libya, which continued until May 1959. Air Charter still operated government support flights to Woomera and Christmas Island, with Tudors and newly acquired turboprop Britannias.

Troops carried during July 1957 – June 1958: 137,821 by air (BIATA)

1959

May   Hunting-Clan awarded the Far East contract, flying Britannias six times/month.
October   Hunting-Clan wins the Aden, East Africa and Cyprus contracts, taking over from Eagle; to be operated by Britannias.
October   Transair retains West Med contract.

During the year Dan-Air introduced Bristol Freighters on Government services to Woomera, and Air Charter's Tudor operations ceased. Air Charter was bought by Airwork, joining Transair which had been bought out in 1956.

Troops carried during July 1958 – June 1959: by air 142,085 (BIATA)
Troops carried during 1958/59: 136,700 by air, 323,500 by sea (Estimates Committee)

1960

October   Nigerian independence; the end of West Africa contracts.
October   New trooping contract awarded to Silver City between Manston, Kent and points in Germany. Fifty flights/month with Hermes.

British United Airways was formed in July, amalgamating Airwork, and its subsidiaries, with Hunting-Clan. The newly formed airline held all the major contracts: West Med, Aden, East Africa, Far East. The UK base for these trooping flights was consolidated at Stansted. Eagle still held the Medair contract, with its Vikings now based in Malta. The RAF took over some freight services to the Far East with its newly delivered Britannias.

Troops carried during April 1960 – March 1961: 171,138 by air (BIATA)
Troops carried during 1959/60: 134,400 by air, 298,500 by sea (Estimates Committee)

1961

September   Cunard Eagle awarded West Med contract, with DC-6As.
October   German trooping flights awarded to British United Airways, with Viscounts, to add to all its other contracts.

Troops carried during 1960/61: 172,400 by air, 225,000 by sea (Estimates Committee)

1962

June   Cunard Eagle awarded major Woomera support contract, with DC-6s, to Adelaide.

September   RAF takes over Gibraltar flying, with Comet C.2s. Cunard Eagle retains the Malta flying, which is consolidated with the Medair service, and now operates with Viscounts.

Otherwise, British United retains all the major contracts; Far East flights are now running at 15/ month.

Troops carried during 1961/2: 283,900 by air, 148,000 by sea (Estimates Committee)

1963

No changes. British United's flights to Germany now running at thirty/week.

Troops carried during April 1963 – March 1964: 425,362 by air (BIATA)

Appendix 2
Government Statements on
Civil Aviation Policy Since October 1951

GOVERNMENT STATEMENTS ON CIVIL AVIATION
POLICY SINCE OCTOBER, 1951

Date		Reference
	The Conservative pledge of 1951 stated:-	"Britain strong and Free" 1951
1951	"For Civil Aviation we favour a combination of public and private enterprise". This policy was re-affirmed by S.of S. for Co-ordination of Transport, Fuel and Power in the Civil Aviation Debate in the House of	H.A.(52) 37 P.1. para. 3 Hansard House of Lords 5th Dec. 1951
5th Dec.	Lords of 5th December, 1951. "Our main policy is clear and simple. It is that we favour a combination of public and private enterprise in whatever way is in the best interests of British civil aviation.	Vol. 174. Col. 820

Turning to the private operators, I would remark that their position is now, as I have said, happier than it was. This is largely due to the growth of charter work and of work for Government Departments, which has been increased by recent contracts for carrying troops by air - a most valuable business for them. The private operators have also been allowed to get a foothold - though only a small one - in the field of the scheduled services. But there are some of us who feel that the private operator can play a more important part in the development of civil aviation, and this is a subject to which we shall give close considera-tion. All I can say now, is this. It is the intention of the Government to help forward the sound development of civil aviation, to reduce the cost of air transport to the taxpayer and to give greater opportunities to private enterprise to take part in air transport development, without in any way impairing the competitive strength of our international air services. The precise methods and arrangements for giving effect to these intentions can be decided only after consultation with all the interests involved. The Corporations have established an important position in the highly competitive field of international air transport, and it is the intention that they should retain that position. For that reason we have no intention of undermining the existing international networks of the Air Corporations, B.O.A.C. and B.E.A. However, there are also other ways of expanding our air transport effort, and we shall

<u>Date</u>		<u>Reference</u>

<u>Date</u>

1951
(Cont'd.)

explore directions in which it is possible
to provide opportunities for the private
companies to play a valuable part in
this expansion.

5th Dec.

We realise that the role of the
private operators was enlarged in 1950
by the noble Lord, Lord Pakenham when he
extended the period for which private
companies might be granted permission
to operate scheduled services from two
years to five years, and that about
seventeen such services are in being.
However, to continue granting more of
these long-term associate agreements,
as they are called, while policy is
being reviewed, might prejudice the
pattern of future development. The
Minister has therefore decided that
for the time being existing agreements
coming up for renewal shall not be
extended beyond March, 1953, nor shall
new agreements be granted extending
beyond that date. That will give
them an opportunity of thoroughly
overhauling the whole situation and of
dealing with new agreements and the
extension of the old ones simultaneously. There may be some
independent companies whose plans for
the future are based on getting longer
term agreements, and the Minister is
making it quite clear to them that the
present restriction is solely to
allow breathing space for working out
future plans."

1952

26th Feb.

The Minister of Civil Aviation
presented a paper to the Home Affairs
Committee giving his views on the
opportunities which could be afforded
to private companies "to play their
part with the Air Corporations….
in future air transport development".

H.A. (52) 37

Home Affairs Committee invited
the Minister of Transport and Civil
Aviation to consult the interests
affected with a view to further
working out of policy proposals. The
results were presented to the
Committee – approved and Minister
authorized to make an early statement
to Parliament

H.A. (52) 6th Mtg.
n. 3. p.4.
Con. 1.

13th May

H.A. (52) 63

16th May

H.A. (52) 13th Mtg.
Min.

<u>Date</u>

1952

(Cont'd.)

27th May

<u>Reference</u>

C.(52) 176

        The Minister's statement on the
Government's policy on civil air
transport; (made to both Houses).

        "It is the policy of Her Majesty's
Government, as has been stated, to
combine the activities of the
Airways Corporations and the
independent companies in the way
which will best serve the interests
of British civil aviation and of all
users of their services.

        We recognise that the Airways
Corporations have established themselves well in the international
field. We shall do all we can to
encourage this.

        On the other hand, we seek to
improve the position of the
independent companies, which with
few exceptions lack long-term security
and opportunities of expansion. They
cannot establish their position if
they cannot plan firmly ahead. We
therefore intend to give them more
scope and security, while, at the
same time, not increasing the cost of
civil aviation to the taxpayer.

        We have therefore decided that
the development of new overseas
scheduled services shall be open to
the Corporations and independent
companies alike. Associate agreements for new routes will normally be
granted for seven-year periods with
extension to 10 years in special
cases. This should give private
firms sufficient security for
capital outlay and expansion, such as
seasonal inclusive tours and services
at cheap fares not directly competitive with the Corporations to places
within the Colonial Empire. Charter
operations are in the main the
domain of the independent operator.
The Corporations will keep the right
to engage in charter work in those
cases where they have special
facilities. They will not, however,
maintain aircraft specifically for
charter work.

        United Kingdom internal services
present a special problem. Their
cost to the taxpayer is considerable.
We are still examining the best way of
dealing with this. At the same time
we are considering how best to meet
the needs of Scotland. The Channel
Islands and the Isle of Man also

C.C.(52) 56th Cons,
Min. 3
Hansard Vol-501.
Col~ 1152
27th May, 1952

1952

27th May

present their special problems. In
the meantime, British European Airways
will continue to operate their existing
network. Internal services additional
to those of British European Airways will.
be made available to private operators
for long-term periods.

The Air Transport Advisory Council
will be ready to receive during this
summer applications not involving subsidy for these and for new overseas
services in time for the policy to take
effect in 1953. The companies will
continue to operate scheduled services as
associates of the Corporations, but
under a modified form of agreement.
Terms and conditions of service must be
not less favourable than those reached
through the machinery of the National
Joint Council for Civil Air Transport.

Under this policy, which has been
framed after consultation with the many
interests affected, the public and private
sectors of the industry can both make
their best contributions to the development of British civil aviation.

The availability of aircraft is of
the utmost importance, and one of the
reasons why we are now giving private
companies long-term security is to
enable them to raise the capital to get
the aircraft required.

I was very anxious to make
a statement on the very limited
field in which we are able to make
a decision, in order that private
operators and others should have
confidence as to the future."

16th July

In the Debate on Civil Aviation
in the Committee on Supply, the
Minister of Transport and Civil Aviation
repeated his assurance of 27th May
regarding charter work. He said "I
repeat what I said in the House on
27th May, that the two Corporations
will not keep aircraft specifically
for charter purposes, though I think no
one would resent their using those
planes which they have got and which are
specially suitable, during the off
seasons when there is no other employment for them. I hope this will
reassure all of those who are concerned
about charter development that the
field is almost entirely open to the
private operators, and we wish them
every possible success in that field."

Date	Reference

1952

In his reference to Internal United Kingdom Services the Minister said.

16th July

"The present position with regard to the internal services is this. All internal services that are additional to services now carried out by B.E.A. are, of course, open to private operators and will remain so under the new machinery, which I will come to shortly, of the A.T.A.C. which we hope will be licensing operators all over the world in a very few months' time.

All existing internal services at the moment are reserved to B.E.A., but if operators come forward with worth while propositions, I as Minister will be very glad indeed to welcome and consider them. I think this is a function that ought properly to fall on the Minister and not on the A.T.A.C."

When the Minister of Transport and Civil Aviation referred to the International routes he said. "As the Committee knows, the existing international passenger services run by the Corporations will be preserved, but the Corporations will no longer be protected against competition over what might be called their planned routes, but only over their existing routes.

The new terms of reference to the Air Transport Advisory Council will make this absolutely plain."

On the subject of Tourist Class fares the Minister stated

"To the private operators we can say that we believe, that there is a very great field indeed open to them in the future. We look with confidence to their taking full advantage of the field of third-class travel... This is the field in which the private operator can play a large part. If there is any other way in which we can help them to do this work, this Government have every intention of adopting it."

Regarding Freight the Minister assured the House. "I have the authority of both Chairmen to say that the Corporations will not apply to the A.T.A.C. for all-freight services on any new routes for one year, unless considerations of national importance require them to do so. This will give independent operators an opportunity to

Date		Reference
1952 (contd.)	apply for long-term routes in this field without any counter-claim from the Corporations for a period of a year,	
16th July	which will give those people coming new into the business a chance to get started."	
1953	Minister of Civil Aviation presented a memorandum to the Home	H.A.(53) 70
20th July	Affairs Committee in which the possibilities for obtaining Capital Finance for the Independent Civil Airline Companies was examined. The Chancellor of the Exchequer had already arranged that Banks be told of the Government's attitude to the extension of credit to "hire purchase" firms (in respect of any bona fide contract for the purchase of aircraft.	H.A.(53) 70 p.2 sub-para.(i)
24th July	At its 18th Meeting the Home Affairs Committee invited the Minister of Transport and Civil Aviation to further discuss with Defence and Service Ministers the feasibility of Long-Term Trooping Contracts. (To enable the Independent Operators to raise capital without other Exchequer Assistance) and report back to the Committee.	H.A.(53) 18th Mtg. H.A.(53) 18th Mtg. Min. 1 p.3. Con.(2) H.A.(53) 70 p.2. new para. sub-para.(ii)
25th Nov.	Referring to the Minister's statement in May, 1952 the Joint Parliamentary Secretary of the Ministry of Transport and Civil Aviation said:- "The intention which my Rt. Hon. Friend announced to the House on 27th May, 1952, that the corporations would not maintain aircraft specifically for Charter work naturally precludes them from tendering for regular trooping flights but they are not thereby debarred from tendering for ad hoc troop movements."	
1954	Lord Malcolm Douglas-Hamilton gave notice that he would draw	
4th Feb.	attention to need for adequate fleet of Civil Transport Aircraft and move Resolution on going into Committee of Supply on the Civil Estimates for Air.	Hansard Vol. 523 Col. 568
10th Feb.	Mr. Lindgren asked the Minister of Transport and Civil Aviation how far it is the policy of his Department to permit the Air Corporations to offer charter services, on any route.	Hansard vol. 523 Col. 1147 para. 31 para. 32

Date		Reference

1954
(Cont'd.)

10th Feb.

Mr. Lennox-Boyd: "As I have previously informed the House, the chairmen of the Air Corporations have undertaken not to maintain aircraft specifically for charter work, which has always been recognised as the domain of the independent companies and only incidental to the main business of the Corporations as operators of scheduled services. Subject to the limitations which this principle implies, the Corporations are free to tender for charter work including ad hoc trooping operations. The Corporation chairmen recently informed me that they did not understand that charter work included trooping, but I see no reason to modify long established Government policy in this respect".

15th Feb.

Mr. Beswick asked when it became a matter of policy that freight should be the responsibility of the independent operators. Mr. Lennox-Boyd: "In my view and the view of the Government, there is no question of a change of policy. It has been the view throughout that the service which independent operators and the Corporation can provide should be complementary more than competitive. I may add that I also pointed out in a letter to the chairman of B.O.A.C. on 2nd March that if the Corporation could satisfy the A.T.A.C. of the validity of its claim to operate an all-freight service in addition to the capacity provided by Airwork, whose application had already been approved, there was nothing in the terms of reference of the A.T.A.C, that would prevent them from recommending it".

Hansard Vol, 523 col. 1648 2nd para.

1955

23rd Feb.

At a Meeting in February, 1955 Ministers agreed that, in order to enable Independent Civil Airline Companies to purchase, without direct financial assistance from Exchequer, suitable aircraft on loans with advantageous terms the Ministry of Supply was to order three Bristol Britannia 250's, and put out to tender. The successful tenderer. to take over the aircraft as soon as possible.

E.A.(55) 7th Mtg. Item 4 of 23.2.55

7

Date		Reference
1955 (Cont'd.)	The Economic Policy Committee approved these decisions with slight amendments e.g. long-range aircraft	E.A.(55) 7th Mtg. Min. 4 p.6.
23rd Feb.	and shorter term Air Trooping Contracts (a). The Minister of Transport and Civil Aviation was invited to consider with interested parties, in consultation with the Treasury, timing, terms and period of long-term trooping contracts (b).	P.7. (a) para.2 sub-para. (c) (b) p.7 Con. (1)
15th Feb.	The Chancellor of the Exchequer stated that whilst agreeing to purchase of Bristol Britannia 250's (to relieve unemployment in Northern Ireland) he reserved his position on the terms on which they be made available for Trooping, but in spite of this reservation, was in favour of going out to tender as soon as possible.	E.A.(555) 34 p.1 para. 4
3rd May	Ministers and Officials met under Ministry of Defence Committee on "Air Trooping" and agreed on terms but the length of trooping contracts was left as "alternative periods up to seven years".	Misc./M(55) 47 Rev.)p.3 Con. (3)
	The Election Manifesto of 1955 stated "Air Transport gives us new highways. Experience has shown that a blend of public and private enterprise is best for this service... we shall ensure that their (the Corporation) relationships with independent operators are developed in the interests of travellers, trader and taxpayer".	Conservative Election Pledge of 1955 (not attached) E.P.(55) 61 p.2 para.3 C.A.P.(56) 3 p.1 para. 1
17th Nov.	A Review of Civil Aviation Policy by the Minister of Transport and Civil Aviation quotes the 1955 Conservative Election Manifesto and reviews the difficulties.	E.P.(55) 61 p. 2 para. 3
	New points brought out are:- Necessity for legislation to free Independent Airline Companies and to bring about a balance between Air Corporations and Independent Airline Companies which could not be radically altered in the event of a change of government. The memorandum closes with the proposal that a Small Ministerial Committee be set up,	P.1 para. 1 sub-para. (c) Civil Aviation Act, 1949 Air Corporation Act, 1949 Section 24 Sub-para, (d) After P.7 Appendix D.)

Date		Reference

1955
(Contd.)

7th Dec.
An approach to the Prime Minister with a view to the setting up of a Civil Aviation Committee was proposed by the Chancellor - in consultation with the Minister of Transport - and was agreed.

E.P.(55)
12th Mtg.,
Min.1,P.12
Conclusion (2)

20th Dec.
In the Debate on the Reports and Accounts of the Air Corporations referring to the Independent Airlines the Joint Parliamentary Secretary to Ministry of Transport and Civil Aviation (Mr. Profumo) said: "They too have had a successful year during which all their activities have in fact increased, as compared with the previous year, by percentages even greater than those of the Corporations. Independent companies are now tending to concentrate more and more on regular operations, including both scheduled services and regular air trooping, which is carried out wholly by the independent companies. These together now constitute a large part of their total activities.

Air trooping has continued to increase throughout the past year as more aircraft, some of them of more modern types, have been employed on this work. It now accounts for about 67 per cent of the total operations of the independent companies...

The independent companies have also taken full advantage of the increased opportunities made available to them since 1952 to operate scheduled services as associates of the Airways Corporations. Under the law as it at present stands, the existing networks of the Corporations are fully protected, and this inevitably places some limit on the opportunities available to the independent companies."

Mr. Profumo referred to the Conservative Election Manifesto of 1955 and said: "To the extent to which the companies concerned, not forgetting the great shipping interests, can help to shape this end by freely conceived co-operation, so much the better. But there should be no doubt about the Government's long-term intentions. In the interests of the industry it is essential that aviation policy should transcend party differences, and I firmly believe we can arrive at a pattern for development which will remain unchanged even if - as I venture to suggest is unlikely - Governments change."

Page 1,
paras. 5 and 6

<u>Date</u>		<u>Reference</u>

<u>Date</u>
1956

23rd July   The Report of the Civil Aviation   C.A.P.(56) 3
Committee admitted the "fundamental dilemma"
of conflicting Governmental interests and
finally recommended, as the only hope
for further expansion of the private
airline companies, that an approach be
made to corporations and companies
with a view to extending the existing
type of collaboration.

2nd Nov,   In the Debate on the Air   Hansard Vol. 558,
Corporations Account the Minister of   Col. 1774
Transport and Civil Aviation said:
"The independents, too, have been
playing their full part .... In this
expanding world, therefore, they are
finding their niche, which is what the
Government wishes them to do. I think
that their limited opportunities - and I
am sure that the House understands that
they are limited opportunities - have
paid off ...... Before I leave this section,
I might mention another interesting point.
I refer to a new piece of enterprise, the
combined air-coach services which have been
so popular, to the Continent."

In the same Debate the Joint   Hansard Vol. 558,
Parliamentary Secretary to Ministry of   Cols. 1842-1843
Transport and Civil Aviation
(Mr. Profumo) referring to the progress
of the Independent Airlines said:
"At the same time, I think I should say
a word about the independent air operators.
My hon. Friend the Member for Gosport and
Fareham (Dr. Bennett) asked whether we
would try to elucidate our attitude. He
mentioned long-term trooping contracts and
suggested, quite rightly, that if we were
able to give contracts of much greater
length it would be possible for the
independent operators to buy more up-to-date
aircraft and to plan efficiently.
That is all very well, but my hon.
Friend will realise how difficult it is to
see ahead as far as seven years from the
point of view of trooping contracts to any
part of the world. At the same time my right
hon. Friend and I have this matter very much
in mind, and we are extremely pleased to note
what progress the independent companies have made.
Although the opportunities which have been
available to the independents since 1952 have
necessarily been limited, they have taken full
advantage of them, and they have rapidly built
up their traffic within the sphere open to them.
This is the case not only in charter work and
not only in colonial coach services...

Date		Reference
1956 (Cont'd.) 2nd Nov. (Cont'd.)	My right hon. Friend and I are confident that there is a great deal of service which the independent operators can render without damaging or harming the Corporations and without damaging or harming all those thousands of people who work in civil air transport and who have such a great love for it. The Government welcome the progress which has been made by the independent companies in recent years, and will continue to foster their development in every possible practical way."	
1957 3rd Jan,	The Minister of Transport and Civil Aviation referred to inability of Official Committee on Civil Aviation to find a solution to the problems and spoke of investigating the possibilities of a mixed corporation composed of Independent Companies and Corporations and/or a merger of the four major independent operators. These proposals on later consideration proved to be impracticable.	C.A.P.(57) 1 C.A.P.(56) 3 C.A.P.(57) I p.I., para. 5 C.A.(57) 1st mtg. p.1., 2nd para.
3rd Jan.	Refers to importance of Bingley Report to Chiefs of Staff as regards air trooping problems.	C.O.S.(57) 33
5th Feb.	The Minister of Transport urged action as shipping firms, financial backers of the major airlines were pressing for discussion on the Government's "undertakings" and stated he must be able to give an assurance to the independent airline companies of trooping contracts and Colonial Coach Services or face an accusation of breach of faith in this matter.	C.A.(57) Ist Mtg, P.2., para. I
	The Committee invited the Minister of Transport in consultation with interested Departments to circulate papers clearing up difficulties for independent airlines on Colonial Coach Services and Trooping Contracts.	C.A.(57) 1st Mtg. C.A.(57) 1st Mtg., Con.(2) Con. (3)
9th May	In the Debate on Air Estimates the Secretary of State for Air stated: "In discussing Transport Command, we must not overlook the importance of maintaining a strategic reserve of airlift in the field of civil aviation, which is done, as hon. Members know, by giving civil charter companies contracts for regular trooping for all three Services in peacetime... On scheduled civil air lines, the policy of the Government has been to invite the independent civil operators to carry out the air movement task.	Hansard Vol. 569, Cols. 1191-2

11

Date		Reference
1957 (Cont'd.) 9th May (Contd.)	Under this arrangement, Transport Command is free to concentrate on its operational role of being ready to pro vide air movement support for the Services. The Corporations are able to concentrate on the highly competitive task of operating world-wide scheduled services. And, last but by no means least, the trooping work is of great value to the independent companies, whose civil opportunities are necessarily limited. At present, the carriage of military personnel represents about 65 per cent of their passenger-carrying activities." and says: "We are, examining at the moment the future of the three Britannias which are being built to the order of the Ministry of supply. As the Committee will know, these aircraft were ordered for use on trooping, particularly to the Far East. We hope that in spite of the cuts in the size of the forces it will be possible to provide a task on which these aircraft can be employed and we intend to invite tenders from the independent operators for these tasks in the very near future."	
29th May	The Minister of Civil Aviation informed Cabinet of the recommendation of Air Transport Advisory Council to remove restrictions limiting independent airlines to the use of sub-standard aircraft. Cabinet authorised the informing of Government supporters in the House of the intention of implementing this recommendation.	C.C.(57) 43rd Cons. (Min. 10)
	The Minister of Civil Aviation also told Cabinet he was looking into longer-term contracts for trooping and hoped to make a statement to Parliament in the near future about future policy on Independent airlines.	HANSARD Vol. 572, Col. 40 (Written. Ans.) C.C.(57) 43rd Cons.
26th June	The Minister of Transport and Civil Aviation said that the Air Transport Advisory Council's recommenda-tions "will now free the Colonial Coach operators from some of their present restrictions and will give them, on their existing Colonial Coach routes a continuing share in the future operation of low-fare services."	Hansard Vol. 572 Written Ans. Col. 40

Date		Reference
1957 (Cont'd.) 24th July	In an oral answer to Mr. Bellinger's question on trooping contracts the Secretary of State for Air (Mr. Ward) said: "The Government's broad policy has always been that the Corporations should concern themselves primarily with the operation of scheduled services. The Corporations have undertaken not to maintain aircraft specifically for charter work, so we do not invite tenders from them for long-term trooping contracts."	
31st July	A few days later Mr. Ward replied to Mr. Lipton's similar question. "The current contract for air trooping to the Par East and the new contracts which will replace it next September are all long-term contracts and the Corporations were not therefore invited to tender for them."	Hansard Vol. 574, Col. 1255
1958 19th Feb.	The Joint Parliamentary Secretary, Ministry of Transport and Civil Aviation said his Department welcomed the Private Member's Motion of 28th February, 1958 as giving an opportunity for a useful debate.	L.C.(58) 5th Mtg., Min,1(1) Hansard Vol. 583, Col. 790

In his summing up at this Debate Mr. Neave said: "I think today's debate shows that the Government's air services policy is not far wrong, since it is suggested on the one hand that we have been too generous to the independent companies, at the expense of the Airways Corporations, while on the other hand we are accused of not giving to the independent companies a large enough share of the traffic. The criticisms suggest that we have, in fact, achieved a fair and reasonable balance."

The Joint Parliamentary Secretary in referring to the question of Air Freight said: "It was hoped that the independent companies would be able to develop vigorously from this country all-freight services, which up to that time had been rather neglected. Unfortunately, I do not think the prospects have proved as good as we expected. The carriage of freight by air is still relatively expensive, and unless the goods themselves are valuable, the extra cost can be justified only if it brings some additional advantages."

13

Date

1958
(Cont.d,)   In mentioning trooping he
                       stated: "Our view is that the main
19th Feb   business of the Corporations is
(Contd.~   scheduled operations and that the
                       independent companies are more suited
                       in many ways to charter operations and
                       to trooping movements. That has been
                       our reaction to the problem for some
                       time. At present, discussions are
                       still proceeding on the whole subject
                       of trooping." and ends by saying:
                       "we shall try to give the independents
                       a fair crack of the whip"
                           The House on this occasion took
                       note: "Of the contribution being
                       made by United Kingdom independent
                       operators in the field of air transport,
                       and is of the opinion that the potential
                       future growth of world air traffic gives
                       scope for an accelerated expansion in
                       association with or complementary to but
                       not to the detriment of that of the
                       national corporations."

                                    -14-

Appendix 3
The Development of
Britain's Independent Airlines

This fine diagram, drawn by Ron Davies for his seminal *History of the World's Airlines*, published by Oxford University Press in 1963, charts the evolution of Britain's major independents. It is typical of Davies's work: he prided himself almost as much on his artistic talents as on his writing and research skills, and it displays his best qualities, painstakingly thorough, original, beautifully executed.

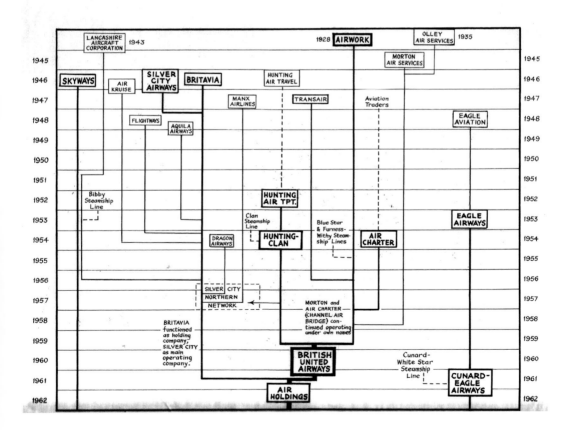

Appendix 4
Lord Brabazon and the Tudor

After the disappearance of the Tudor IV *Star Ariel* on 17 January 1949, the second BSAA Tudor to be lost within a year in unexplained circumstances, Lord Pakenham asked Lord Brabazon to inquire into the possible causes of the crashes and report back as quickly as possible. Brabazon formed a committee to investigate various aspects of the aircraft's design and manufacture, which in turn was broken down into five subcommittees, each tasked with a separate area of investigation:

(1) Structure and Materials
(2) Investigation into Previous Tudor Defects, Examination of Condition of Existing Tudor I and Tudor IV Aircraft, Constructional Investigation from the Point of View of Engineering Practices
(3) Systems and Dinghy Installation
(4) Explosions and Fire, Noxious Gases, Explosive Decompression, Lightning and Static Discharge
(5) Power Plant

Each subcommittee presented its findings and comments in a common format, and after some 'very real hard work', the main committee submitted its report at the end of the following month, February 1949. The report was not published, and it appears that one section covering two paragraphs from subcommittee (4) is missing from the archives,[1] although there is no note to suggest that the paragraphs have been redacted. After he read the report, Lindgren told the House of Commons on 1 March 1949: 'The decision not to bring the Tudor back into service was made only late yesterday, following the receipt of the reports of Lord Brabazon and the five committees which have been considering the problem and also the report of the inspector on the investigation of accidents.'[2]

Brabazon was unable to deduce precisely the causes of the two accidents from the reports of the five subcommittees, but suggested various possibilities:

The Main Committee has evaluated these reports and considers that the possibilities can be placed in three categories:-

1. Conditions which could possibly lead to a sudden catastrophic accident.
2. Conditions which could possibly lead to a sudden catastrophic accident but on which the evidence suggests improbability.
3. Conditions which, if not rectified, might lead to an accident, but not of a sudden catastrophic nature.

Category 1.

1. Explosion of hydraulic fluid spray passing through the cabin heater (experiments proceeding.)
2. The failure of the bolts at the tailplane centre joint (experiments proceeding).

Less Probable

3. Operation of the Methyl bromide fire extinguisher producing dangerous fumes which, if of sufficiently high concentration, could impair the efficiency of crew members in quite a short space of time.
4. Fire in the engine nacelle (Exhaust system is unsatisfactory and panels behind exhaust have been found buckled; these defects offer a number of possibilities of disaster).
5. The possibility of the forward freight door opening resulting in the ejection of a crew member or a piece of bulky freight into the propeller.
6. Auto-Pilot failure (experiments continuing).

Category 2.

1. Complete failure and detachment of propeller.
2. An uncontrollable fire at a power plant.
3. Failure of an incorrectly heat treated spar joint link plate.
4. A minor fire under the floor destroying the main petrol cross feed pipe.

Category 3.

1. Fatigue failure of the screw fitting at the rear end of the push/pull rod in the elevator control.
2. Fatigue failure of link rods to balance tabs leading to flutter of control surfaces.
3. Loosening of rivets at tailplane centre joint.
4. Damage to control tubes at rear end of fuselage due to mechanics standing on them.
5. Fire from a slow leak of hydraulic or de-icing fluid.
6. The possibility of whole or partial seizure of the aileron hinges due to the effect of a lightning strike.

Brabazon allowed Avro, the manufacturers, to attach their comments to his report. 'With certain exceptions,' they said 'we agree with the assessment of the risk as set out in Lord Brabazon's Interim Report.'

The report illustrates the problems, and dangers, of converting aircraft built for warfare, like the Lincoln bomber, into civilian transports. 'We agree that it ought to be possible to trace the history of all vital parts,' admitted Avro: 'It was part of the policy governing Tudor construction to use proved Lincoln material, some of which was not identifiable due to the wartime relaxation of the requirement governing such precautions.' What was acceptable, just, for RAF crews, did not transfer to airline operations.

All the piping (of the hydraulic system) is of light alloy…It is generally accepted that light alloy piping is rather more prone to failure by splitting or breaking than the steel and Tungum used for the high pressure lines of most British aircraft hydraulic systems. Light alloy was approved for the Tudor because it had proved satisfactory on the Lancaster and because of the weight saving effected in comparison with the stronger materials.

There was a scary incident involving the auto-pilot.

One of the two B.S.A.A. Captains whom we interviewed had experienced an auto-pilot failure, in which the aircraft was caused to bunt. The pilot was thrown to the roof but he held on to the control column and must have been able to exert sufficient backward pull to remove the downward acceleration, because he came back to his seat and was then able to cut out the auto-pilot and bring the aircraft back to level flight.

What if that had happened at 2,000 feet on the way from the Azores to Bermuda, and the pilot had being incapacitated?

The first subcommittee was concerned about the tail unit, which 'had not been adequately stressed for asymmetric load and the treatment of the centre joint of the tail plane was not satisfactory'. It pointed out that there had been a number of failures of tail plane joint bolts in other Avro aircraft, Lancasters, Lancastrians and Yorks. There was evidence of high frequency vibration, undetectable through the controls, which 'would cause fluctuating stresses in the elevator and the tail plane and in the rear end of the elevator control system'. Avro disagreed: 'We do not consider that the evidence available, whether from calculation or from experience, justifies the inference that [structural failure of the tailplane] is a probable, or even a possible, cause of catastrophe.' Further tests were to be conducted, resonance testing and tail unit strength tests being the priority.

When subcommittee (2) came to discuss working practices at the manufacturer's, it could not disguise its dismay: 'The impression was formed…that very little pride of workmanship exists,' and went on to comment,

Nuts, washers, bolts, swarf and rags, not to mention liquid, dust and grit, fall through this mass of machinery and are extremely difficult to retrieve, but there is hazard from the fire angle and also jamming of chain and sprocket systems.…There is evidence of much damage having been done by maintenance personnel in this region due to trampling on formers and pressure against piping.

The subcommittee inspected Tudor I G-AGRJ and found 420 faults, but 'these are mainly of a minor nature and are no more than one expects to find on the modern complicated aeroplanes'. Somehow I did not find that very reassuring. The subcommittee also inspected Tudor IVs G-AGRH and G-AGRF, both of them converted from Tudor Is, and found one issue, a hydraulic leak in the belly of G-AGRF, which it considered might have had immediate catastrophic results. With access to existing reports – 'These technical records are very cryptic and frequently do not disclose the exact nature of the trouble' – it noted other matters regarded as unsatisfactory and which, if uncorrected, might have led to a catastrophe, like 'air to air cooling fairing cracked', 'power plant cowling fasteners broken and incorrectly marked for locked position', 'deterioration of tanks and fittings' to name but three. Trouble regions were: propeller spinner back plate retaining studs shearing; magneto failure; fuel and heating systems; auto-pilot; instruments; access door locking arrangements. The cabin heater installation did not sound promising:

> The work of installing the heater unit is a trying and difficult task and a not too conscientious workman might, with some excuse perhaps, be inclined to use undue force with consequent risk of damage to the unit or accessories or nearby services. There are too many wire looms in the vicinity of the heater outlet pipe and the actual wiring in connection with the unit is somewhat ragged.

Avro accepted the dangers of the heating system: 'The present form of heating system is unsafe in a cabin which contains any inflammable fuel, especially if the fuel is under pressure.'

Subcommittee (3) also regarded the heating and ventilation system as a major hazard:

> The danger arises from the presence of the Cabin Heater unit and the lay-out of the air circulations system. Failure of an hydraulic pipe could result in several gallons of the fluid being sprayed into the fuselage in a few seconds, and the resulting air/fluid mixture exploded by contact with the hot surfaces of the combustion heater.

Nor were the fire-extinguishing measures altogether satisfactory:

> The components and system are generally satisfactory, but the use of methyl-bromide is strongly deprecated. Discharge of the extinguisher bottle for the cabin-heater compartment, or of the crews' hand-operated extinguishers, will cause a concentration of methyl-bromide sufficient to give severe toxic effects, combined with anaesthesia, to the occupants within one or two minutes of exposure.

And the electrical system was not much better:

> The electrical system on this aircraft appears to be a direct development of 2-pole Lancaster wiring with certain sections of negative wiring omitted and the aircraft structure substituted. The adoption of this policy has resulted in a very undesirable wiring system employing several complex negative systems supplied by single large cables to the structure....The installation of the wiring is poor and cables are not adequately secured adjacent to terminals, etc.; one case in point is the wire to the circulating fan which runs several feet unsupported. Further, the system appears difficult to inspect due to its inaccessibility....The system employs quite a large amount of electrically unprotected cabling.

Avro agreed, up to a point: 'It is evident that the electrical installation received consideration in the general design of the aircraft unworthy of its importance to the extent that accessibility suffered.'

Auto-pilot failure had been considered at the enquiry on the loss of *Star Tiger*.[3] There was a large discrepancy between calculations made by the RAE for the Brabazon report, which seemed to indicate the possibility of height loss between 2,600 ft and 3,200 ft in 10 seconds, a severe loss of altitude. Yet the Court investigation had recorded a 'much gentler manoeuvre than the above, the figure quoted being 35 ft. loss of height in 5 seconds, 105 ft. in 9½ seconds'. Brabazon concluded:

> We are not yet able to say whether malfunctioning of the auto-pilot can give rise to catastrophic loss of control or structural failure and it is recommended that the work necessary to establish this be pursued vigorously. The probability should not be dismissed lightly on the grounds the human pilot can override

the auto-pilot since in the case of a "bunt" he may be thrown to the roof and unable to reach the controls in time.

The report recommended that pilots should be strapped in at all times.

There was some discussion about the emergency dinghies, which it was thought would prove difficult to release, and possible decompression of the fuselage. The latter was discounted, as the windows and doors were so small, but the subcommittee accepted that failure of the forward door, followed by ejection of a crew member if he happened to be standing there, could damage the inboard propeller.

The report, even at this interim stage, and still awaiting further results from the strength and other tests on the tail unit, was enough to ground the 'thin' Tudor Is and IVs. When Laker reintroduced them into service, early in 1954, *The Aeroplane*[4] explained the changes Air Charter and Aviation Traders had to make for the ARB to grant the type a new Certificate of Airworthiness:

> In modifying the Tudors, it was first felt necessary to remove all the equipment which might have contributed in any way to the two unexplained accidents, and to replace it with selected material. Another aim was to "add lightness" by the removal of all non-essential accessories, such as brackets, fittings and various odds and ends, and this was done to such good effect that about 2,000 lb. of "variable purpose" equipment was removed from the first aircraft.
>
> All light alloy piping in the hydraulic system is removed and replaced by Tungum pipes, and repositioned where necessary to avoid electric cables. The combustion heater and its associated equipment is removed, and replaced by tubular electric heating elements which have proved entirely satisfactory in the Tudor 2, G.AGRY. Also removed is the ventilation recirculation air fan and equipment, the pressure refuelling system and the cabin pressurization system. This limits the Tudor's operating ceiling to below 10,000 ft., whereas its former most economical altitude was about 20,000 ft. A new ventilation system, utilizing an external air scoop, has been installed. The hydraulic fluid and water tanks have also been repositioned beneath the pilots' seats, and the redisposition of weight gives an increased loading flexibility within the comparatively narrow limits of C.G. movement. The redisposition of electrical and radio equipment is also calculated to reduce the fire risk.
>
> Particular attention has been paid to emergency equipment, and an extra escape exit is incorporated. The former Merlin 621 engines…have been brought up to Merlin 623 standard, providing slightly more power. All single piece de Havilland airscrews are replaced by the split-barrel type, and the main landing gear wheels changed to the latest Shackleton-type units.

Despite his best efforts, Laker could not get the War Office to agree to allow passengers to fly on the type, and so had to content himself with modifying the available aircraft, which he called Super Traders, for use as freighters by the Air Ministry. It is also a matter of record that, to Laker's great distress, two Super Traders crashed in 1959: G-AGRG, on take-off from Brindisi in January; and G-AGRH, one of the aircraft mentioned above, near the summit of Suphan Dag in Turkey in April. The remaining aircraft had all been withdrawn from service by October, and were subsequently scrapped.

Glossary of Terms

AAJC	Associated Airways Joint Committee
AOC	Air Operator's Certificate
AOG	Aircraft on Ground
ARB	Air Registration Board
Argonaut	Canadair C-4
ATAC	Air Transport Advisory Council
ATLB	Air Transport Licensing Board
BAC	British Aircraft Corporation
BBC	British Broadcasting Corporation
BEA	British European Airways
BIATA	British Independent Air Transport Association
BKS	Independent airline, named for the initials of its three founders
BOAC	British Overseas Airways Corporation
BSAA	British South American Airways
BUA	British United Airways
BUAF	British United Air Ferries
BWIA	British West Indian Airways
CAA	Central African Airways
CAP	Committee on Civil Aviation (notes to chapters)
CI	Channel Islands
CM	Cabinet Meeting (notes to chapters)
CP	Cabinet Paper (notes to chapters)
Dakota	Douglas DC-3
DH	de Havilland
Douglas DC-3	Dakota
Douglas DC-4	Skymaster
Dragon Rapide	de Havilland DH.89
EA	Economic Policy Committee (notes to chapters)
Elizabethan	Airspeed Ambassador
GWR	Great Western Railway
HA	Home Affairs Committee (notes to chapters)
Halton	Handley Page Halifax
HC	House of Commons debate

Herald	Handley Page Herald, also known as Dart Herald
HL	House of Lords debate
HMG	His (or Her) Majesty's Government
HP.42	Handley Page airliner type
HS	Hawker Siddeley
IATA	International Air Transport Association
ITC	Inclusive Tour
KLM	Royal Dutch Airlines
MEA	Middle East Airlines
MP	Member of Parliament
RAeS	Royal Aeronautical Society
RAF	Royal Air Force
Rapide	de Havilland DH.89
RAS	Railway Air Services
Skymaster	Douglas DC-4
TNA	The National Archives
Wayfarer	Passenger carrying version of Bristol Freighter
WP	War Cabinet Paper (notes to chapters)

Notes to Chapters

Chapter 1: Managing Somehow to Muddle Through

1. Synopsis of Progress of Work done in the Department of Civil Aviation: 1 May 1919-31 October 1919 Cmd. 418
2. House of Commons Debate 11 March 1920 vol 126, column 1622
3. Captain Olley, *A Million Miles in the Air*, 1934, 103-4
4. *Imperial Airways Gazette* April 1934
5. Report on Government Financial Assistance to Civil Air Transport Companies, 1923 Cmd. 1811
6. Sir Philip Sassoon, HC Deb 17 March 1936 vol 310, 271
7. A. J. Quin-Harkin, *The Journal of Transport History*, 1st series, vol I, no.4 (1954), 197-215
8. HC Deb 16 December 1919 vol 123, 311
9. Gordon Pirie, *Air Empire*, Manchester University Press, 2009
10. Report of the Committee of Inquiry into Civil Aviation and the observations of H.M. Government thereon: Air Ministry, 1938 Cmd. 5685 (Cadman Report) Appendix L
11. Report of the Committee to consider the development of civil aviation in the United Kingdom. 1937 Cmd. 5351 (Maybury Report)
12. Reports on the Progress of Civil Aviation, 1933 and 1935
13. *Shell Aviation News*, December 1935
14. Maybury Report, 1937, 19
15. *The Aeroplane* 31 January 1934
16. Maybury Report, 22-23
17. HC Deb 30 May 1934 vol 290, 173W
18. House of Lords Debate 21 November 1934 vol 95, column 67
19. England-Scandinavia Civil Air Transport Services, 1936 Cmd. 5203
20. HC Deb 18 November 1936 vol 317, 1776-7
21. HC Deb 05 May 1937 vol 323, 1149
22. HC Deb 20 December 1934 vol 296, 1329
23. *The Aeroplane* 28 September 1938
24. C. H. Barnes, *Shorts Aircraft since 1900*, Putnam 1967, 313
25. Brian Cassidy, *Flying Empires*, 1996, 187
26. Ibid. 188
27. HL Deb 15 April 1943 vol 127, 275-7
28. Civil Aviation Statistical and Technical Review, 1937

29. *Shell Aviation News*, April 1938
30. Gordon Pirie, 'Passenger Traffic in the 1930s on British imperial air routes: refinement and revision', *Journal of Transport History*, March 2004
31. Civil Aviation Annual Report, 1938
32. HC Deb 09 March 1939 vol 344, 2396
33. Robin Higham, *Britain's Imperial Air Routes*, 1960, 228
34. C.P. 76 (37), 27 February 1937
35. Ibid.
36. Ibid.

Chapter 2: Ominous Skies
(with acknowledgment to Harald Penrose)

1. *Flight* 21 May 1936
2. HC Deb 21 March 1935 vol 299, 1467
3. Sir Peter Masefield, Chartered Institute of Transport, Brancker Memorial Lecture 1951
4. *The Aeroplane* 20 October 1937
5. Maybury Report, 1937
6. *The Aeroplane* 5 January 1938
7. *The Aeroplane* 27 October 1937
8. *The Aeroplane* 5 January 1938
9. HC Deb 17 November 1937 vol 329, 417
10. *The Aeroplane* 5 January 1938
11. HC Deb 17 November 1937 vol 329, 464
12. Ibid.
13. Cadman Report, 1938 Cmd. 5685
14. Norman Hulbert, HC Deb 16 March 1938 vol 333, 462
15. *The Aeroplane* 4 May 1938
16. HC Deb 16 March 1938 vol 333, 441
17. Ibid. 435
18. C. H. Barnes, *Handley Page Aircraft since 1907*, 1976, 325
19. HC Deb 16 March 1938 vol 333, 449
20. Ibid. 451
21. HC Deb 17 November 1937 vol 329, 437
22. *The Times*, 4 May 1938
23. HC Deb 28 March 1938 vol 333, 1783
24. HC Deb 14 December 1938 vol 342, 2009-10W
25. HC Deb 18 May 1938 vol 336, 476
26. HC Deb 11 November 1938 vol 34, 454
27. HC Deb 10 July 1939 vol 349, 1913
28. Ibid. 1833
29. Ibid. 1860-1
30. Ibid. 1918
31. René Francillon, *McDonnell Douglas Aircraft since 1920*, 1979, 309

32. Higham, *Britain's Imperial Air Routes*, 309
33. HC Deb 03 September 1939 vol 351, 295-6

Chapter 3 Civilians in Wartime

1. Sir Kingsley Wood, HC Debate 07 March 1940 vol 358, 704
2. Wing Commander Wright, HC Deb 04 March 1942 vol 378, 758
3. *Merchant Airmen*, 1946, 107
4. *Flight* 7 March 1940
5. HC Deb 30 April 1940 vol 360, 558W
6. John Stroud, *Railway Air Services*, 1987, 70
7. Report on the Progress of Civil Aviation, 1939-1945, MCA, Appendix A Table 4
8. Captain E. E. Fresson, *Air Road to the Isles*, second edition, 287-8
9. Sir Archibald Sinclair, HC debate, 11 March 1941 vol 369, 1183-4
10. Lord Apsley HC debate, 11 March 1941 vol 369, 1207-8
11. HC Deb 17 Dec 1942 vol 385, 2121
12. John Stroud, *European Transport Aircraft since 1910*, 1966, 329
13. Francillon, *McDonnell Douglas Aircraft*, 251
14. *Merchant Airmen*, 140-1
15. Harold Balfour, *Wings over Westminster*, 1973, 201
16. W.P. (44) 268 27 May 1944
17. HL Deb 12 Oct 1944 vol 133, 504
18. HC Deb 17 Dec 1942 vol 385, 2123
19. HC 17 Dec 1942 vol 385, 2151
20. HC Deb 01 June 1943 vol 390, 102
21. HC Deb 11 March 1943 vol 387, 964
22. HC Deb 01 June 1943 vol 390, 50
23. British Overseas Airways Corporation: Further Correspondence February - March, 1943. Cmd. 6442
24. Longhurst, *Nationalisation in Practice*, 53
25. Letter to *The Aeroplane* 12 May 1944
26. Report on the Progress of Civil Aviation, 1939-1945, MCA, Appendix D
27. HL Deb 12 October 1944 vol 133, 521
28. International Air Transport, Air Ministry, 1944, Cmd. 6561
29. W.P. (44) 508. 8 September 1944
30. HC Deb 14 March 1944 vol 398, 123
31. W.P. (44) 585 23 October, 1944
32. HC Deb 20 March 1945 vol 409 cc646-773
33. Longhurst, *Nationalisation in Practice,* 77
34. Geoffrey Mander, HC Deb 06 June 1945 vol 411, 1007
35. HC Deb 20 March 1945 vol 409, 682
36. War Cabinet W.P. (43) 537. 3 December 1943
37. Brabazon to Balfour, 25 October 1943, quoted in Longhurst, 159
38. HC Deb 26 January 1945 vol 407, 1215

39. *The Aeroplane* 7 September 1945
40. C.P. 222 12 October 1945
41. C.P. 221 11 October 1945
42. Letter to Lord Winster from the Secretary, Parliamentary Labour Party 18 October 1945
43. C.P. (45) 245 24 October 1945
44. HL Deb 01 November 1945 vol 137 cc623-48
45. HL Deb 06 November 1945 vol 137, 665
46. British Air Services, December 1945 Cmd. 6712
47. HC Deb 24 January 1946, cc313-438
48. HC Deb 06 May 1946 vol 422, 671
49. C.P. (46) 110 14 March 1946
50. HL Deb 25 July 1946 vol 142, 971
51. HL Deb 23 July 1946 vol 142, 827
52. HL Deb 25 July 1946 vol 142, 973
53. C.P. 222 12 October 1945
54. C.M 46 25th Conclusions 18 March 1946

Chapter 4 Meddle and Muddle

1. HC Deb 24 January 1946, 325
2. A. J Jackson, *Avro Aircraft since 1908*, 374
3. *Air Transport and Airport Engineering*, March 1947
4. HL Deb 26 November 1946 vol 144, 354
5. *Flight* 27 June 1946
6. *Aeronautics* April 1946
7. *Aeronautics* December 1946
8. *The Aeroplane* 24 May 1946
9. Fresson, *Air Road to the Isles*, second edition, 350
10. *Flight* 31 July 1947
11. *Flight* 17 July 1947
12. *Flight* 31 July 1947
13. *Air Transport*, November 1946
14. HC Deb 24 April 1947 vol 436, 1308
15. *Air Transport*, August 1946
16. *Flight* 6 March 1947
17. HL Deb 21 January 1948 vol 153, 503
18. BOAC Annual Report and Statement of Accounts 18 December 1947, 6
19. HC Deb 07 July 1948 vol 453 cc349-51
20. Higham, *Imperial*, App. VII Table III
21. *Air Transport and Engineering* March 1947
22. *The Aeroplane* 14 November 1947
23. HL Deb 21 January 1948 vol 153, 556
24. HC Deb 26 February 1948 vol 447, 2195
25. Ibid., 2138

26. *International Aviation*, 6 June 1947

27. Interim report of the committee of enquiry into the Tudor aircraft, Cmd. 7307, 1948

28. HL Deb 21 January 1948 vol 153, 522

29. HC Deb 18 February 1948 vol 447, cc1138-42

30. Report of the Court investigation of accident on the Tudor IV Aircraft *Star Tiger* G-AHNP on the 30th January, 1948, 1948 Cmd. 7517

31. *Flight* 7 October 1948

32. HC Deb 26 February 1948 vol 447, 2247

33. *Flight* 3 June 1948

34. *The Aeroplane* 21 May 1948

35. HC Deb 26 February 1948 vol 447, 2184-5

36. *The Aeroplane* 28 May 1948

37. HL Deb 21 July 1948 vol 157, cc1101-71

38. *Flight* 29 July 1948

Chapter 5 Along the Corridor

1. Quoted in *The Aeroplane* 31 December 1948

2. HC Deb 30 June 1948 vol 452, 2216

3. *Airports & Air Transportation*, March 1949

4. TNA AIR/10573

5. Arthur Pearcy, *Berlin Airlift* 1998, 77

6. *Airports & Air Transportation*, April 1949

7. *The Aeroplane* 6 May 1949

8. HC Deb 16 May 1949 vol 465, 20

9. HC Deb 29 June 1949 vol 466, 1305

10. HL Deb 20 July 1949 vol 164 cc274-301

11. TNA BT245/103

12. HC Deb 24 May 1950 vol 475, 2200

13. HL Deb 02 February 1949 vol 160, 463

14. HC Deb 15 March 1950 vol 472, 1092

15. HL Deb 02 February 1949 vol 160, 493

16. HL Deb 06 December 1950 vol 169, 799

17. *Flight* 8 December 1949

18. HC Deb 13 December 1949 vol 470, 2614-5

19. HL Deb 17 June 1952 vol 177, 219

20. *Flight* 26 May 1949

21. *The Aeroplane* 28 October 1949

22. HC Deb 09 December 1949 vol 470, 2328

23. HC Deb 06 July 1950 vol 477, 741-2

24. HC Deb 19 March 1951 vol 485, 2119

25. J.E.D. Williams, *The Role of Private Enterprise in British Air Transportation*, RAeS Lecture, 15 March 1967

26. HL Deb 05 December 1951 vol 174, 841

27. Lord Salisbury, HL Deb 06 December 1950 vol 169, 794
28. HL Deb 06 December 1950 vol 169, 812
29. Ibid. 807-8
30. *The Aeroplane* 3 June 1949
31. *The Aeroplane* 29 June 1951
32. *The Aeroplane* 28 September 1951
33. HC Deb 14 March 1951 vol 485 cc1532-3

Chapter 6 Basking in Pale Sunshine

1. HC Deb 05 December 1951 vol 494 cc2357-8
2. HC Deb 27 October 1953 vol 518, 2705
3. Douglas Wybrow, *Air Ferry*, 2
4. *The Aeroplane* 19 January 1951
5. HL Deb 05 December 1951 vol 174, 850
6. Ibid. 822
7. Ibid. cc834-8
8. HL Deb 21 March 1972 vol 329, 625
9. HC Deb 27 May 1952 vol 501, cc1152-3
10. Cabinet Papers; C. (52) 176)
11. HL Deb 17 June 1952 vol 177, 226
12. Report of ATAC 1951
13. HC Deb 29 October 1952 vol 505, 1960
14. Ibid. 1977
15. HC Deb 05 April 1954 vol 526 cc8-9W
16. HC Deb 15 November 1954 vol 533 c76
17. ATAC Report for Year ended 31st March 1956
18. BEA Annual Report and Accounts for the year ended 31 March 1959, 28
19. HC Deb 28 February 1958 vol 583, cc 768-793
20. HC Deb 09 May 1956 vol 552 cc1212-4
21. Quoted in *Flight* 30 March 1956
22. HC Deb 24 October 1956 vol 558 c38W
23. HC Deb 27 January 1958 vol 581, 51-2
24. Report from the Select Committee on Nationalised Industries - The Air Corporations HC 213 1959
25. Ibid. para 217
26. HL Deb 13 December 1956 vol 200, 1132
27. *Flight* 6 December 1957
28. BIATA Annual Report 1956-57
29. HL Deb 11 December 1957 vol 206, 1074
30. HC Deb 28 February 1958 vol 583, 767
31. Select Committee, op. cit. para 164
32. Board of Trade, The safety performance of United Kingdom airline operators: special review, 1968

33. HC Deb 28 February 1958 vol 583, 782
34. HC Deb 20 July 1959 vol 609, 972

Chapter 7 A New Charter

1. HC Deb 15 February 1960 vol 617, 958
2. HC Deb 02 March 1960 vol 618, 1225
3. *Flight* 26 February 1960
4. *The Aeroplane* 26 February 1960
5. HC Deb 02 March 1960 vol 618, 1232
6. HL Deb 26 May 1960 vol 223, 1327
7. *Flight* 27 July 1961
8. HC Deb 02 March 1960 vol 618, 1248
9. HC Deb 15 December 1959 vol 615, 1312
10. *Flight* 1 April 1960
11. Air Transport Licensing Board, Annual Report to 31 March 1961
12. *Flight* 29 June 1961
13. HC Deb 19 October 1961 vol 646, 342
14. HC Deb 23 November 1961 vol 649, 1574
15. Ibid. 1606
16. *Flight* 27 September 1962
17. *BOAC News* 6 June 1962
18. Cabinet C. [62] 87) 29 May 1962
19. *BOAC News* 6 June 1962
20. HC 240 Report from the Select Committee on Nationalised Industries - B.O.A.C. 1964, Q1221
21. HC Deb 06 November 1962 vol 666 cc805-903
22. *Flight* 18 April 1963
23. HC Deb 17 June 1963 vol 679 6W
24. Sixth Report of ATLB, to 31 March 1966
25. *Journal of the Royal Aeronautical Society,* April 1981
26. C.P. (63) 14, 12 November 1963
27. HC Deb 02 November 1956 vol 558, 1776
28. C.P. (63) 14, 12 November 1963, Draft Cmnd.
29. Corbett Report, 1963, unpublished
30. C.P. (13) 17, 18 November 1963
31. HC 240 1964 Select Committee Q394
32. HC 240 1964 Select Committee Q320
33. The Financial Problems of the British Overseas Airways Corporation, MoA, 20 November 1960, para 51
34. HC 240 1964 Select Committee Q293
35. HC Deb 02 December 1963 vol 685, 898
36. Statutory Instrument 1963 No. 1978: the Civil Aviation [Licensing] [Application to Colonial-Registered Aircraft] Regulations 1963
37. HC 240 1964 Select Committee Conclusions para 319

Appendix 4 Lord Brabazon and the Tudor

1. TNA DR 11/154
2. HC Deb 01 March 1949 vol 462 cc192-325
3. Report Tudor IV Aircraft *Star Tiger*, 1948 Cmd. 7517.
4. *The Aeroplane* 26 February 1954

Bibliography

C. F. Andrews, *Vickers Aircraft since 1908*, Putnam, 1969

Christopher Balfour, *Spithead Express*, Magna Press Leatherhead, 1999

Harold Balfour, *Wings over Westminster*, Hutchinson & Co., 1973

C. H. Barnes, *Bristol Aircraft since 1910*, Putnam, 1964

C. H. Barnes, *Handley Page Aircraft since 1907*, Putnam, 1976

C. H. Barnes, *Shorts Aircraft since 1900*, Naval Institute Press, 1967

Victor F. Bingham, *Handley Page Hastings & Hermes*, GMS Enterprises, 1998

Peter M. Bowers, *Boeing Aircraft since 1816*, Funk & Wagnalls (Putnam), 1968

Lord Brabazon of Tara, *Air Transport & Civil Aviation 1944–45*, Todd Publishing, 1945

Lord Brabazon of Tara, *The Brabazon Story*, Heinemann London, 1956

Alan Bramson, *Master Airman* (Donald Bennett), Airlife, 1985

Peter Brooks, *The World's Airliners*, Putnam, 1962

Brian Cassidy, *Flying Empires*, Queen's Parade Press, Bath, 1996

Peter Clegg, *A flying start to the day*, Peter Clegg, 1986

Peter Clegg, *Flying against the elements*, Peter Clegg, 1987

Peter Clegg, *Rivals in the North*, Peter Clegg, 1988

Peter Clegg, *Sword in the Sky*, Peter Clegg, 1990

Peter Clegg, *Wings over the Glens*, GMS Enterprises, 1995

Douglas Cluett, *Croydon Airport 1928–1939*, London Borough of Sutton, 1980

Commercial Motor, *Air Transport Manual*, Temple Press, 1934

A. C. Critchley, *Critch!*, Hutchinson, London, 1961

Colin Cruddas, *In Cobham's Company*, Cobham plc, 1994

Tom Culbert, *PanAfrica*, Paladwr Press, 1998

Keith Dagwell, *Silver City Airways: Pioneers of the Skies*, History Press, 2010

R. E. G. Davies, *British Airways, An Airline and its Aircraft, Vol. 1: 1919-1939*, Paladwr Press, 2006

R. E. G. Davies, *De Havilland Comet*, Paladwr Press, 1999

R. E. G. Davies, *History of the World's Airlines*, Oxford University Press, 1964

J. A. Daynes, *Wartime Airmails - The Horseshoe Route*, Chavril Press, Perth, 1992

Neville Doyle, *The Triple Alliance*, Air-Britain (Historians), 2002

A. B. Eastwood, *Piston Engine Airliner Production List*, T.A.H.S., 1996

Robert Finch, *The World's Airways*, University of London Press, 1938

René Francillon, *Lockheed Aircraft since 1913*, Putnam, 1987

René Francillon, *McDonnell Douglas Aircraft since 1920*, Putnam, 1979

E. E. Fresson, *Air Road to the Isles*, David Rendel, 1967

J. M. G. Gradidge, *The Douglas DC-3 and its predecessors*, Air-Britain (Historians), 1984

C. G. Grey, *History of the Air Ministry*, George Allen & Unwin, 1940

John Gunn, *The Defeat of Distance: Qantas 1919-1939*, University of Queensland Press, 1985

John Gunn, *Challenging Horizons: Qantas 1939-1954*, University of Queensland Press, 1987

John Gunn, *High Corridors: Qantas 1954-1970*, University of Queensland Press, 1988

Guy Halford-MacLeod, *Britain's Airlines Volume 1 1946–1951*, Tempus, 2006

Guy Halford-MacLeod, *Britain's Airlines Volume 2 1951–1964*, Tempus, now History Press, 2007

John F. Hamlin, *The de Havilland Dragon/Rapide Family*, Air-Britain (Historians), 2003

Robin Higham, *Britain's Imperial Air Routes 1918 to 1939*, G.T. Foulis , 1960

Robin Higham, *Speedbird: The Complete History of B.O.A.C.*, I.B. Tauris, 2013

Roderic Hill, *The Baghdad Air Mail*, Edward Arnold, London, 1929

Mike Hooks, *Croydon Airport*, Chalford, 1997

Francis E. Hyde, *Cunard and the North Atlantic 1840–1973*, Humanities Press NJ, 1975

A. J. Jackson, *Avro Aircraft since 1908*, Putnam, 1965

A. J. Jackson, *British Civil Aircraft 1919-1972 Vol 1*, Putnam, 1959

A. J. Jackson, *British Civil Aircraft 1919-1972 Vol 2*, Putnam, 1960

A. J. Jackson, *British Civil Aircraft 1919-1972 Vol 3*, Putnam, 1960

A. J. Jackson, *De Havilland Aircraft since 1909*, Putnam, 1962

David Jones, *The Time Shrinkers*, David Rendel, 1971

Derek A. King, *The Bristol 170 Freighter, Wayfarer & Superfreighter*, Air-Britain (Historians), 2011

O. J. Lissitzyn, *International Air Transport and National Policy*, Garland Press NY, 1983

John Longhurst, *Nationalization in Practice*, Temple Press, 1950

Peter J. Lyth, *Studies in Transport History - Air Transport*, Scolar Press, 1996

Peter J. Marson, *The Lockheed Constellation Series*, Air-Britain (Historians), 1982

Bernard Martin, *The Viking, Valetta and Varsity*, Air-Britain (Historians), 1975

Keith McCloskey, *Airwork: a history*, History Press, 2012

Tony Merton Jones, *British Independent Airlines 1946–1976*, T.A.H.S., 2000

Kenneth Munson, *Airliners from 1919 to the present day*, Peerage Books, 1972

Peter Newberry, *The Vectis Connection*, Waterfront, 2001

Gordon Olley, *A Million Miles in the Air*, Hodder and Stoughton London, 1934

Susan, Ian Ottaway, *Fly with the Stars - British South American Airways*, Sutton Publishing, 2007

Martin Painter, *The DH.106 Comet: An Illustrated History*, Air-Britain (Historians), 2002

L. G. S. Payne, *Air Dates*, Heinemann London, 1957

Harald Penrose, *British Aviation - Widening Horizons 1930-1934*, H.M.S.O., 1979

Harald Penrose, *British Aviation - Ominous Skies 1935-1939*, H.M.S.O., 1980

Harold B. Pereira, *Aircraft Badges and Markings*, Adlard Coles, 1955

Mike Phipp, *The Brabazon Committee and British Airliners 1945-1960*, Tempus, 2007

Gordon Pirie, *Air Empire: British Imperial Civil Aviation 1919-1939*, Manchester University Press, 2009

Welch Pogue, *Airline Deregulation Before and After*, National Air and Space Museum, 1991

Taffy Powell, *Ferryman, from Ferry Command to Silver City*, Airlife, 1982

John Provan with R. E. G. Davies, *Berlin Airlift: The Effort and the Aircraft*, Paladwr Press, 1998

John Pudney, *The Seven Skies*, Putnam, 1959

Vladimir Raitz, *Flight to the Sun* (with Roger Bray), Continuum, London and New York, 2001

Anthony Sampson, *Empires of the Sky*, Hodder and Stoughton London, 1984

Kenneth R. Sealy, *The Geography of Air Transport*, Hutchinson University Library London, 1957

Lord Sempill, *International Air Transport 1947*, Todd Publishing, 1947

Graham M. Simons, *Western Airways*, Redcliffe Press, 1988

Basil Smallpeice, *Of Comets and Queens*, Airlife, 1980

Martin Staniland, *Government Birds*, Rowan and Littlefield, 2003

Eric Starling, *The Flight of the Starling*, Kea Publishing, 1992

Chris Sterling, *Commercial Air Transport Books*, Paladwr Press, 1996

Chris Sterling, *Commercial Air Transport Books Supplement*, Paladwr Press, 1998

John Stroud, *Annals of British & Commonwealth Air Transport*, Putnam, 1962

John Stroud, *European Transport Aircraft since 1910*, Putnam, 1966

John Stroud, *Jetliners in Service since 1952*, Putnam, 1994

John Stroud, *Railway Air Services*, Ian Allan, 1987

John Stroud, *Soviet Transport Aircraft since 1945*, Funk & Wagnalls, 1968

T. Sykes, *The DH.104 Dove and DH.114 Heron*, Air-Britain (Historians), 1973

John W. R. Taylor, *ABC Civil Aircraft Markings*, annual, 1950 – 1963, Ian Allan

John W. R. Taylor, *Air Transport before the Second World War*, New English Library, London, 1975

Oliver Tapper, *Armstrong Whitworth Aircraft since 1913*, Putnam, 1973

Owen G. Thetford, *ABC of Airports and Airliners*, Ian Allan, 1948

Miles Thomas, *Out on a Wing*, Michael Joseph, 1964

Thomson & Hunter, *The Nationalized Transport Industries*, Heinemann London, 1973

Robert Wall, *Brabazon: The World's First Jumbo Airliner*, Redcliffe Press, 1999

Stephen Wheatcroft, *Air Transport Policy*, Michael Joseph, 1964

Stephen Wheatcroft, *The Economics of European Air Transport*, Harvard University Press, MA, 1956

Douglas Whybrow, *Air Ferry*, Tourism International, 1995

J. E. D. Williams, *The Operation of Airliners*, Hutchinson, London, 1964

W. E. Wynn, *Civil Air Transport*, Hutchinson, London, 1946

Journal Articles

George Cribbett, *Some International Aspects of Air Transport*, Royal Aeronautical Society, 1950

L. T. H. Greig, *The Economics of Air Line Operation*, Royal Aeronautical Society, 1936

B. K. Humphreys, 'Nationalisation and the independent airlines', *Journal of Transport History*, 1976

B. K. Humphreys, 'Trooping and British independent airlines', *Journal of Transport History*, 1979

Peter J. Lyth, 'A Multiplicity of Instruments', *Journal of Transport History*, 1990

J. W. F. Merer, *The Berlin Air Lift*, Royal Aeronautical Society, 1950

Henry Self, *The Status of Civil Aviation in 1946*, Royal Aeronautical Society, 1946

Stephen Wheatcroft, *Licensing British Air Transport*, Royal Aeronautical Society, 1964

J. E. D. Williams, *The Role of Private Enterprise in British Air Transportation*, Royal Aeronautical Society, 1967

Myles Wyatt, *British Independent Aviation - Past and Future*, 20th Brancker Memorial Lecture, 1963

Reports

A.T.A.C. Annual Report of the Air Transport Advisory Council 1/6/47-31/3/61, H.M.S.O.

A.T.L.B. Annual Reports of the Air Transport Licensing Board 1961 to 1972, H.M.S.O.

B.E.A. Report and Accounts 1949 to 1963, H.M.S.O.

B.I.A.T.A. British Independent Air Transport Association Annual Reports 1951 to 1967

B.O.A.C. Report and Accounts 1949 to 1963, H.M.S.O.

B.S.A.A. Report and Accounts 1947 to 1949, H.M.S.O.

HMG, British Overseas Airways Bill, amended in the Select Committee, and on re-committal, 1939

Air Ministry Cmd. 1739, First Report on Imperial Air Mail Services, H.M.S.O., 1922

Air Ministry Cmd. 1811, Report on Government Financial Assistance to Civil Air Transport Companies, H.M.S.O., 1923

Air Ministry, Annual Reports on the Progress of Civil Aviation, H.M.S.O.

Air Ministry, Reports on the progress of civil aviation , H.M.S.O.

Air Ministry Cmd. 5203, England-Scandinavia Civil Air Transport Services, H.M.S.O., 1936

Air Ministry Cmd. 5351, Report of the Committee to consider the development of Civil Aviation in the United Kingdom, H.M.S.O., 1937

Air Ministry Cmd. 5685, Report of the Committee of Inquiry into Civil Aviation, H.M.S.O. , 1938

Air Ministry Cmd. 6442, BOAC Further Correspondence February - March 1943, H.M.S.O., 1943

Foreign Office Cmd 6614, International Civil Aviation Conference, Chicago Cmd 6614, H.M.S.O., 1944

Foreign Office Cmd 6747, Bermuda Agreement between USA/UK, H.M.S.O., 1946

HMG/MCA Ministry of Civil Aviation, Cmd 6605, British Air Transport March 1945, H.M.S.O., 1945

HMG/MCA Ministry of Civil Aviation, Cmd 6712, British Air Services December 1945, H.M.S.O., 1945

HMG/MCA Ministry of Civil Aviation, Draft Civil Aviation Bill, Lords Amendments July 1946, 1946

HMG/MCA Ministry of Civil Aviation, Report 1946 and 1947, H.M.S.O., 1948

HMG/MCA Cmd. 7517 Report of the Court investigation on the accident to Tudor IV Aircraft *Star Tiger* G-AHNP 30 January 1948, H.M.S.O.

HMG/MCA DS 43225/1, Report on the Progress of Civil Aviation 1939-1945, an unpublished document, Ministry of Civil Aviation

Ministry of Information, *Atlantic Bridge*, H.M.S.O., 1945

Ministry of Information, *Merchant Airmen*, H.M.S.O., 1946

Ministry of Supply Cmd. 7307, Interim report of the committee of enquiry into the Tudor aircraft, H.M.S.O., 1948

Ministry of Supply Cmd. 7478, Final Report Committee of Enquiry into the Tudor aircraft, H.M.S.O., 1948

Ministry of Aviation, The Financial Problems of BOAC 20 November 1963, H.M.S.O., 1963

House of Commons, paper 98, Second Report from the Select Committee on Estimates Session 1947-48, H.M.S.O., 1948

House of Commons, HC 213, Report from the Select Committee on Nationalised Industries: The Air Corporations, H.M.S.O., 1959

House of Commons, paper 49, First Report from the Estimates Committee Trooping: Session 1961-2, H.M.S.O., 1961

House of Commons, HC 240, Report from the Select Committee on Nationalised Industries: B.O.A.C., H.M.S.O., 1964

Index